Goldwater Girls to
Reagan Women

Goldwater Girls to Reagan Women

GENDER, GEORGIA, AND THE GROWTH OF THE NEW RIGHT

Robin M. Morris

The University of Georgia Press
ATHENS

© 2022 by the University of Georgia Press
Athens, Georgia 30602
www.ugapress.org
All rights reserved
Set in 10/13 Kepler Std Regular by Kaelin Chappell Broaddus
Printed and bound by Sheridan Books, Inc.
The paper in this book meets the guidelines for permanence
and durability of the Committee on Production Guidelines for
Book Longevity of the Council on Library Resources.
Most University of Georgia Press titles are
available from popular e-book vendors.
Printed in the United States of America
26 25 24 23 22 P 5 4 3 2 1

Library of Congress Cataloging-in-Publication Data

Names: Morris, Robin M., 1975– author.
Title: Goldwater girls to Reagan women : gender, Georgia, and the growth of
    the New Right / Robin M. Morris.
Description: Athens : The University of Georgia Press, 2022. |
    Series: Since 1970 : histories of contemporary America |
    Includes bibliographical references and index.
Identifiers: LCCN 2022015993 | ISBN 9780820360676 (hardback) |
    ISBN 9780820360690 (paperback) | ISBN 9780820360683 (ebook)
Subjects: LCSH: Women—Political activity—Georgia—History—20th
    century. | Women, White—Political activity—Georgia—History—20th
    century. | Conservatism—Georgia—History—20th century. | Republican
    Party (Ga.)—History—20th century. | Political culture—Georgia—
    History—20th century. | Social values—Political aspects—Georgia—
    History—20th century. | Georgia—Politics and government—1951–
Classification: LCC HQ1236.5.U6 M66 2022 | DDC 320.082/09758—dc23/
    eng/20220521
LC record available at https://lccn.loc.gov/2022015993

For Mom and Dad

CONTENTS

ACKNOWLEDGMENTS

This book began with a simple question, "Why did the ERA fail?" Thanks to the help, patience, and kindness of many, I learned that while the answer was not simple, it was fascinating. So many people helped me peel the layers, taking what I thought was a late-1970s question back a couple of decades.

My first step was an email to my former boss and former Georgia state representative, Cathey Steinberg. In high school, I worked on her campaign and interned for her when I was in college. Thankfully, she remembered me nearly twenty years later. I asked Steinberg, the former sponsor of the ERA in the Georgia legislature, who had been her biggest obstacle. She replied with one name: "Dunaway." Like any historian with a nugget of hope, I was off. At the time, I was one of few researchers to look at Kathryn Dunaway's unprocessed papers at Emory University, where I soon realized that hers amounted to much more than a STOP ERA story.[1] I have been fortunate to study women who, I believe, knew they were making history and saved everything in hopes someone would come looking. I thank them for saving it and their families for recognizing the stacks of papers in mom's house as the treasures they really are.

Past Georgia Federation of Republican Women president Millie Rogers introduced me to Lee Ague Miller. As I asked question after question, an exasperated Miller said, "I wish I hadn't given all those boxes away in the 70s!" Boxes? What boxes? Just about every archivist in Georgia got an email from me the next day. Finally, I tracked those boxes down at the Georgia Archives. Not only had they not been processed, I even got to rip off the tape that had sealed them.[2] While I may be the first to tell Lee Ague Miller's story, I know more scholars and activists will find uses for her papers.

I owe much to the archivists who recognized the value of preserving the papers of housewives who labored as unpaid political organizers. Randy Gue, Kathy Shoemaker, and the entire staff of Rose Library at Emory University stand out for preserving these papers, even granting me space to sit with Lee Wysong as we looked through Dunaway's papers together one day. The staff of Georgia Archives displays a great dedication to preserving the state's history, even through budget battles that have challenged their very ability to remain open. Morna Gerrard and Hilary Morrish from the Special Collections department at Georgia State University Library demonstrate a strong commitment to preserving and sharing the stories of women in Georgia history. I thank Morna for giving a home to Lee Ague Miller's papers and oral histories and for preserving the many stories of the Georgia women's movement.

One of the unexpected joys of this research has been visiting numerous presidential libraries, each with a distinct personality and a rich archive. Many times, I would show up with the intention of looking at one collection but end up looking at three or four more after a knowledgeable archivist took an interest. Employees of the National Archives and Records Administration preserve our nation's history and are eager to help spread the stories. Archivists at the Eisenhower, Nixon, Ford, Carter, and Reagan libraries all contributed knowledge of their collections to this research. The Eisenhower Foundation and the Gerald R. Ford Presidential Foundation generously awarded me travel grants to visit their archives, allowing me to understand how the local grassroots corresponded to the national story.

I had the honor to interview Lee Ague Miller, Lee Wysong, Phyllis Schlafly, and other women who appear in these pages. Miller, Wysong, and Schlafly have since passed, and I am so grateful to have recorded their stories. Hearing them firsthand brought the archives to life and allowed me to provide a more textured account. In fact, everyone I interviewed was generous with memories and time. So much so, that I encourage readers to find someone to interview about their first vote, the evolution of their political views, and any other story they are willing to tell. So many stories, especially women's stories, will never be known because nobody asked for them. Many of the seemingly small details about women's organizing—what they wore, gifts they gave, and how they used shoeboxes—brought this part of history to life for me. I found the women as grateful for a chance to tell their story as I was that they trusted me to listen.

Writing is a solitary activity that requires a great deal of support, and I have been blessed with a championship team. Glenda Gilmore knew this was a book back when I thought it was just a question. I am so grateful I stumbled into her office with the blessed combination of arrogance and naivete of a first-year college student, and even more thankful that she has continued to mentor me. Any use of the passive voice that remains in this text is my fault alone and does not reflect Glenda's influence.

I have faked sympathy when others complain about nightmare dissertation committees because I had a dream committee consisting of Glenda Gilmore, Beverly Gage, and Joanne Meyerowitz, who guided the work that became the foundation for this book. They read numerous drafts, filling pages with questions and comments that challenged me to be clearer and stronger.

The people at the University of Georgia Press have been patient as I completed this final manuscript during a pandemic. I am grateful for the grace and guidance of Mick Gusinde-Duffy, Beth Snead, and the rest of the press's crew.

I have benefitted from the generosity of many organizations. The Yale Graduate School of Arts & Sciences funded a year of research that allowed me to travel to archives and collect oral histories. Radcliffe's Schlesinger Library funded my participation in a valuable workshop considering post-1960s histories. I was fortunate to be placed into Robert Self's workshop, where I met Claire Potter, Chris Huff, and others who have pushed this work forward. The National Endowment for the Humanities funded the summer seminar on Gender, the State, and the 1977 International Women's Year Conference, hosted by Leandra Zarnow and Nancy Beck Young at the University of Houston.

A sabbatical from Agnes Scott College freed me from teaching and service for a semester, allowing me to indulge in research and writing. The James T. and Ella Rather Kirk Fund at Agnes Scott supported me in my first year of teaching there, giving me an opportunity to present early stages of this research to the community. I am grateful to have landed at Agnes Scott, with wonderful colleagues in the History Department—Mary Cain, Yael Manes, Shu-Chin Wu, Reem Bailony, Katharine Kennedy, and Kristian Blaich. I also thank my students, who read drafts as assignments and gave strong feedback. I appreciate your editing with the sharp eye of an undergraduate student, asking questions and making connections I otherwise would have missed. I am honored to have you as my students and I am proud of your work.

Numerous friends and colleagues read drafts—in whole or in part—and provided valuable feedback. Françoise Hamlin, Marjorie Spruill, Claire Nee Nelson, Katherine Mellon Charron, Alison Collis Greene, Elizabeth Gillespie McRae, Tammy Ingram, Jason Morgan Ward, Keri Leigh Merritt, Kelly Ball, and Cornelia Lambert all generously read drafts. I also want to thank anonymous readers of this work and related articles whose questions pushed my work in helpful directions. My writing group has witnessed this project move from seminar paper to book and they are a big part of asking the questions that kept expanding my own understanding of the history. Francesca Ammon, Catherine McNeur, Julia Guarneri, Sara Hudson, Kathryn Gin Lum, and Helen Curry are the best of editors and the best of friends.

I am certain that I have omitted names, for which I apologize. I thank everyone who has read drafts, endured a conversation where I worked through an idea, asked a conference question, or showed interest in this project.

Perhaps more than anyone, my family deserves a gratitude I can never fully express. My sister Rebekah has endured endless conversations, to the point where she finally sent me cross-stitched encouragement to finish. Mom took toddler me to vote, ushering me behind a curtain like the Wizard of Oz and pulling levers that made the world run. Mom and Dad indulged me when I learned that watching debates meant a later bedtime. In high school, they let me borrow the car to go work on campaigns. My parents raised a political nerd and never tried to make me a princess, for which I am ever grateful. They have also provided unlimited dog-sitting during my research trips and, so far, have always given my dog back. For all their love, tolerance, encouragement, patience, and investment in me, I offer the small return of dedicating this book to Tommye and Bob Morris.

ABBREVIATIONS

CCFRW	Cobb County (Ga.) Federation of Republican Women
GFRW	Georgia Federation of Republican Women
EAC	Educational Advisory Committee
ERA	Equal Rights Amendment
GOP	Grand Old Party, another name for the Republican Party
IWY	International Women's Year
IWY CRC	International Women's Year Citizen's Review Committee
NAACP	National Association for the Advancement of Colored People
NFRW	National Federation of Republican Women
NOW	National Organization for Women
OLAE	Operation Lend-An-Ear
RNC	Republican National Committee
STOP ERA	Stop Taking Our Privileges Equal Rights Amendment
WNDC	Women's National Democratic Club
WIG	Write-In Georgia, gubernatorial campaign for Ellis Arnall, 1966

Goldwater Girls to Reagan Women

"First, Take a Shoebox"

When she had a campaign to organize, Lee Ague rummaged through her closet for an old shoebox. She filled it with index cards, each with the name and contact information of one voter in her precinct. Next, Ague plastered campaign bumper stickers on her children's strollers and canvassed her neighborhood, putting a face to every name. Each time she contacted a voter, she wrote more information on her card. She recalled, "I could say, 'Susie, how's your daughter? Last time we talked, she had the measles.'" Ague boasted 98 percent turnout from her first shoebox and still, sixty years later, remembered the woman who had pneumonia and was too sick to vote.[1] Every card in Lee Ague's shoebox led to a ballot box.

Later, whenever anyone asked Lee Ague Miller to teach them her successful campaign strategies, she began, "First, take a shoebox."[2] That mundane item, which any woman could find in her closet, represents an apt place to open this history of women's work building the New Right. The movement depended on ordinary women's volunteer time and their everyday tools of shoeboxes, telephones, coffee cups, and cakes.

As a repurposed household item, a shoebox stores family photos, transforms into children's art projects, and can even serve as a small filing cabinet to organize a campaign. Lee Ague believed politics—like shoeboxes—should be easily accessible and inside every home. As she introduced the Republican Party to the Atlanta suburbs in the early 1960s, she strategically used metaphors to reinforce politics as women's work, akin to baking, gardening, or grocery shopping. When she moved to Cobb County, Georgia, in 1963, Ague struggled to find a Republican community. She decided to build one. By 1965, she was accepting awards for leading the nation's fastest-growing federation of Republican women. By the end of the 1960s, Lee Ague divorced and remarried, becoming Lee Miller. While her name changed, her dedication to the Republican Party and women's grassroots organizing remained steadfast.

Everyday acts of women have political meaning. In Georgia in the 1960s, brewing a pot of coffee could constitute a political act, depending on who drank it and with whom. Hundreds of women found their way to the Republican Party over a cup of coffee in a neighbor's living room. Baking a cake, likewise, was a political act when that dessert ended up on the desk of a state legislator on the day of the vote on the Equal Rights Amendment. Index cards in a shoebox and bakery receipts are political artifacts as much as national party polling data. Pollsters and party leaders assumed men set the political course for the household, leading them to overlook women's acts steeped in political significance. Women in this book brought the GOP home over dinner conversation and took politics to the pulpit by sharing anti-ERA pamphlets with ministers. This book shows that southern white women were, in fact, at the fore of right-wing activism.[3]

Lee Ague lit a spark in a state that was ready for political realignment. Women eagerly joined local Republican women's clubs as soon as they organized. Over the 1960s and 1970s, the main period covered here, Georgia's conservative women grew to take leadership roles in local clubs, state meetings, and national campaigns. The title of this book reflects that growth. Between 1964 and 1966, they were new to Republican Party politics, taking the roles of "Goldwater Girls," "Go Bo Girls," and "Victory Girls."[4] Through their time in the Republican Party, coinciding with a peak of activism in the women's movement, conservative women also matured as political actors. By the 1970s, they no longer identified as "girls," having matured into women with their own politics. No longer simply cheerleaders for a candidate, they began to influence policy and campaign strategy. By the final pages of the book, some of the women had moved from volunteer work to paid political positions.

The following chapters tell the story of conservative women's work in Georgia spanning the years from the founding of the Georgia Federation of Republican Women (GFRW) in the early 1950s through the defeat of the Equal Rights Amendment (ERA) in 1982. This book sits at the intersections of political history and social history, southern history and national history. By recognizing conservative women's grassroots organizing, a more complete understanding of southern political realignment and women's dynamic conservatism takes shape. The local story of voter recruitment and grassroots lobbying in the South provides critical grounding for the national story of the New Right.

Situating the story at the state level is also essential. A study of state-level leadership provides a window through which to view state leaders' relationship with national organizations like the National Federation of Republican Women (NFRW) and Stop Taking Our Privileges Equal Rights Amendment (STOP ERA), while also examining how they translated the message to women in neighborhoods and communities. In both GFRW and STOP ERA, local women were only a few phone calls away from national leadership. Further, my research reveals the centrality of women to party building at precinct and district levels in Georgia. National conservative leaders did not recruit new voters. Local women carried national messages into their communities and, more importantly, educated voters on conservative issues.[5]

From the 1950s through the 1980s, conservative white women gradually shifted southern race-based conservatism into a family-values brand that found a place in national political dialogue. They, along with thousands of other women throughout the Peach State, had been building a women's network for conservative causes. They contributed significantly to the political realignment of Georgia and to the growth of the New Right nationally. Throughout Georgia, conservative women hosted teas, conducted phone surveys, and engaged voters at church meetings and grocery stores and in other daily interactions. While men ran for office and conducted major fundraising campaigns, women grew the Republican voter base one person and one bake sale at a time. Those voters comprised the electorate that moved Georgia out of the Democratic "Solid South" and into the emerging New Right of the national Republican Party. By the 1970s, the women who built the GOP in Georgia would lead national conservative campaigns. They also stared down pro-ERA president Jimmy Carter, defeating the amendment in Carter's home state at a time when the president needed a policy victory.

Though this narrative begins with African American women organizing Republican politics in Atlanta, most of the story focuses on white women in the suburbs. The timeline of this study coincides with years of southern party realignment, national civil rights movements, and widespread women's movements. In the 1950s, African American women of the Metropolitan Club in Atlanta promoted the Republican Party as the party of civil rights. Ten years later, they struggled against new white Republican converts who saw that securing the future of Massive Resistance politics—organized efforts to resist desegregation—lay in the party of Barry Goldwater. Indeed, the story of Black Republicans in Georgia at this time follows that of Black Republicans nationwide: their numbers grew smaller, and white conservative voices began to drown them out. Yet in Georgia as nationwide, some African American women stayed in the party, fighting hard to connect the GOP with the Black community and vice versa.[6]

The GFRW offers a valuable organizational vehicle to examine substantial changes through these years. Membership in a local Republican women's club automatically included membership in the NFRW. Georgia's Democratic women did not have a national network equal to the NFRW. The National Federation of Democratic Women was not established until 1971, long after Republican women had already been organized nationally.[7] The national network and mentorship sustained Georgia's new Republican clubs as they established a presence and learned strategy.

Most of the women in this book were white, middle-class homemakers. Their opponents at the time often mistakenly dismissed them as uneducated, though most held at least a high school diploma and many had obtained some higher education. While many of these women were stay-at-home mothers during their years of political activism, nearly all had worked for a wage prior to motherhood. They had finally attained the class status to stay home just as parts of the mainstream women's movement argued for expanding women's roles in the workforce. Feeling their choices questioned, these conservative women set about arguing for the value of the stay-at-home mother. They also asserted a political identity of mothers as the protectors of home, an identity with a long tradition in American politics.[8] As organizers, white conservative women held critical roles as the moral center and the volunteer lifeline of family-values politics.

Investigating the shift of southern conservatism from 1950s to 1980s, this book also challenges the prevailing view of the southern strategy of the Republican Party. In *The Emerging Republican Majority* (1969), Nixon strategist Kevin Phillips located the future of the GOP in southern states, declaring, "Together with the Heartland, the South is shaping up as the pillar of a national conservative party."[9] He believed that the Civil Rights Act of 1964 and the Voting Rights Act of 1965 instigated "a sharp conservative trend among hitherto populist Southern poor whites."[10] Thus, his book mapped out a national Republican strategy not only to win southern elections, but to position the region as an indispensable stronghold.

Kevin Phillips was late. Perhaps we should not be surprised that a political professional believed his was the original idea of a southern strategy, but it is time to set the record straight. By the end of 1964—five years *before* Phillips articulated a southern strategy for readers nationwide—local women had already planted chapters of the GFRW in urban, suburban, and rural districts. They did not simply register Goldwater voters for one election; they organized Republican voters for years to come. After Goldwater's selection in 1964 as the party's nominee for president, the women's groups continued to meet and strategize for the 1966 Georgia gubernatorial election. Had Phillips looked at the local level or at women's work, he would have seen that southerners already stood in the midst of a Republican revolution.

Political scientists Angie Maxwell and Todd Shields have tackled Kevin Phillips's blind spots in *The Long Southern Strategy*. Their rich analysis challenges Phillips's timeline, and they argue that we must consider the long story of southern white voters in order to understand their political realignment. Moreover, the Nixon southern strategy in 1968 was grafted on to existing southern politics of race, religion, and gender, all forces undergoing rapid changes. Phillips's strategy assumed a stagnant southern political culture that outsiders could shape. Maxwell and Shields understand the region as vibrant and already changing long before and after Nixon.

Importantly for the following chapters, Maxwell and Shields recognize the value of examining women's work: "These anti-feminist southern white women have too often been missed, and yet they are the bridge between the racial appeals of the original Long Southern Strategy and the political ascent of the Christian Right."[11] Their statistical studies provide stunning data sets to support their thesis. *Goldwater Girls to Reagan Women* uses the Georgia story to support the thesis that women are the bridge between Massive Resistance and Christian Right conservatisms.

Reagan political strategist Lee Atwater explained the effect of the southern strategy on political communication: "You start out in 1954 by saying, 'N**ger, n**ger, n**ger'. . . . By 1968, you can't say 'n**ger'—that hurts you. Backfires." South Carolinian Atwater explained the lesson the GOP learned: "So you say stuff like forced busing, states' rights, and all that stuff." Yet behind the coded language, he continued, "You're getting so abstract now [that] you're talking about cutting taxes, and all these things you're talking about are totally economic things, and a byproduct of them is [that] blacks get hurt worse than whites."[12] As numerous scholars have begun to demonstrate, while candidates and voters no longer employed the language of race, they still applied the goals of white supremacy.

Many historians agree that race alone cannot explain the partisan shift and that we should also look at suburbanization and the role of class. Historian Matthew D. Lassiter argues that Nixon's focus shifted from the overtly racist politics of anti–civil rights legislation that had worked for Goldwater toward a "suburban strategy." Lassiter emphasizes the creation of the middle-class suburban South and places the roots of modern southern conservatism in the postwar class mobility of these white families living in the suburbs. In a study of Atlanta, historian Kevin Kruse skillfully shows the interplay between the white working class and white middle and upper classes. After showing that the growth in Atlanta suburbs was indeed a mix of white flight from Atlanta and new arrivals to the region, Kruse argues that "segregationist phrases, such as 'freedom of choice' or 'neighborhood schools,'" joined the traditionally segregationist rhetorics to unite white suburbanites ideologically.[13]

If Lassiter is correct that a focus on "top-down 'Southern Strategy'" obscures the critical story of suburban, middle-class voters, then such a top-down analysis likewise misses the convergence of southern local and national politics that revolved around gender. When those "white flight" refugees or new arrivals to the Sunbelt South settled in the suburbs of Atlanta, Augusta, or Savannah, they likely had a visit from a member of the local chapter of the GFRW. Examining white backlash alone does not provide sufficient understanding of why southerners eventually moved to the GOP, since *both* state parties vied for the segregationist vote. Race is certainly a central component to southern conservatism, but on its own it remains insufficient for appreciating how the region went over to the Republican Party. Placing the 1960s white backlash in conversation with 1970s anti-feminism reveals a connection that illuminates another path that allowed for the South's transition into a bastion of the GOP.[14]

The rise of the Christian Right did not come through Atwater's replacing race with the economy as the narrative focus, but with anti-feminists replacing racism with family values as a rallying cry. Rather than racist Massive Resistance chants, women began to talk about abortion, motherhood, and home. To untrained ears, the new conservatism sounded color-blind, but southerners knew that gender and race have always been two sides of the same Jim Crow coin.[15] As a rich historiography reveals, calls for the protection of white women propped up white supremacy even as they restricted white women to the immobility of a pedestal. Privileged white women learned to reshape that pedestal into a podium from which they could challenge the status quo while promoting the politics that would benefit them. Through campaigns for suffrage, Confederate monuments, revisionist education, and segregation, southern white women justified their organizing in terms of motherhood and women's duty to protect children. By the 1970s, after significant advances in civil rights, they understood that they could no longer organize campaigns around the protection of white womanhood—but they subtly rearticulated the same premise by demanding respect for mothers and protection for families.[16]

Throughout the period of this study—from the 1950s through the early 1980s—Georgia women led in New Right organizing. In 1953, African American women in Atlanta formed one of the few southern federations of Republican women. Over the next decade, the state's sunbelt economy pulled new residents to Georgia, including women like Lee Ague who had experience with Republican politics in other states. These new Georgians planted a new GFRW, one not rooted in the aspirations for civil rights of their Black Republican predecessors. By 1965, Atlanta's suburban Republican women's clubs were the fastest-growing in the nation—rapidly outpacing all the other southern-state federations. That growth and organization positioned them in the next decade to lead in national conservative movements like anti-busing and anti-ERA campaigns. While Georgia's male political figures of these same years garnered more attention—Lester Maddox, Jimmy Carter, Newt Gingrich, John Lewis—unrecognized women worked behind the scenes, shaping Georgia politics from the living room to the precinct and eventually to the White House.

As the story proceeds, the women build confidence in their political work and grow their numbers as the state shifts more and more toward the GOP. By the end, the women are successful and accomplished organizers, though still unsung for their work in establishing Republican strength in the region. Chapter 1, "The Two Party Tea Party" examines how white conservative women organized for Barry Goldwater in 1964 and used that great momentum to lead a conservative takeover of the previously moderate GFRW. Long before the post-2008 Tea Party political movement, Lee Ague created what she called the "Two Party Tea Party" as a social avenue to introduce Democratic women to the Republican Party and its ideas. Because white Goldwater voters lived in all corners of the state, GFRW chapters organized in rural, urban, and suburban areas. The GFRW grew so rapidly during the period that the NFRW created a prize to recognize such amazing development and to spur more laggard states into friendly competition.

Chapter 2, "The Go Bo Girls," follows the GFRW as it turned the Goldwater momentum toward the 1966 gubernatorial campaign of Bo Callaway. Elected in the 1964 Goldwater wave, Howard H. "Bo" Callaway became the first Republican to have a real chance at winning statewide office since Reconstruction. However, this campaign pitted him against famed Democratic segregationist Lester Maddox. The 1966 Georgia gubernatorial race thus provides an interesting study of the tension between the racist right of Maddox and the newer, more polished, though still segregationist conservatism of Callaway.[17] GFRW volunteers conducted thousands of phone surveys of voter attitudes in order to shape Callaway's messaging. They continued the work of hosting teas, recruiting voters, and staffing county-fair booths. Additionally, Bo's wife, Beth Callaway, hit the campaign trail with Lee Ague at her side. Ague balanced her role as women's outreach director for the campaign with her goal of organizing more GFRW clubs.

By 1967, Georgia had the largest NFRW membership among southern states. Chapter 3, "Fighting Factions," focuses on the internal politics of the NFRW and the organization's presidential election. This election divided the federation into moderates and conservatives. The fallout and bitterness of that divide spilled over to affect group members at the personal, local, and state levels. This chapter tells the story of that fork in the road for Georgia's Republican women. After spending the previous five years adding to its numbers, the GFRW lost membership over the national divide. The final four chapters follow the two roads that diverged from that party split.

Chapter 4, "Thousands of Mothers Make a Movement," stays with Lee Ague and the women who remained with the GFRW to examine members' rise to national leadership. Georgia women created the national campaign Operation Lend-An-Ear, which surveyed citizen concerns about education and shared the results with the White House. Repackaging Massive Resistance as freedom of choice, GFRW leaders pioneered a meaningful modification in the rhetoric of new conservatism. Significantly, they used the guise of concerned mothers to conduct a survey that they presented to respondents as nonpartisan. The White House took note.[18]

The final three chapters follow those conservative women who left Republican party organizing to join Phyllis Schlafly's grassroots STOP ERA and Eagle Forum organizations. Schlafly hand-picked her longtime friend Kathryn Dunaway to lead the movement in Georgia. Applying methods used successfully in her previous ten years of GFRW activism and combining them with Schlafly's new gendered language, Dunaway and her network successfully defeated the ERA in Georgia.

Chapter 5 tells the story of the early years of STOP ERA in the Peach State, and how adherents to the cause followed Schlafly's lead in creating an antifeminist presence at the state capitol building and articulating the arguments against the ERA. Chapter 6 shows how the movement matured as Georgia women deployed femininity as a tactic to prevent ERA ratification. Dressing demurely to demonstrate their status as ladies, they plied the lawmakers with baked goods to reinforce the message of their duty to protect the home. Chapter 7 follows the Georgia women as they took their state anti-ERA campaign to national battlefields and fought the International Women's Year conference. They also stared down pressure from the White House as Jimmy Carter, Georgia's native son, pushed for a critical domestic policy victory. The women of STOP ERA were well organized and strong-willed. Fighting what they viewed as an encroachment on extant legal and socially sanctioned protections for women, they forged a new conservatism within the state that moved political rhetoric further from its overtly racist roots and toward a more palatable message of family values.

Goldwater Girls to Reagan Women ends with the defeat of the Equal Rights Amendment and the election of Ronald Reagan in 1980. The conclusion follows some individual women's stories for a few more years to show their continued commitment to and engagement with Republican politics. While they started in 1964 as new volunteers knocking door-to-door, the women reached the level of paid positions in politics and a seat at the table with leaders hashing out campaign strategy. Republican women have won elected office at all levels. They, like all Georgia Republican officeholders, stand on the shoulders of the women in these pages.

The GOP Has Been Asleep

Mrs. Hattie Greene took the occasion of the Abraham Lincoln birthday dinner in 1954 to announce that women "are going to resurrect the Republican Party" in Georgia. She proclaimed that "women have decided to give all" to awaken "the Republican Party that has been asleep for 20 years."[1]

The previous year, Greene had joined eight other women in the Auburn Avenue neighborhood of Atlanta to establish the Metropolitan Republican Women's Club. White women had tried, unsuccessfully, to charter clubs in the state during the previous decade, but only Greene's club thrived.[2] Thanks in part to Greene's and other African American clubwomen's labor, women did revive the Republican Party in Georgia. The GOP that grew up in Georgia, though, did not fulfill Greene's vision of getting "better jobs, in and out of government, for Negroes."[3]

The nine original Metropolitan Club members were African American women living and working in Atlanta's Auburn Avenue neighborhood. Club history records that the women recognized a need for "a new organization and a necessary change" in Georgia politics, especially one that would encourage "participating in the Republican Party and two-party politics."[4] The women cited the 1952 election of African American educator W. C. Ervin to the Augusta School Board as inspiration to organize Republican women across the state.[5] Unable to meet the requirements for statewide status, the women of the Metropolitan Club applied first for single-club membership. The NFRW based state organization on the number of organized counties, meaning that 95 of Georgia's 159 counties would need chapters—an unimaginable goal in a Jim Crow, one-party state.

As educated, upper-class, and politically active urban citizens, the women of the Metropolitan Club were some of the few registered African American voters in Georgia. Some, like Hattie Greene, came from families who had been active in the Republican Party since Reconstruction. Many held degrees from the colleges of the Atlanta University system. Some of the women were business owners themselves, while others were wives of business owners. Their educational, professional, and social status allowed the women independence from any ties to a white boss or banker who might be able to intimidate them from voting or activism. Unable to vote in the all-white Democratic primaries, the women of the Metropolitan Club turned to the Republican Party as a means of political participation and protest in a state controlled by the whites-only Democratic Party.[6]

In 1953, the same year the Metropolitan Republican Women's Club was chartered, Hattie Greene and two other members traveled to the nation's capital for the annual meeting of the NFRW, putting them among "approximately 30 Negro women" of the hundreds of attendees from around the nation. Other African American women came from New Jersey, Texas, Illinois, Ohio, New York, and California—Greene, Mrs. Birdie Wallace, and Mrs. W. A. Scott were the only African American attendees representing the Deep South.[7] By identifying themselves as "Mrs.," these women claimed a title of respect likely denied to African American women in most Georgia political meetings.

The Atlanta women marveled at the integrated events planned, including a visit to the White House, where the First Lady greeted them. Later, they attended a luncheon at which President Eisenhower emphasized women's roles in his campaign. Senator Margaret Chase Smith, the only woman in the Senate, introduced the six Republican women then serving in the House of Representatives. Eisenhower had recently nominated an African American woman as assistant to the secretary of the Department of Welfare, and one of the attendees from Chicago marveled, "Lincoln, here we are! You gave us our freedom and Eisenhower has given us equality under law!"[8]

Excluded from the Democratic Party, generations of Georgia's African American business leaders clung to the Republican Party for a voice. While not central players in the national GOP, these African American women had a place at the table. The First Lady hosted them at the White House when the Georgia Democratic Party would not seat them at all.

African American women organizing the GOP in Georgia faced obstacles of racism, sexism, and partisanship; all the power structures in Georgia sought to prevent their progress. Reporting to the Republican National Committee (RNC), Greene wrote that "there is tremendous work to do . . . but a small group of Republican women here are determined." She told national GOP leadership that the women would require "yours & God's help."[9] In asking for "a word" in person with NFRW leadership, she wrote, "We are fighting hard & persistently, but we have problems here that require personal advice & help in our struggles for 'More in '54.'"[10]

The women of the Metropolitan Club were well connected within Atlanta's

African American community. Marian Scott's husband, W. A. Scott, founded the *Atlanta Daily World*, the city's African American newspaper and a strong Republican voice. The women met at Frazier's Café Society, owned and operated by club officer Evelyn Jones Frazier. The restaurant was a center of the city's African American life, with a hall big enough to accommodate wedding receptions, dinner, dancing, banquets, and, eventually, NAACP and Metropolitan Club meetings and banquets. Frazier was an alumna of Morris Brown University and a member of Big Bethel AME Church, placing her in elite circles in the city. Her husband, Luther, helped run the restaurant when he was not chauffeuring golfer Bobby Jones.[11]

True to Hattie Greene's promise that the women would awaken the Georgia GOP, the women continued organizing in the state and with other state organizations. In 1955, the NFRW planned a regional meeting of southern Republican women in New Orleans. The event marked the first time that the Republican women "have gone into the Deep South for a conclave." The NFRW hoped to double its membership to one million by the 1956 campaign season and looked to the South for its potential new members.[12] After the NFRW amended its rules to base membership on congressional districts, of which Georgia had only ten, rather than counties, Georgia could qualify. By 1957, enough clubs organized so that the Georgia Federation of Republican Women affiliated with NFRW, one of the last southern states to do so.[13] The African American women of the Metropolitan Club were at the fore of organizing the GFRW throughout the state.

By 1960, an interracial group of Georgia Republican women worked together to support the presidential campaign of Richard Nixon. Mrs. Lottie Harris joined a white woman, Mrs. John Pendergrast, to present plans for campaign activities at a meeting of Republican women at the Phyllis Wheatley YWCA just a couple of weeks before the election.[14] As Democrats in the state legislature plotted to keep Georgia politics all white, a group of interracial Republican women strategized to maintain GOP leadership in the White House. Unable to affect the private-club structure of local and state politics, the Republican women began with the White House in the hopes that they could bring change from the national level down to the local.[15] The Republican Party was the only partisan space for women to work for civil rights. Metropolitan Club vice president Mrs. J. V. Harris explained that the national GOP stood for "the emancipation of the Negro. A Negro can't be a Democrat in Georgia."[16]

While white Democratic women supported local and state campaigns in Georgia and elsewhere, they did not enjoy the national network that characterized the NFRW. The Democratic Party did not have an organization equal to the NFRW until decades later. Founded in 1927, the Women's National Democratic Club (WNDC) was a social club first and political club second. It was simply a physical space open to women residing in or visiting Washington, D.C. In contrast, the NFRW began in 1937 with chapters in eleven states and eighty-five member clubs. None in that first year were southern. While the WNDC did not allow its first African American member until 1955, the NFRW welcomed four "colored women's clubs" at its inaugural meeting.[17]

While the GOP welcomed African American members, the South remained inhospitable to the Republican Party. Georgia's GOP was especially late. Neighboring Alabama had an active Republican Party that ran viable candidates for governor in 1954 and Senate in 1960. Tennessee voters even sent two Republican congressmen to Washington. Five other southern states ran Republican candidates that won up to a third of the total vote. Southern Republicans did not win often, but they showed on the ballot in all but the deepest South states of Georgia, Mississippi, and South Carolina. The first real toehold southern Republicans found came in presidential elections. Dwight Eisenhower pulled 48.1 percent of the southern vote in 1952 and slightly more than that in 1956. He carried Florida, Tennessee, Virginia, and Texas in both elections and added Louisiana in 1956.[18]

Though Metropolitan Club members might overcome restrictive voter laws and register as Atlanta voters, they were still limited by the county-unit system. Under this system, counties received unit votes in the all-white Democratic primaries, similar to the national electoral college system. The eight most populous counties received six votes each. The next thirty had four votes each. The remaining 121 counties, the state's least populated, each had two votes. In 1960, this resulted in rural counties, which had 32 percent of the population, having 59 percent of the vote. Urban areas, in contrast, had 41 percent of the population but only 12 percent of the vote. The tiny Georgia GOP's power largely lay in these underrepresented urban areas. Until 1962, state elections operated on a county-unit system that heavily favored rural districts. Federal courts ruled the county-unit system unconstitutional even as suburban areas boomed. Over the next few years, three factors—African American registration, the end of the county-unit system, and growing suburbanization—cracked open an opportunity for the development of a two-party system in 1964.[19]

As the women of the Metropolitan Club worked to bring together the African American community and the Republican Party at the ballot box, another movement developed just north of the city. Georgia's population was shifting with the booming Sunbelt economy, bringing new residents—and new voters—to the region. Hattie Greene's prophecy would soon be fulfilled: women would resurrect the Republican Party in Georgia. But Hattie Greene and her friends would have to fight for their place in it.

CHAPTER 1

The Two Party Tea Party

Lee Ague did not want her street widened. She and her husband Bob had chosen a house in a quaint neighborhood in Smyrna, Georgia. They imagined their two children, ages three and two, romping in the yards with all the other children of young families. The Agues had just relocated from the Washington, D.C., suburbs to the Atlanta area with Bob's job at the U.S. Department of Health, Education, and Welfare. This was their first time living in the Deep South. In this suburban Atlanta neighborhood, they felt at home with the other young white veterans' families.[1]

When the Cobb County Commission sent notice of plans to widen the quaint street, the Agues felt their new dreams threatened. County commissioners of the fast-growing suburb planned the area's first divided highway straight through the Spring Street neighborhood, a route Lee Ague suspected the commissioners had chosen with the expectation of little organized resistance from a "nice docile group of young ladies . . . and not a high-income area." From experience, though, Lee knew that the anger of mothers was a fierce tool. She invited her new neighbors for coffee, cramming everyone into her small living room, where the women decided to make an appointment with the commissioners.

Still, Ague worried that the elected men might easily dismiss a bunch of housewives. She decided, "We need to be somebody or have some name that when we go to talk . . . we're somebody, not just a group of little housewives."[2] She had a plan. Lee Ague also had connections. Before moving to Georgia, she had been active in the Martha Washington Council of Republican Women. She knew she needed just ten members paying dues of $1.00 each in order to become an official NFRW club. Quickly finding ten mothers in the neighborhood willing to fight the road project with her, Ague formed the Cobb County Federation of Republican Women (CCFRW).[3]

As the women squeezed into in Lee Ague's living room, they speculated that it would be the first time commissioners had met with Republicans, since the GOP did not have any noticeable presence in Cobb County. They put together their case: if the road project went through, no other housewives or mothers would feel comfortable moving to that suburb. While presenting themselves as a partisan group, they shaped their message as one of interest to all mothers and, thus, all taxpaying families. Eventually, with the name of the NFRW and the political message of motherhood, the women won their fight to keep their street quaint.

Equally important, they established themselves as a political entity in Cobb. They sent press releases to ensure that the news of CCFRW reached area readers of the *Atlanta Constitution, Atlanta Journal, Smyrna Herald,* and *Marietta Daily Journal.*[4] They quickly shifted from being a neighborhood ladies' group to a strong voice for women's conservatism. Getting the word out that they were organized attracted other conservative women and shot up a flare to the Democratic Party that they had competition.

The story as Ague recounted it omits the deep Republican roots of the original CCFRW members. Like Ague, several of the women were longtime Republicans, though new to Georgia. Ague, a native New Yorker, cast her first vote in 1952 for Dwight Eisenhower because "I loved what he had done in the war . . . and that he could use his expertise in managing a war to help manage our country." She graduated from the University of Wisconsin Law School and went to work as an attorney with the antimonopoly division of the Federal Trade Commission. There, as one of the only female litigators, she had a salary lower than her secretary's.[5] Ague brought her experiences as an organizer and a government employee to the Republican desert of Georgia. Member Edna Kinsman was raised in St. Louis, Missouri, and had lived in Toronto, Indianapolis, San Diego, Milwaukee, and Philadelphia before moving to Smyrna. Another founding member, Clara Curtis, was born in New York and lived in Arizona prior to settling in Cobb County. A native Georgian, Marjean Birt spent many years in Pennsylvania before returning to her home state. While in Pennsylvania, Birt first joined the Republican Party and rose to hold several leadership positions in the Erie Council of Republican Women.[6] Unlike others who had spent their lives in the South, these women had lived places with vibrant two-party systems where they had exposure to and, more importantly, experience with the Republican Party. As the group grew, they attracted lifelong southerners, but the founders of the Cobb County Federation overwhelmingly represented new and returning Georgians.[7]

Ague long believed in the power of women as a political force. Before moving to Georgia, she consulted for the fledgling Arkansas Republican Party, reminding the male leadership, "Don't underestimate the importance of womanpower on the precinct level. Women not only have more of the time required to keep the precinct under control than do men, but more often than not prove to be more zealous." Reframing negative gender stereotypes as political strengths, she asserted, "As a gossipy, phone-happy, coffee drinking lot, they are innately better equipped to spread the 'good word' more abundantly."[8] When the Agues settled in Georgia, Lee set about proving that women could build a political party. She argued, "Women are the backbone of the Republican Party," the part that held everything else up.[9] As she grew the women's group in Cobb, Ague continued to emphasize the traits of "womanpower" and expanded the organization through phone trees, coffee meetings, and social events—taking women's traditional spaces and making them training grounds.

While the Cobb County Federation of Republican Women celebrated its victory over road-expansion plans, the national party buzzed over the 1964 primary race for its presidential nominee. The moderate and liberal factions of the GOP, including the Metropolitan Club in Atlanta, supported New York governor Nelson Rockefeller. The conservative wing—including the CCFRW—actively pushed the candidacy of Arizona senator Barry Goldwater. Both men were hawkish on Cold War politics but differed significantly on domestic issues. As governor of New York since 1959, Rockefeller successfully pushed the passage of laws banning discrimination in private housing, promoted affordable housing for poor and often minority citizens, and forced unions to open their ranks to nonwhite members.[10] Goldwater preached a conservatism based in strong national defense with all other powers returned to the states. His 1960 bestseller *The Conscience of a Conservative* offered up Goldwater's conservatism in ten concise chapters. He upheld the constitutional rights of the individual above all else, though his chapter on state's rights asserted, "I deny that there *can* be a conflict between State's Rights, properly defined—and civil rights, properly defined." Goldwater declared, "I am firmly convinced—not only that integrated schools are not required—but that the Constitution does not permit any interference whatsoever by the federal government in the field of education."[11] These lines struck a chord with white southern voters and politicians who had resisted integrating schools since the Supreme Court's 1954 *Brown v. Board of Education* decision. In the midst of the Massive Resistance to school desegregation, Goldwater even visited Georgia in September 1960 to drum up support for Richard Nixon's presidential campaign.[12] Four years later, Goldwater's own candidacy would do a great deal more toward establishing a Republican Party challenge to Democratic dominance in the South.

In 1964, the Georgia Republican Party—like the national party—splintered into moderate and conservative factions. As the Fulton County GOP convention neared, longtime party leaders began to notice a change in the makeup of the Georgia party. In a letter to Atlanta's daily African American newspaper, Dr. Lee R. Shelton, vice president of the Fulton GOP, wrote, "The proportion of Negroes in the Fulton County Republican Party has fallen due largely to a disproportionate increase in the number of white voters. The majority of the new white Republicans were attracted to the party by the Goldwater-type conservatism." He asked newly registered African American voters to come out in support of the GOP with the hopes of defeating the faction that supported states' rights in matters of civil rights.[13] As the Goldwater wing gained traction in Georgia, longtime Republicans, many of them African Americans, began to lose control over their once small party. Long the sole women's club recognized by the national party, even the Metropolitan Club began to feel squeezed by white suburban women who were just finding the GOP through Goldwater's campaign.

A few days before the Fulton County Republican Convention on February 22, 1964, the African American women of the Metropolitan Club announced a planning meeting at Frazier's Café Society. The *Atlanta Daily World* ran a front-page announcement of the club meeting to encourage broad participation. Club women, along with many other of the city's Republicans, worried that an "alien, racist group" threatened to gain control of the state GOP. For years in Georgia, the Republican Party had been the party more likely to support civil rights—or at least not to oppose them violently. As the candidacy of Barry Goldwater loomed, Fulton County Republicans worried that they could lose their political home and their civil rights. Black leaders penned a press release titled "Urgent Plea to Help Save the Republican Party in Georgia." They denounced the Goldwater faction, writing, "we cannot abide in a narrowly based party of the radical right, affected by racism and fanaticism." They called the conservative wing of the party "a threat to our successful, two-party grass roots development." Current and former state and county women's federation leaders added their names to the document.[14]

That year's Fulton County GOP convention was the largest in the organization's history, with nearly fifteen hundred registered delegates present at the Atlanta Municipal Auditorium. Attendees voted 704 to 457 for Goldwater, despite what the *Atlanta Daily World* called the overwhelming opposition of "the large number of Negroes who attended the usually integrated convention." Republican and African American businessman T. M. Alexander explained, "[Goldwater] unfortunately gives the impression that he is not concerned with the aims and aspirations of the Negro people." He continued, "It is no secret . . . that a majority of Negro Republicans and Democrats would favor Gov. Rockefeller." A police officer working at the event noticed the change in the size of the crowd and the composition of the delegates from past years, saying, "I can remember twenty years ago when there were only a handful of participants, but you had Negroes attending." In a compromise, moderate Republicans kept control of the Fulton County Party in exchange for the delegates' votes for Goldwater "until released by the senator." Moderates hoped that Rockefeller would take the lead in the national convention vote and their delegates would be free to vote for him after Goldwater's concession. They saw the Georgia party shifting rightward but hoped that the national party would remain in the center. Locally, some African American Republicans retained positions of leadership in the county organization. Delegates elected eight African American Republicans—including Metropolitan Club members Evelyn Frazier and Lottie Harris—to the thirty-seven-member Executive Committee. While they faced a hard fight, these moderate, longtime Republicans would not surrender their state or their party to Goldwater Republicans.[15]

On July 2, President Lyndon Baines Johnson signed the Civil Rights Act of 1964, legally ending the practice of segregation in public spaces and outlawing discrimination on the basis of race, national origin, religion, and sex. Not two weeks later, Senator Barry Goldwater accepted the Republican nomination for president of the United States. Goldwater had been one of six Republicans to join the southern Democrats in voting against the Civil Rights Act. With Goldwater at the top of the ticket, Georgia was ripe for a Republican revolution, and Lee Ague's CCFRW was one of the few organized conservative GOP groups at the time. Other new party converts might attend local conventions, but Ague knew the deep investments required to maintain momentum.

As the summer of 1964 began, Ague celebrated, noting in the organization's newsletter that "summertime is such a wonderful time for politics." The Cobb County Republican Party opened its headquarters and CCFRW women provided the volunteer labor to keep its doors open. She saw casual meetings of neighbors doing yardwork and backyard cookouts as opportunities for voter education. Every time a woman was outside, she had an opportunity to be a "clothesline philosopher" and bring Republican politics to her neighbors. As women planted their flower and vegetable gardens, she reminded them to "PLANT the seeds of Republicanism and watch them GROW."[16] In autumn, Ague compared political work to the seasonal task of baking apple pie— "To the winning ingredient of Republicanism, add that spice of Republican thought throughout the State, blend well, pop into the oven, and voila!—a unified and responsible voice for all Republican women in Georgia."[17] Using the language of women's domestic work such as laundry, gardening, and cooking, she couched political goals in familiar terms, giving women the message that growing the party took the same type of care as growing flowers. Like those tasks, political work was never done. Clearly, politics was women's work.

Her labor paid off in the summer and fall of 1964. Shortly after Goldwater accepted the Republican nomination, CCFRW membership had swelled from the original ten women in her living room to sixty-three. CCFRW president Ague credited Goldwater's campaign for their numbers and hoped to keep the momentum growing to Election Day and beyond. She did not address the party's earlier factional conflict but kept her tone supportive of Goldwater.

Ague structured the CCFRW to be a social outlet as well as an educational and political group. The Episcopalian Ague adopted evangelism in her political work, telling members, "You reach out with your right hand, get one friend. Bring 'em in. Bring 'em with you to the next meeting. Reach out with your left hand and get a friend.... We'll double and triple our membership." By the time of the November election, the CCFRW claimed 101 members.[18]

The most popular outreach program for the CCFRW was the Two Party Tea Party, so named for its purpose of introducing women from solidly Democratic areas to the message of the Republican Party. Since the GOP had not been an option in most elections in county voters' memory, the CCFRW emphasized educational programming. The name "Tea Party" harkened back to the American Revolution and the image of patriots taking a stand against oppressive government practices. As a familiar event in itself, a tea party could introduce lifetime Democratic women to the Republican Party. Tea parties were also the provenance of women who did not have to go to a workplace, and who likely could employ someone to care for the children while they attended social events.[19] The phrase generated ideas of patriotism, class, and a white woman's social place.

As Ague developed the Two Party Tea Party, she penned instructions for hostesses: "Our ultimate goal is to encourage and ensure the growth of the Two Party System in Georgia." For any concerned hostesses, she assured them, "The name ... is symbolic—and accordingly, the refreshment served doesn't have to be Tea."[20] Whether over tea, coffee, or punch, the themes of patriotism and freedom of voter choice had to be on the program. Two Party Tea Parties became a signature program of the Georgia Federation and Republican campaigns for the next few years.

In building the Cobb County Federation and branding the GOP statewide, Ague emphasized free enterprise and Cold War foreign policy. Even before Goldwater's nomination, Ague used the May 1964 newsletter to remind women to focus on building the two-party system above all else. She argued that the principles of "free enterprise and a strong dynamic of foreign policy" should appeal to "people in all walks of life, regardless of race, color, or creed." She warned further, "Factionalization is Fractionalization.... As a responsible Republican, refuse to write off the vote of any group—any individual—any Republican."[21]

After Goldwater's nomination, the political rhetoric in the state focused on civil rights and integration, but Ague did not rely on that message to grow the party. Of course, Georgians were well aware of Barry Goldwater's opposition to the civil rights bill, but they also knew their own state Democratic leadership's record against the legislation. The only place where Georgians would find support for civil rights was at the top of the ballot with Lyndon Johnson. Otherwise, race was not an overt platform for difference between the state parties. Therefore, the CCFRW packaged their product as anti-communist, free enterprise, and voter choice. State Republicans also hoped to attract voters who had opposed Roosevelt's New Deal and were likely to oppose Johnson's Great Society proposals. Under Goldwater, the southern Republicans attracted voters not only because of his support of states' rights, but also because of his opposition to increased federal programs.

CCFRW campaign activities director Hope Ayo kept members busy. She recruited women to be Victory Girls, who "appear in uniform and escort our candidates to various functions." Victory Girls became a staple of the group for the next few years. The club stressed that the position was open to all women, coaxing that "You do not have to be a beauty queen." Volunteers did have to provide their own uniforms, but any potential Victory Girl could find the fabric and patterns on hold at Wayne's Fabric Store.[22] The navy-blue skirt and blue-and-white-striped vest identified the women as Victory Girls and also as members of the Federation of Republican Women. As the group grew, women also wore these uniforms to general Republican events in addition to candidate rallies. In October 1964, for example, the Victory Girls welcomed Indiana congressman Don Bruce at the Atlanta Airport and took him to his speaking engagement at the Marietta Country Club.[23] Women provided the first impression of the Republican Party both for Georgians and for national party officials. When not in uniforms, members could still identify as Georgia Republicans by wearing—or even selling—elephant charms or "Rain Hats in the plastic elephant case."[24]

The CCFRW grew so rapidly that the national organization created an Exemplary Award to recognize the club in the fall of 1964.[25] The club, not yet a year old, already outnumbered the membership of the rest of Georgia's local federation chapters combined. The Cobb County women knew the entire state could share their success if they just used the same methods. As the women continued to organize their local precincts, Ague set her sights on expanding the GOP throughout Georgia and electing Barry Goldwater in November.

With her local CCFRW club thriving, Ague volunteered to organize the statewide canvass of voters for the Georgia for Goldwater campaign, adopting the slogan, "A Knock on Every Target Door Will Win in '64."[26] As state canvass chair, Ague spread her message and her movement across county lines. In neighboring Douglas County, Katherine Gunnell headed the Draft Goldwater movement early in 1964 and became the co-chair for the county's Goldwater for President Committee. Gunnell's team of six women covered the county and, she boasted, "put our county in the Republican column for the first time."[27]

While Ague emphasized a Goldwater victory, she also worked with other state Republican organizations in order to boost the party's reputation. She and Georgia Republicans coordinated with GOP leaders in other Deep South states to create a strategy to crack the Solid South. She collected training materials from Alabama's MORE (Mobilization of Republican Enterprise) campaign that described the South as "America's Political Opportunity Number 1." The message of that campaign included, "After 100 years of Democratic loyalty, our section is still the poorest in the nation. After 100 years of Democratic loyalty, our schools in the Deep South stand at the bottom. After 100 years of loyalty, the flower of our youth must go North for job opportunities."[28] The materials focused on economic opportunity and building the two-party system without ever mentioning the swirling civil rights struggles. Since Democrats had held local, state, and national seats since Reconstruction, the Democratic Party itself was the target. In framing the struggle as economic and placing the South in a national context, the Republican literature emphasized the South as a vibrant part of the nation rather than arguing for regional exceptionalism. Years before Nixon's southern strategy, southerners launched their own Republican strategy.

Ague recognized her goal as putting "Georgia . . . into the Republican WIN column!" In addition to organizing for Goldwater at the top of the ticket, she and her volunteers spread the word about local and state Republican candidates for office in every district. She told a meeting of Cobb County Republicans, "Even if you are outnumbered by Democrats and lose, it is still vital to lose by as little as possible." Of course, any victory should be by as wide a margin as possible. She trained her volunteers for the long marathon of changing Georgia politics, not merely the sprint to Goldwater. She challenged canvass volunteers to rally the grassroots to vote in numbers that would firmly establish the Republican Party as an undeniable power in Georgia for years to come.[29]

Copying the Two Party Tea Party message she had used so successfully with the CCFRW, Ague stressed that volunteers and voters did not have to be Republicans to vote for Barry Goldwater. The native New Yorker organized what she called a "true Georgia 'Y'all Come'" atmosphere—"If you believe in what we believe in, y'all come!"[30] In Georgia, an outsider spreading conservatism was an organizer, not an agitator. Ague did not expect the state to vote straight-ticket GOP overnight but hoped that Barry Goldwater would simply be the gateway Republican vote for Georgians. Ague later remembered that the 1964 vote "opened the door for them . . . [to] vote Republican because we believe in what Goldwater's saying."[31] The candidate was the crucial factor, but the grassroots organization supporting him in Georgia allowed the enthusiasm to spread like political kudzu through the state. By the November 3 election, Ague's canvassers would reach over three hundred thousand Georgia voters.[32]

In rallying volunteers, Ague stressed the importance of accurate data. The numbers from the canvass determined the strategy for local, state, and national efforts for the Goldwater campaign. Ague selected a canvass chairman in every county targeted by the Goldwater team as well as all other counties with any Republican presence. As is clear from archives of Ague's written communications with them, despite the gendered term, the canvass "chairmen" did not have to be male. County chairmen organized precinct teams of volunteers who tallied the likeliest areas of GOP votes.[33] They were a part of a national effort to elect Goldwater—and this southern state that had not voted Republican in almost a century was being taken seriously by the national office.

Throughout September, Ague traveled to each of Georgia's ten congressional districts to run canvass-volunteer training. In one week, she traveled to Statesboro, Albany, Griffin, Athens, Valdosta, Rome, and Augusta—"zigzagging" the state from north to south and east to west. Volunteers collected weekly data, sending reports back to Ague so she could measure progress and identify any troubling trends. Ague forwarded statewide numbers to the national Goldwater for President office. District and state campaign teams used the weekly updates to strategize. Ague went home to Smyrna as often as possible and took her two children with her when she could. However, as a working mother, she also relied on her husband and employed a maid to assist in caring for the family.[34]

Training for canvass volunteers in every district started on September 16 —the deadline for new voter registration. Ague and her team shifted focus from registering new voters to educating existing voters about the Republican ticket.[35] Ague encouraged door-to-door canvassing rather than telephone contact. She led training for Republican district chairmen in canvass management and volunteer recruitment, and suggested that the chairmen identify recruiters who were involved in other community volunteer work. Good prospects and places to find them, she wrote, included "the PTA, church circles, doctors' wives, engineers' wives, lawyers' wives, bowling leagues, etc." Volunteers went out in pairs armed with a map, a card file of registered voters, precinct reporting sheets, and a flashlight. They took note of all "brass collar Democrats" so no one else would waste time on those who could not be led away. Canvass pairs went up and down a street, knocking on doors and marking down names of the "GOLDWATER VIPs—the Goldwater Voters in the Precinct." If no one answered, the volunteers left a card with the district chairman's contact information in case the voter had questions, needed a ride to vote, or wanted to volunteer. The door-to-door work ended in the final week of October. Volunteers dedicated the five days before the election to compiling telephone lists of Goldwater voters, each of whom would get a call from a GOP canvasser on Monday, November 2, or on Election Day, November 3. Wanting no surprises, Ague pushed her team to identify every Goldwater voter and then to confirm that each one would make it to the polls.[36]

In early October, Ague was astonished to learn about trouble in the Ninth District, even though Cherokee County ran in the high-sixtieth percentile for Goldwater.[37] Jack Prince was the Goldwater chairman and also the district's Republican candidate for the U.S. House of Representatives. A young professor named Newt Gingrich managed Prince's campaign. A month earlier, Ague asked Gingrich to combine the canvass efforts of the Goldwater and the Prince campaigns. Gingrich, however, asserted that Prince would outpoll Goldwater, thereby offering to allow Goldwater to ride on the congressional candidate's coattails. Worrying Gingrich had not trained his volunteers well, Ague kept her own team.[38] Gingrich's boast turned out to be hot air. Ague's numbers proved correct: Goldwater carried the district while Prince lost in a wave of split-ticket voting. Ague succeeded, however, in establishing a new chapter of the GFRW in the Gainesville home of Mrs. Jack Prince and reported ten new Republican women ready to grow another club in the Ninth District.[39]

While the CCFRW turned to economic language to support Republican candidates, elsewhere voters confronted civil rights. African American organizers were determined to get more voters to the polls. In 1964, the Georgia Voters League, NAACP, Southern Christian Leadership Conference, and Student Nonviolent Coordinating Committee ran registration drives to sign up African American voters throughout the state. African American Republican leader John H. Calhoun reported that, as of mid-May 1964, approximately 275,000 African Americans were registered to vote in the state, representing about one-fifth of the state's total voters. In 1956, only 157,000 African American Georgians had registered. Calhoun's Statewide Registration Committee reported, "With a majority population in some 30 to 40 counties, increased citizenship education at both local and state levels will make the Negro votes more potent."[40] It was clear that many Georgia counties maintained practices—legal or not—that effectively excluded African Americans from elections.

The conservative white leadership that had recently taken over the Georgia Republican Party did not recognize African Americans as important potential voters, despite the integrated history of the GOP in Georgia. In the final week of the canvass, Wilcox County for Goldwater chairman Ralph Sutton reported that his team had polled 2,348 voters, with 2,263 declaring for Goldwater and only 175 for Johnson. He added, "This does not include 413 Negroes."[41] In Wilkinson County, located in central Georgia with a significant African American population, canvasser Carolyn Wynn Smalley reported that the county seat, Irwinton, had 450 Goldwater voters, 100 for Johnson, and 50 undecideds. No other part of the county was even that close, except perhaps Bethel, which she did not count since it was "All Negro."[42] In northeastern Clarke County, Mrs. Lee Wash reported her numbers with the understanding that "this is allowing for not contacting Negro voters and for the very large number of voters for which we can find no telephone or street listing."[43] White canvassers discounted African American voices easily because they did not expect those votes to count on November 3. The passage of the Civil Rights Act of 1964, they assumed, would increase African American voting just as much as schools had desegregated in the decade since the Supreme Court decreed it—negligibly, if at all.

In southern Clinch County, the canvass chair reported "1,100–1,200" of the county's "1,700–1,800" votes would go for Goldwater as of October 14. With just four days before the election, the county's Goldwater for President organization planned a "fish fry . . . at which time we will have as our main speaker the Hon. Marvin Griffin, former Governor of Georgia."[44] A staunch segregationist, Griffin broke with the national Democratic Party in order to support Goldwater. Most other state Democratic leaders remained loyal and did not endorse Barry Goldwater. Neither did they endorse Lyndon Johnson. Most notably absent from Johnson's Georgia campaign were the state's popular Democratic U.S. senators, Herman Talmadge and Richard Russell, neither of whom campaigned for either presidential candidate.[45] State Senator Jimmy Carter pleaded with the powerful Russell to make appearances on Johnson's behalf, but Russell went on a European vacation instead. Later, Russell refused the First Lady's request that he accompany her during a campaign visit to Georgia. Russell did release a letter stating his intent to vote a straight Democratic ticket, but he did little beyond that.[46]

CCFRW women sponsored a booth at the Cobb County Fair in September. They distributed "buttons, balloons, bumper stickers, bottle caps, and brochures" for Goldwater as well as all local and state Republican candidates. CCFRW organizer Hope Ayo reported, "The Democrats had a booth close to us and it was an encouraging sight to see their booth so deserted." She celebrated that they "showed the people of Cobb County in a big way that the Republicans are here to stay!"[47] Wearing their blue-and-white uniforms, the Victory Girls strolled throughout the fairgrounds introducing candidates, distributing information, and building excitement every night. While they increased recognition for the candidates, the easily identifiable uniforms also branded the Georgia Federation of Republican Women.

More and more younger women volunteered as Goldwater Girls. Many of them not old enough to vote, they were part of the national effort to excite conservative American youth. Goldwater Girls dressed identically all across the nation. They wore navy-blue or yellow skirts, white button-down shirts, and a gold kerchief and cowboy hat to play up the Western identity of the candidate. The kerchief was tied on the right to emphasize the conservative leanings of Goldwater.[48] At the Cobb County Fair, the Goldwater Girls sang every night, like the mythical sirens pulling voters to their booth to learn more about the new Georgia GOP.[49]

White girls had long been a rallying symbol for Civil Rights opponents. In the 1957 Little Rock Central High School desegregation battle, opponents distributed pins showing the silhouette of a teenaged white girl followed by a National Guardsman pointing a bayonet at her back.[50] In the era of Jim Crow, protection of white women from African American men served as the justification for countless murders and other acts of violence against African American men.[51] The presence of the young, white Goldwater Girls served as a not-so-subtle reminder of that historic connection between beliefs about both white female purity and African Americans.

As head of the state canvass, Ague regularly examined the data to determine which of Georgia's 159 counties to target. She looked for high population and voter turnout. Her volunteers examined files of the Georgia secretary of state to identify counties likely to vote for GOP candidates. Using the data from past elections and current registrations, she identified a target number of Republican votes required for each county to land Goldwater in the win column.[52] Ague condensed the information to one sheet per county and distributed her advice and clear goals to her canvass coordinators. Through her meticulousness and her growing knowledge and experience, she reduced the lofty goal of making Georgia a truly two-party state down to easily understood plans and steps. Ague's ability to combine strategic vision with tactical know-how was invaluable to the volunteers setting out to educate and persuade voters, and to the party.

Even while it was imperative to achieve short-term victories, in counties that remained heavily Democratic, volunteers still pushed for Republican gains. In Clarke County, a woman reported that the "figures do not approach the assigned quota for this county," but that "we have a definite organized Republican Party in Clarke County now and that it is an organization which can be built upon for future use."[53] While one Georgia for Goldwater slogan was "Why Not Victory?," some county organizers found a real victory in getting a Republican Party established at all. If they could not win in 1964, then at least they would lay a foundation for 1966 and 1968. Even while Ague strategized to keep voters and volunteers in the GOP column for the upcoming election, she was—along with others—articulating and pursuing a long-term vision.

Across the South, prominent lifelong Democrats began switching to the Republican Party, attracted by Goldwater's local-control conservatism, which contrasted sharply with Lyndon Johnson's civil rights and Great Society programs. Perhaps the most famous Southern Democratic Party defector was South Carolina senator Strom Thurmond, who declared his allegiance to "the Goldwater Republican Party" in September 1964. Thurmond warned that if the Democrats did win the election, "freedom as we have known it in this country is doomed, and individuals will be destined to lives of regulation, control, coercion, intimidation, and subservience to a power elite who shall rule from Washington."[54] Importantly, Thurmond declared his allegiance to the party of Goldwater, indicating that he—and the South—could just as easily switch again if moderates regained control.

Closer to home, south Georgia's former congresswoman Iris F. Blitch declared her own support of Barry Goldwater. The Homerville, Georgia, housewife first won election to the state legislature in 1946 as a Talmadge Democrat. In 1954, she squeaked out a victory in the Democratic primary—the only election that mattered then—and left her Clinch County home to represent Georgia's Eighth District in the U.S. Congress.[55] She served four terms until her retirement for health reasons in 1962. In office, Blitch was a strong anticommunist and segregationist. When she pledged her support for Goldwater, Blitch said the Republican presidential candidate was the only one to offer people "a choice between a more and more centralized state and the complete dignity of the individual." The former Democratic national committeewoman continued, "Had there been any place else to go, I would have left the Democratic Party long ago." Finally, Blitch pledged, "From this day forward, my political allegiance will be with the Republican Party."[56]

Blitch even declared her interest in running for the Republican nomination for her former U.S. House seat in 1964, but the party chairman of the Eighth District had no interest. By the time Blitch expressed her aspiration in September, a district official maintained, "It's too late to raise all that money and begin getting five per cent of the names of voters on a petition" needed to get her name on the ballot.[57] That year, no Republican opposed the Democrat in the Eighth District. Leaders instead directed their energies toward the presidential campaign. Georgia's Republican women, for the time, would focus on getting men elected rather than running themselves.

By the week before the election, Lee Ague's team of canvassers had contacted 267,795 likely voters and determined that 152,592, or 57 percent of them, pledged for Goldwater. More voters claimed to be undecided than were

Johnson voters—59,906 to 50,009.[58] Ague reported, "In my travels through-out Georgia as State Canvass Chairman, I have found an overwhelming sentiment for the Republican ticket. However, sentiment and feeling do not win elections. Ballots do!"[59] Days before the November 3 election, she outlined Operation Win, which consisted of three straightforward goals:

1. Find the Goldwater voters
2. Get the voters to the polls
3. Count those Goldwater ballots

She shifted the canvassing volunteers onto the "vote-getting crew" that would observe the polls and make sure their confirmed Goldwater voters showed up.[60] Rallying her core of women volunteers, Ague emphasized, *"We Can Win With Womanpower!"*[61]

The NFRW offered incentives to members who volunteered time canvassing for votes. The "inner-circle pin" went to any woman who gave one hundred hours to door-to-door canvassing for voter registrations, votes, or campaign donations. As additional incentive for Georgia Republican women introducing the GOP to a Democratic state, Ague personally offered a five-dollar award for the "most interesting or most humorous story of your canvassing efforts." Women who stayed home could earn the black-and-gold "live-wire pin" for a hundred phone calls. Two hundred calls earned the "gold-finish pin." Any member who hosted a Two Party Tea Party that introduced at least twenty women to the Republican Party was eligible for the NFRW's special "party-giver pin." The Cobb County group planned an awards banquet the next month, an evening dinner at the Marietta Country Club where the husbands could join in celebrating their wives' commitment to the new GOP.[62]

Ague asked her trusted friend and CCFRW officer Clara Curtis to serve as state Election Day chairman, organizing the efforts to make sure all the identified Goldwater voters made it to the polls. Curtis organized local telephone committees and Victory Squads to provide rides to the precincts. The final days of the statewide canvass involved hundreds of thousands of phone calls to identified Goldwater voters. On Monday, November 2, volunteers called each Goldwater voter with a reminder of the polling place location. The afternoon of Election Day, November 3, voters received a follow-up call to confirm they had voted and had not had any trouble doing so. Those who had not voted by 4:30 p.m. received a personal visit from a member of the Victory Squad, who would remind citizens of the importance of voting and offer an immediate ride, babysitter, or both in order to get another Goldwater vote counted by the 7:00 p.m. closing time. Wanting to keep women on the phones or monitoring the polls, Ague suggested that Victory Squads consist of students participating after school or men who could leave work early.[63] Electing Republicans would be a family affair.

Once they got the voters to the polls, Goldwater supporters had to ensure that the votes were counted. The GFRW was on the lookout for any fraud. Days before the election, one volunteer reported, "We have found an alarming number of dead persons" still on the voter lists of Clarke County.[64] Having learned the history of voter fraud in Georgia, Ague emphasized the final component in Operation Win: "After the polls close, then be sure the ballots are properly counted. Don't depend on somebody else to do this." Ague advised county and district GOP volunteers to assign "ballot security officers on duty at the polls so that there are no irregularities in polling."[65] Every precinct had one assigned ballot-security monitor to report irregularities to the district ballot-security officer. Ague reminded volunteers to be aware of absentee ballots as potential sources of fraud. In order to get a fair election, she stressed that every Republican volunteer must ensure "that every step in handling, counting, tabulating, and reporting election be watched."[66] Georgia Goldwater campaign chairman Ralph Ivey encouraged, "Assure honest election with honest count."[67] Ague emphasized, "election frauds occur when no one watches!"[68] Working her home precinct in Cobb County, Clara Curtis perched herself on the ballot box, white go-go boots swinging, and told the precinct chairman she would accompany him and the ballot box to lunch if he tried to take it. When the ballots were counted, that precinct went for Goldwater.[69]

The day after the election, the *Atlanta Constitution* headline blared, "Republican Captures State for First Time." Though Goldwater lost the national election, he won the state and the local headlines. The newspaper's political commentator Reg Murphy wrote, "Sen. Barry Goldwater won Georgia and smashed a century-old tradition Tuesday." Of the metro Atlanta counties, DeKalb went for Goldwater while Fulton went for Johnson. Nearly all the white vote in Fulton went to Goldwater. Murphy reported that a record "81.8 per cent of the Negro registration in Fulton turned out" and that "virtually all of the 48,700 Negroes voted for Johnson."[70]

In addition to Georgia, Barry Goldwater carried four other Deep South states and his home state of Arizona. Despite the national loss, Georgia Republicans celebrated a major victory. Ague recorded that Goldwater carried 111 of the 159 counties, resulting in a 53.9 percent Goldwater tally. In 1960, Republican candidate Richard Nixon had won only 37.4 percent of the state's votes.[71] She wrote, "This is what we had all been working for. This was the mandate 616,000 Georgia voters gave the Republican Party. This was VICTORY!"[72] She did not even mention the fact that their candidate had actually lost the national election. Even Barry Goldwater recognized the significance of the state's vote and thanked Ague for her efforts while celebrating the cause of creating a two-party system in Georgia.[73]

Women of the Third District had the most to celebrate. Not only had their district voted for Goldwater, but they also elected Howard H. "Bo" Callaway as the first Georgia Republican sent to Congress since Reconstruction. While Goldwater carried the Third District by 62.7 per cent, enough voters stayed with the party down the ticket so that 57.2 per cent voted for Callaway. Bo Callaway joined a Republican freshman class with other new Deep South party switchers from Alabama and Mississippi. They joined Virginia, North Carolina, Florida, and Tennessee in sending Republican representatives to Congress.[74] The women's Republican strategy for the South was already underway. Four years later, Nixon's more widely recognized "southern strategy" in his 1968 presidential campaign would follow the trail Ague, Curtis, and so many other Georgia women blazed.

Callaway ran on the slogan "Strength for Georgia" and set five goals for his congressional term: "The repeal of the Civil Rights Bill; The return of the right of voluntary prayer to our schools; A fair and effective farm program; A foreign policy based on strength and not weakness; and The establishment of an effective two party system in the state."[75] He warned third-district voters that congressmen, especially freshmen, voted with their party leadership. Although southern Democrats had opposed the Civil Rights Act of 1964, Callaway still linked the unpopular bill to the national party. Bo Callaway also rode on the Republican coattails of Barry Goldwater, who had famously opposed the Civil Rights Act, while Democratic candidates had to walk careful lines between state and national party platforms.[76]

Offering an alternative to the nearly century-long tradition of Democratic representation, Callaway continued, "The time has come when the South can no longer follow the leadership that spurns us. The Republicans want us. The National Democrat Party has kicked us in the face." Voting Republican would strengthen the South's political standing, he said, because the Democrats would fight to keep voters and the Republicans would fight to take them: "We will be in the best bargaining position of our lives." By playing the national parties off one another, Callaway told voters that the South would win "more industry, more water development, a stronger highway system which we badly need."[77] In addition to opposing the Civil Rights Act, Callaway provided another convincing argument for voters to follow his move to the Republican Party.

Immediately after the November election, Lee Ague set about converting Goldwater clubs into active Federation of Republican Women chapters. First, though, she had to replace the moderate white and African American Republicans of the existing GFRW leadership. Ague set up a rival GFRW and appealed to the national organization to recognize the new group as the true state organization.

Ague organized a statewide meeting of conservative GFRW clubs for November 23, 1964, just weeks after Goldwater's Georgia victory, setting the stage for a showdown among the party women's leadership. The previous leadership had kept the state federation so small, she maintained, that it had not even existed in Cobb County, which now led the state in membership. Two of the officers, including outgoing GFRW president Rita Creson, were not members of local clubs. Ague criticized the GFRW leadership, saying, "Although Republican activity was at its peak in Georgia in 1964, the Federation did nothing to increase its membership or to encourage new clubs."[78] She did not mention that the GFRW leadership had earlier supported Nelson Rockefeller and hoped that Goldwater would eventually lose the nomination. Unsurprisingly, these old-guard Republican women did not actively organize for the very conservative Goldwater's campaign.

To disguise the racial politics and draw attention away from the turn to the right, leaders of new GFRW clubs began to gripe about inefficiency in the state leadership. Nancy Stephens of the new Clayton County FRW sent her club's dues, membership, and by-laws to Creson, but "never even received the courtesy of a reply." Ague accused the old GFRW leadership of wanting to keep power in a few hands. While she claimed that "the rift came, not as a result of an ideological split ... but rather as an outgrowth of frustration," she also accused the leadership of not working "for the Republican Party's nominee."[79] She drew the lines for a months-long battle for the title of official GFRW.[80]

Officers of Republican women's clubs all over Georgia withdrew from the existing GFRW in order to affiliate with Ague's "newly formed Georgia Federation of Republican Women." Some sent notice of their change of affiliation to NFRW president Dorothy (Dottie) Elston. The president of the Muscogee County FRW charged that the old GFRW had held a meeting "illegally called and illegally conducted" and had refused representation to qualified delegates. Muscogee withdrew and rejoined under Ague's rival GFRW, "which we believe to be the true and legal representative of the Republican Women of Georgia."[81] Mrs. Hallie M. Kendall from the south Atlanta suburb of College Park wrote Elston to express support for Ague's breakaway group: "Since the Republicans won in Georgia, I hope we can go on from there. But, this enthusiasm will die a-borning without the proper leadership and organization."[82] Ague's record on the Goldwater campaign had demonstrated her qualifications. Women from the county federations of Cherokee, Jefferson, Hall, Gwinnett, Douglas, and Richmond, in addition to other local clubs, contacted Lee Ague directly to let her know of their decision to join her organization. She forwarded their national dues of ten cents per person to the NFRW, as if she already operated the official state federation.[83]

With so many clubs seceding from the old to join the new, Ague's faction became the only one that could meet the NFRW qualifications of clubs in 75 percent of the state. Stepping in to mediate, NFRW president Dorothy Elston called for a reorganization meeting of the Georgia Federation to be held on February 20, 1965. The NFRW temporarily suspended recognition of both GFRW factions. NFRW second vice president and southern regional coordinator of NFRW Constance Armitage oversaw the meeting of over two hundred Georgia Republican women. A year earlier, Ague supported both Elston and Armitage in their NFRW campaigns, predicting their term would bring two years of "GOProductivity" for southern growth.[84]

Attendees at the state reorganization meeting wrote new by-laws. They agreed to a statewide convention a couple of weeks later at which members would vote on the by-laws and new officers. GFRW could then reapply for national recognition. To prevent any last-minute effort to swing votes, only groups chartered and recognized by NFRW by February 15, 1965, would be able to vote in elections for new officers.[85] Ague tossed her hat in the ring for GFRW president with the campaign promise that "by the end of 1965, our State membership will exceed 2,000." However, she warned that if "the 'do-nothings' . . . regain control . . . we will surely lose the gains we made in 1964, and slide to defeat in 1965 and 1966."[86]

White conservative women planted local groups all over Georgia before the February deadline. In north Georgia, the Lookout Mountain FRW reported seventy-five members when it applied for club status in January 1965. The Atlanta suburb of Tucker reported fifty charter members. Neighboring Gwinnett County began with twenty-five women while Troup and Coweta counties reported numbers in the thirties.[87]

In an important coming-out moment for the Republican women, *Atlanta Constitution* writer Reg Murphy dedicated an entire column to the GFRW feud. He announced, "The hair-pulling is almost over in the Georgia Federation of Republican Women. The newcomers have won. The women who formed the group back in 1956 have lost and know it." Despite the exclusion of old-guard members from any leadership positions, an anonymous Atlanta GFRW founder assured Murphy, "We will remain in the federation. We have worked for it since 1956—and we remain Republicans." Murphy reported Ague's likely victory as just another conservative triumph in a region that seemed to be shifting not only away from the Democratic Party, but specifically toward what he identified as "Goldwater-oriented Republicans." The real victors, though, according to Murphy, were the "long-suffering husbands" who now might be able to enjoy "warm dinners" once their wives returned from battle.[88] Despite reducing the women to negative stereotypes of hair-pulling, squabbling, husband-starving women, Murphy ultimately acknowledged the rising political power of Georgia's GOP women.

Atlanta's Fulton County FRW perhaps walked the most challenging line. The African American founders of the Metropolitan Club lived in Fulton. Membership across the county had nearly doubled from thirty-six before the elections to seventy-one by February 1965. While other local federations were just forming, the Fulton club established a History Committee to record their club's achievements of the past decade. In between state meetings of the new and old GFRW, the Fulton County FRW inaugurated its own newsletter, *GOPeople*. The board chose that name to represent the many members of their club, for "without you, our people, we would have no ties and no splits, no reason for being, no growth, nor even our Republican Party." President Nancy Geiger carefully recognized the contributions of each faction—founding and growth—alongside the reality of the splits occurring within the group at that moment. Geiger called for unity and respect for the sake of the party: "We have gotten this far not by independent action alone, but by independent action teamed with full cooperation and communication. Our right hand and left hand must work in one accord." As the old GFRW battled with the new, Fulton County Republican women hoped that conservatives and moderates would learn to work together for the sake of the party.[89]

Former GFRW president Mrs. W. C. (Ruby) LeShanna of Fulton County lamented the fractured state of the organization and lashed out at the movement to reorganize the group: "Splinter organizations are destructive influences and can only result in decay of the moral fiber of our party." Sensationalistic stories like Reg Murphy's in state newspapers particularly frustrated her as she explained, "Differences may certainly be aired in meetings, but when we emerge we must be united and pledged to promote the Republican cause." She hoped for healing and encouraged that the GFRW "must solidify itself and be broad based enough to be inclusive without being exclusive." She reminded moderates to continue working for the future of the party: "How can we rebuild our party nationally and maintain the great strides we have made in the south?"[90]

Clara Curtis headed up the Lee Ague for President Committee.[91] Ague ran on the slogan "Let Us Build" and set the goal of "a concrete structure of trained Republican womanpower throughout the state of Georgia, ready, willing, and educated to serve as needed."[92] Curtis sent a letter to all existing state federations, asking, "Why shouldn't there be a Women's federation in each county? If anyone can bring this about, Lee Ague can."[93] Most of the clubwomen already believed in her promise since she had organized them just a few months earlier.

Conservative Republican organizers within the state assumed Ague had enough support to win, but did not want to take any chances. Keeping the momentum of conservative victory rolling, they planned a dinner with Barry Goldwater for the evening after the GFRW reorganization meeting. Fliers reminded women, "Many of your husbands will be interested in attending the Columbus meeting and staying until Saturday night," when a couple could join Barry Goldwater for dinner with a fifty-dollar donation. With such incentive, a husband might not object to his wife spending a weekend away from home and, indeed, might even join her.[94] Even Rep. Bo Callaway came to the GFRW meeting and addressed the audience. He, too, stayed for dinner with Goldwater the next night and sat at the head table—the Georgia party's only elected representative in the federal government sitting alongside the man whose coattails he had ridden.[95]

On March 6, 1965, the factions of the GFRW gathered in Columbus. As in any good showdown, the vote happened at noon. That morning, Ague supporters caucused at the nearby Martinique Motel to strategize and then enter the meeting as a united front. Ague's strategy worked, and the newest clubs of the GFRW had enough votes to elect her their new state president. The relatively new Georgian and Goldwater organizer beat her more centrist Republican opponent and former GFRW president, Halcyon Bell, by a decisive 77–14 in the only contested election on the slate. Mrs. Bootsie Calhoun of Augusta became first vice president. Virginia Estes of Columbus accepted the position of second vice president, with Kathryn Dunaway of Atlanta as third vice president.[96] All the new officers were white women from the conservative and pro-Goldwater slate. In appreciation of her service, the Cobb County Federation presented Lee Ague with a gold charm in the shape of Georgia. The Republican outsider had quickly become an insider and influencer in Georgia politics.[97]

Vastly outnumbered, African American women found themselves without a political home. Mary Ruth King, a delegate from the African American Metropolitan Club of the GFRW, rose to ask for clarification of the word "conservative" and spoke about "what can and should be done to help with the Negro vote." There followed a "very good discussion" in which "almost everyone" participated, though it did not alter the all-white leadership of the organization.[98] The minutes do not specify what any of the proposals were, nor who spoke in the conversation. Back in Atlanta, Mary Ruth King and her Metropolitan Club colleagues continued to negotiate the ever-narrowing path of being African American, Republican, and women in Georgia.

Prior to the 1964 campaign season, the GFRW had only fifteen clubs in eleven counties. In the year since the CCFRW stopped the road project in Smyrna, the Georgia Federation of Republican Women had grown to include over fifteen hundred members in sixty-nine clubs in forty-one counties. The GFRW took forty women from Georgia to the NFRW meeting in April 1965—up from ten women the year before. They networked with Republican women from all over the nation and showed off Georgia with door-prize donations, including a week's vacation at Jekyll Island, flight bags from Eastern and Delta Airlines, peanuts, pecans, and five hundred "See Rock City" birdhouses.[99] They had established the Republican Party as a contender in Georgia elections. Now they had to convince national Republicans that Georgia's success was not just a blip on the GOP radar. With a state win in the presidential race, a Georgia Republican in congress, and hundreds of new party members across the state, the GFRW looked forward to the 1966 midterm elections.

CHAPTER 2

The Go Bo Girls

The 1964 Republican victories in Georgia made Lee Ague excited about the future. As always, she reminded GFRW members that they could not rest: "1966 is such an important year for the Republican Party. It will take all of us to make it a victorious year." She hoped for more congressional seats—and the governor's mansion most of all. Upon assuming leadership of the GFRW, Lee Ague set the goal of establishing a chapter in each of the state's 159 counties—even deep into the rural Democratic strongholds.[1] With the county-unit system abolished, each vote counted. Even a handful of voters in staunchly Democratic rural counties could help elect a Republican governor.

Still, the challenge loomed: Would southerners cast Republican votes without Barry Goldwater? Certainly, Goldwater's anti–Civil Rights Bill vote had won him the support of many southerners. White Georgia Democrats opposed civil rights measures at least as much as Barry Goldwater had, but how would the women define a difference between a Georgia Republican and a Georgia Democrat? This time, the Georgia GOP had to prove that it had loyal Republican voters and not just white-backlash reactionary votes. The best way to demonstrate that it was a permanent force and not a blip was to run a homegrown candidate and win the highest office in the state.

In preparation, women worked through 1965 to craft the southern Republican message, distinct from the traditional pro-segregation message of southern Democrats. To achieve this, Georgia GOP women shifted the rhetoric of southern politics away from race and toward gender. Rather than overtly opposing segregation, they promoted a mother's need to be involved in her child's neighborhood school. The desired effect was still segregation, but the more genteel language allowed white moderates to imagine they were keeping some distance from rabble rousers. Hostesses of ladies' teas looked for voters who would support bake sales, not scream obscenities at schoolhouses.[2]

In suburban Atlanta, the Toco Hills FRW encouraged members to continue hosting Two Party Tea Parties and "invite Republican *and* Democrat women." They also reminded women not to wait for potential party converts to come to them. "The best way to get to know voters is 'knock on doors,'" Toco Hills FRW president Dot Holmes wrote. She warned, though, "Do not contact voters you know are staunch Democrats as we do not want them aroused from their hoped for apathy." The GOP had momentum and womanpower on its side and Holmes reminded the members of their secret weapons: "A friendly greeting and smile will be remembered long after the election and YOU are represent- ing the Republican Party at all times."[3]

In northwest Atlanta, the Cobb County FRW announced an award for the woman who registered the most new Republican voters. Campaign Activities Director Hope Ayo advised, "Register your friend, the couple down the street, the newcomers to the neighborhood, the teenager who just turned 18."[4] In Ful- ton, the county FRW asked their members that February to remember Abra- ham Lincoln's birthday "with a big, fat present—*A New Member!*"[5] Potential Republican voters were, it seemed, everywhere, if the women would just go find them.

In addition to recruiting new members and expanding the party base, the GFRW increased its scope. In February 1965, North Fulton FRW president Kath- ryn Dunaway traveled to Washington, D.C., to testify against disarmament with other NFRW members. Dunaway greeted the Senate Foreign Relations Committee, chaired by Arkansas Democrat William Fulbright, with "saluta- tions from the deep South and from that state, which after 100 years, voted Re- publican again for Barry Goldwater."[6] An Atlanta housewife, Dunaway might not have been an obvious choice to testify before the senators. However, she asserted that the Senate hearing was indeed the proper place for "a mother, a grandmother, and a conservative . . . dreadfully frightened with the trend of Socialism I find in our government." Credentials established, Dunaway con- tinued, "While the U.S. is unilaterally disarming, Russia is building up her nu- clear weapons."[7]

Like many of the newest Georgia Republican women, Kathryn Dunaway was a converted Democrat. Previously, she had volunteered on her husband John's successful 1940 campaign for the Georgia House of Representatives, where he was a member of the Democratic majority. She proudly said that she had voted in "each and every election since 1928," making her part of Georgia's first generation of women voters. Dunaway changed her party affiliation to Republican in 1960, the same year her youngest son graduated from college. A new empty-nester, Dunaway immersed herself in Georgia's emerging Repub- lican scene. In 1963, she founded the North Fulton Federation of Republican Women and set about planting six more local affiliates around the Atlanta suburbs.[8]

During her trip to Washington, Kathryn Dunaway befriended Phyllis Schlafly, one of the rising stars of the conservative wing of the Republican Party and the first vice president of the NFRW. Schlafly testified before the Senate Foreign Relations Committee the day after Dunaway. Schlafly had written a defense of Barry Goldwater, *A Choice Not an Echo*, a bestseller among the Republican Right. Taking its title from a line in Goldwater's announcement of his candidacy, *A Choice Not an Echo* criticized Eastern establishment Republicans for putting forth moderate candidates and neglecting the conservative wing of the party. By the November 1964 election, her book had sold 3.5 million copies and Schlafly had earned fame within conservative circles.[9] Dunaway's friendship with Schlafly connected Georgia's emerging Republican women's organization to the leaders of national conservative circles.

While Kathryn Dunaway became Schlafly's closest ally in Georgia, many more GFRW members also read and repeated Schlafly's far-right rhetoric. Following the success with *A Choice Not an Echo*, Schlafly coauthored *The Gravediggers*, a hawkish warning that while Lyndon Johnson and his administration disarmed the United States, communists gained ground. She cautioned that the Johnson administration's civil rights advances mirrored the agenda of communist appeasement. *The Gravediggers* sold over two million copies. Dunaway cited the book as the source of many of the facts she offered in her Senate testimony.[10]

A copy of *The Gravediggers* also found its way to the president of the Troup County FRW in west Georgia. The club newsletter warned, "It is plain to see that the South is going to be punished for rejecting Lyndon Johnson. The voting rights Bill is the first of the reprisals."[11] The newsletter exemplified the burgeoning right wing within the party, blasting, "Wanted . . . young mothers to take time off from 'Hauling Children' to join the Republican women of Troup County to help assure your child a free country." Fighting the Cold War became just as much a mother's job as carpooling. Taking away any excuses for women not to attend the next meeting, the newsletter promised that "we'll have unsweetened grapefruit juice for all on the new diet." The women could fight communism, save their children, and maintain their figures, all at the same meeting.[12]

When Kathryn Dunaway returned from Washington, she went on a speaking tour to GFRW chapters, repeating her anti-disarmament testimony. "While the U.S. is pouring out billions of dollars in foreign aid," she warned, "more and more of these nations are siding with the communist bloc." Dunaway cautioned women to listen carefully, even in church, for messages of a "peace offensive," which she said was code for disarmament. In these engagements, she not only educated women about Cold War foreign policy, but also exemplified what a dedicated GFRW member could accomplish.[13]

After her tour of local clubs, Kathryn Dunaway won election as third vice president of the Georgia Federation of Republican Women under Lee Ague's presidency. Dunaway added a grandmotherly voice to the gendered fight against domestic and foreign policies. Eventually, her friendship with Schlafly and her commitment to the farthest-right wing of the GOP would lead her away from the GFRW. However, in 1965, Dunaway was still a rising force in the organization.

Whether women were forcefully hawkish or demurely hawkish, the language of politics as a mother's duty pervaded GFRW circles. While the Troup County FRW and Dunaway's own North Fulton organization embraced fearmongering language akin to Schlafly's, most organizations maintained a more toned-down message to invite all women into the clubs. The Cherokee County FRW invited prospective members to a women's activities workshop led by Lee Ague and Mike Hudson, executive director of the Georgia GOP. They encouraged women to get involved: "As an outside 'diversion' or 'recreation' or 'hobby', and certainly as a DUTY, we highly recommend it!"[14] Whether testifying before the Senate Foreign Relations Committee or answering phones at the local GOP headquarters, Georgia women defined motherhood as a political sphere. The "duty" of citizenship overlapped the duties of family. Conservative women defined their activism according to family roles, laying the groundwork for what would develop in the next decade into a gendered politics of the New Right.

While building the Georgia GOP base, Republican women also worked across state lines to secure a strong two-party system across the Deep South. Georgia clubs collected clothes and money for their Republican sisters in Louisiana hit by Hurricane Betsy. Georgia and South Carolina women co-hosted the Deep South federation clubs meeting in the fall of 1965. The program featured NFRW national leaders in a "Womanpower Swap Shop" of organizing ideas. South Carolina senator and leading Republican convert Strom Thurmond delivered the keynote address.[15]

Lee Ague led workshops in Mississippi and Louisiana for the NFRW Countdown to 1966 campaign in addition to the panel on women's activities at a southern campaign managers training. Ague reported that she had created short films for clubs in Mississippi and Louisiana to take around for training purposes after her visit had ended. Ague continued to prove herself a savvy, though unpaid, political strategist who showed other southern states how to copy her award-winning success at growing a state party via a women's organization.[16] That year, Ague reported that she had traveled "more than 25,000 miles" in 1965, growing the GFRW within the state and representing Georgia at national meetings in New York, Colorado, and Washington, D.C.[17]

The work of growing clubs and building interstate networks laid the foundation of Ague's more ambitious goal of a Republican win in the 1966 gubernatorial race. The race was wide open and 1966 would be the first statewide campaign since the Goldwater victory. Georgia Republicans saw their chance, not just to elect a governor, but also to set the state's political agenda, grow the party, and win the state for another Republican presidential candidate in 1968.

Republicans had no clear candidate early on, but the women did not let that slow their momentum. The most prominent Georgia Republican was Congressman Bo Callaway, but leaders had to decide if they should risk losing a congressional seat for a chance at the top position. Callaway had served in Congress for just a year and had built a strong anti-Johnson record—voting against the Voting Rights Act of 1965, a minimum wage increase, and other Great Society programs.

In addition to having no clear candidate, the regionally young party lacked deep pockets. Lee Ague understood that the party's lack of funds opened an opportunity for women. As GFRW president, she committed the members to collecting statewide public-opinion survey data. The women's reports went to the Republican-leaning John H. Friend Company in Mobile, Alabama, for analysis. They measured name recognition for likely Democratic contenders as well as potential Republican entrants to determine where the GOP should focus its resources for the greatest effect.

While the women's volunteerism saved the GOP thousands of dollars, the process of gathering such valuable information put the women at the ground level of the Georgia GOP. Person-to-person phone calls gave the women an edge in learning the opinions and concerns of their neighbors. They did not create their southern strategy from the outside. Rather, Georgia's women were the ultimate insiders—inside churches, homes, schools, and communities.

Insensitive to their volunteer base, the John H. Friend Company's instructions directed women to make most phone calls after 6:00 p.m., when men would be home from work, and to "try to get about two-thirds of your interviews from men, since they are generally more current on political matters at this stage of an election year."[18] This insult did not go unnoticed. Gladys Blackett of Washington Plantation in rural Baker County realized that the company did not know the schedule of farmers, noting that "12 noon is a better time to contact the men than 6pm."[19] Just as Georgia women knew their men's schedules better than the company, they also knew their politics better. Mrs. George Brewton of Martinez, Georgia, asked that the offensive language be taken out of all future instructional guidelines. "Since we are women, often more knowledgeable than the men we are interviewing," she wrote, "and since the compilers of this survey aren't going to consider women as current as men at *any* stage of the campaign, could you remove the insulting language?"[20] Brewton did not expect to alter men's attitudes about women's political knowledge, but she also did not consent to be offended as she conducted her woman's work of campaigning. The women knew their worth, but the men had to catch up.

The first GFRW survey took place on July 6–13, 1965, coinciding with the congressional debate on the Voting Rights Act of 1965. Seventeen months before the election, the women seized on southern white voters' fears about federal intervention in local and state politics. Ague organized the surveys in much the same way as she had organized the Goldwater canvass, with ten district chairmen reporting to her and county supervisors at the next level down. Each district and county supervisor conducted training for volunteers in GFRW clubs.[21] The first survey was door-to-door, building on their experience with the Goldwater canvass. Later, as surveys grew more frequent, the women conducted them almost exclusively over the telephone. By the election, the GFRW had conducted fourteen statewide opinion surveys.

While the bulk of the work came from GFRW members, the women had to appear nonpartisan in order to get the most accurate results. Training materials instructed, "Do not, however, identify the 'client' for this survey, even though you know who the client is." Under no circumstances could they identify themselves as Republicans. The manual reminded them, "*Always remain neutral*."[22] They gathered important information but had to refrain from their previous practice of the persuasive pitch to recruit a new Republican.

Women aimed to interview a range of people who would be classified according to "two primary controls—location of residence and income." The survey forms included boxes to be checked to identify a residence as urban, rural/nonfarm, or rural/farm. Survey choices divided income as less than five thousand dollars per year, five to ten thousand dollars, and over ten thousand dollars—breaking down roughly to lower-to-middle, middle-to-upper, and upper classes. As a state becoming less rural and also less solidly Democratic, these numbers revealed pockets of potential growth for the Republican Party's message of economic conservatism to accompany the racial conservatism of prospective members.[23]

The Friend Company told women conducting door-to-door surveys not to feel uncomfortable asking their neighbors about income. Instructions acknowledged that this was "a rather awkward task," but told the door-to-door volunteers they could easily estimate income through a "visual appraisal" based upon observation of "type of house, neighborhood, late-model higher-priced family automobiles, or vice versa and/or personal knowledge of family and principal wage earner." Later, as the surveys moved to the telephone, women found this the most uncomfortable question. Another survey question inquired about employment, within the categories of professional/white collar, blue collar, service workers, and not employed. Despite instructions to classify housewives as "not employed," several volunteers rebelled and categorized homemakers by their husband's employment status.[24] Class and professional status did not simply belong to the wage-earning man, but also to the homemakers. Though survey-makers did not recognize the critical role of housewives, the women performing the survey—and the labor at home—recognized the economic and political value of homemakers.

Surveys began with open-ended questions like "What do you think are the three most important national issues facing America today?" The next question asked for the three most important issues for the state. The responses, while allowing the subject to speak freely, also revealed issues—in the language of voters—for potential Republican candidates.[25]

Questions then began driving at whether Callaway or any Republican stood a chance in the 1966 statewide races. A little more than a year out, volunteers planted seeds in the minds of voters in hopes of a bumper crop of GOP votes. After assessing if the voter would even entertain voting for a Republican, questions moved toward Callaway's name recognition. Question 7 asked the respondent to identify the current role of potential candidates for each office from a list including many known Democrats who were considering running. Bo Callaway, the only congressman and lone Republican, rounded out the names.[26]

By the completion of the first opinion polls in July 1965, Democrats and former governors Ernest Vandiver and Ellis Arnall had declared their candidacies for governor. By the end of summer, Atlanta restaurant owner and three-time political loser Lester Maddox announced his candidacy for the Democratic gubernatorial nomination. Maddox had lost twice in running for mayor of Atlanta and once in 1962 for the seat of lieutenant governor. Long a thorn in the side of the state Democratic Party, Maddox founded the Georgia Democrats for Goldwater organization in 1964. In August 1965, one month before he declared his candidacy for governor, Maddox picketed the White House in support of states' rights.[27]

His skill at political theater made Lester Maddox a segregationist celebrity even if he was a political loser. When three African American protestors arrived at his Pickrick Restaurant in early July 1964, he chased them off with a pistol. White patrons supported him, threatening protestors with axe handles. Lester Maddox and his pistols and axe handles appeared on the front page of many national newspapers.[28] In August, Maddox decided to close his restaurant rather than comply with desegregation. He called the federal law "involuntary servitude; it's slavery of the first order."[29] Maddox sold his property to Georgia Tech and set about positioning himself as a victim of federal intervention. His demonstration of his commitment to segregation and states' rights became Lester Maddox's basis in running for governor in 1966. However, with three losses in campaigns for elected office in his past, few in

Georgia took Lester Maddox seriously when he announced his candidacy for governor.

State GOP chair G. Paul Jones assured the press that the Republicans would have a gubernatorial candidate. Bo Callaway agreed that the party needed to recruit candidates to keep newly registered Republicans engaged. Jones and Callaway tried to persuade conservative Democratic leaders to switch parties and run on the Republican gubernatorial ticket.[30]

Women of the GFRW were not silent on the Callaway question. Lee Ague expressed her concern about Callaway leaping into the statewide race: "You get a good candidate and you try to spread him too thin. He [Callaway] ... has indicated that he's not interested in a gubernatorial race and that's good enough for me." Republican National Committeewoman Marilu Smith remarked, "[Callaway's] done a marvelous job in the 3rd District and I'd like to see him stay where he is." Smith was the widow of A. Edward Smith, the state's previous Republican candidate for governor, who had died in an automobile accident before the 1962 election. Ague predicted that the GOP would "have a number of candidates" for state offices in 1966 and optimistically added, "If we can elect enough people to office in 1966, we'll have a strong voice in the selection of the [presidential] candidate in 1968."[31]

No matter which Republican ran, Ague promised the women's support. Having planted clubs in all ten districts, she reported that the GFRW women would spend the year "providing a constant source of trained womanpower ... that extra effort that will mean Republican victory across the board in 1966." She did not think twice about committing her members to the "endless, unglamorous tasks which are required to win political campaigns." Ague made sure that party leaders, candidates especially, knew GFRW women were dedicated, educated, and that no candidate could win without womanpower.[32]

Georgia GOP leaders believed they had strong candidates in seven of the state's ten congressional districts. In the other three, state party chairman G. Paul Jones wanted to run candidates who might at least distract strong Democrats from exercising their influence in the governor's race. Jones asked Ninth District chairman John Cauble to look for a "good, attractive, aggressive lady to be nominated ... as a candidate for Congress." Jones conceded that "a male candidate would probably be our best bet ... but in the absence of such a man I think a good, attractive female candidate might make a remarkably strong showing." Cauble may have considered it and would not have had to look far, since his wife Florence was a strong organizer for the GFRW. For the time being—and for the next fifty years—no Georgia Republican woman made a run for the U.S. Congress.[33]

By 1966, some GFRW women had stopped knocking on doors and picked up the phone, allowing them to volunteer from home while children napped or played. A phone survey, by its very nature, lent itself to greater success in areas showing Republican sympathies. The survey company cautioned from the start that urban counties had more telephones. Of Georgia's 159 counties, only nine could claim that 70 percent of housing units had telephones, and those were the urban and suburban counties already more likely to vote GOP. Atlanta suburb DeKalb County led with telephones in 89.3 percent of homes.[34]

More rural women stuck to in-person surveys out of necessity. In Oglethorpe County, women expressed a preference for door-to-door surveying in order to avoid any eavesdropping on party lines.[35] With many households sharing one circuit, party-line phones made it hard to challenge party-line voting. In the north Georgia town of Jasper, Gladys Green reported, "I'm also having trouble getting people to answer my questions because of being on Party line other [sic] being able to listen in."[36]

One woman in southern Echols County struggled to find homes that met her quotas for class diversity. She drove "from Homerville to Statesville, even back-tracked"—a distance of over thirty miles—but found only three homes she assumed to be those of middle-class families. All other homes she saw led her to believe the residents made either over ten thousand or under five thousand dollars a year. She reported that most of the people she did speak to "hedged somewhat," and griped, "Those hard-headed Demos, come what may, are not happy with Johnson—not that I interviewed—but they'd never admit they could be wrong by voting Dem." That frustration appeared in statewide survey results showing a Republican would have to win an overwhelming majority of urban and suburban votes to compensate for the Democratic loyalty of the rural counties.[37]

By the end of March, Ague had recruited 336 women statewide to conduct the surveys. At least 22 women volunteered in each district, with a high of 67 working in Callaway's Third District. Ague asked African American Republican representative Q. V. Williamson for help recruiting nonwhite volunteers, but had not found any by March. Though still organized, the Metropolitan Republican Club did not coordinate with the Goldwater wing that had taken over the state federation.[38]

Survey call sheets included likely African American voters, though the white women rarely took them seriously. Several volunteers reported frustration or obstruction when they did reach an African American voter. The Voting Rights Act of 1965 had only just opened voting to African Americans, but decades of distrust kept African American voters cautious enough to avoid questions. Naomi Roughton in Perry, Georgia, complained that half of her list of names were African American households. Exasperated, she told Ague, "After calling several of the negroes and getting 'Don't know' or 'no answer' to my questions, I gave up. I don't know if it was intentional to have so many negroes on this survey, but I do know it was a waste of time as I did not get any intelligent answers."[39] Jane Pruett in Fulton County complained, "In several instances where it was *very* apparent that I was talking to a Negro they said they were white."[40] Party-line phones made it hard for white subjects to answer questions, but that was not as challenging as crossing the color lines to assess voter attitudes.

A key question for every district read as follows: "On this list are several ways Congressmen sometimes describe themselves. Which one comes closest to the description you would prefer for your Congressman?" The long list of choices included

> Conservative Democrat
> Liberal Democrat
> Moderate Democrat
> Conservative Republican
> Liberal Republican
> Moderate Republican
> Conservative Independent
> Liberal Independent
> Moderate Independent
> Don't Know
> No Answer

Survey instructions did not allow the women to define any of the categories for the respondent, nor was there room for the respondent to explain his or her answer. White voters preferred "Conservative Democrat," but "Conservative Republican" was a strong second choice. The ideological choice of conservatism, then, ranked higher than partisan identification among white voters—revealing a significant opportunity for Georgia political realignment. Among African American voters, however, "Liberal Democrat" was the choice of over half the respondents. Other African Americans answered "Conservative Democrat" or "Don't Know."[41]

Identification with candidates revealed an even greater racial divide. On the question, "If Johnson and Goldwater were again candidates for president, and the election were held today, which one would you vote for?" not a single African American responded Goldwater. The majority of African Americans responded Johnson, though a significant number did not answer the question. An overwhelming majority of white voters in every district responded Goldwater.[42] In this respect, the results suggested a strategy of focusing on white voters and surrendering African American Republicans to the Democratic Party.

The April 1966 survey tested how Bo Callaway might fare in a gubernatorial race against Ernest Vandiver, then the leading candidate. In this version of the survey, the volunteer identified candidates by name only, not party. Callaway fared well among Goldwater voters, not surprisingly, considering he had ridden Goldwater's coattails. However, the numbers also showed Callaway enjoyed name recognition and solid support outside his home district. No other Republican had even shown enough interest to be included in the poll. The women also asked questions to help in the selection of congressional candidates—testing name recognition for Republicans against incumbents and likely Democrats.[43]

Surveys also asked several policy questions to determine voter attitudes. For example, the women asked, "Which of the statements on this card is closest to your opinion on the use of U.S. Military Forces in Viet Nam?," "Do you Approve or Disapprove of the Way the Poverty Program has been administered up to this point?," and opinions on the 1965 Farm Bill. The surveys assessed the most important issues on Georgia voters' minds so candidates could target their messages. Similarly, intending to get at voter attitudes on federal budget choices, the survey asked respondents to "select the most important item" from the following list:

1. Eliminate the Poverty Program
2. Reduce benefits or do away with Medicare
3. Reduce foreign aid
4. Reduce spending on welfare programs
5. Reduce the number of immigrants coming to this country
6. Reduce or remove federal control of voter qualifications
7. Reduce government housing programs
8. Reduce federal aid to education

While the voter could respond "Don't Know" or "No Answer," there was no category for "none of the above." That is, designers of the survey began from the assumption that the voter would support budgetary cuts. The most popular response was a reduction in foreign aid. On this question, Bo Callaway, for example, could see easily that in the Ninth District of northern Georgia his supporters split evenly in supporting cuts to foreign aid, welfare programs, and Johnson's War on Poverty programs. In the Sixth District, representing counties south and west of Atlanta, 35 percent of likely Callaway voters supported cuts to foreign aid. As he developed strategy for a possible gubernatorial run, Callaway knew which issues he needed to emphasize in the remaining months of his congressional term.[44]

Republicans still did not have an official candidate by the June qualifying deadline. Without any prominent Democratic politicians agreeing to switch parties to run for the GOP, Bo Callaway eyed the governor's race much more closely. Formidable front-runner Ernest Vandiver dropped out of the race on his doctor's advice. Callaway, a former Talmadge Democrat, posed a real threat to the state's major political machine. His West Point education and Korean War service shored up his military and foreign policy credentials while his prominent family connections boosted his state business networks. With the Democratic political machine behind him, Callaway would have been set. However, when Bo Callaway switched to the GOP in 1964, he not only surrendered the Talmadge endorsements but made himself a target. Former governor Marvin Griffin later said of the 1966 race, "I hated like thunder not to support Bo ... but he done gone over and got to be a gen-u-wine Republican." Goldwater-supporter Griffin had no problem with Republican presidential candidates but expected state candidates to be Georgia Democrats.[45]

Just as the Republicans did not have a definite candidate, neither did the Democrats. The Georgia Democratic Party spent the spring and summer of 1966 trying to narrow a field of five down to one leading candidate. Meanwhile, Republican women were determined to give whichever Democrat won the party primary in 1966 a real run of it. As Democrats prepared for a runoff, GFRW members surveyed likely voters again. The tally of the June survey results showed Callaway with a two-to-one lead over presumed Democratic candidate and former governor Ellis Arnall. Mocking the Georgia political scene, John H. Friend Jr. began his analysis of survey results with, "In the center ring of the Georgia political arena, the main attractions are Bo Callaway and Ellis Arnall, with Callaway getting top billing." Statewide, Callaway polled at 45.7 percent of likely voters, Arnall garnered 23.9 percent, and 22.7 percent were undecided. That survey question offered only four choices: Callaway, Arnall, Undecided, and No Answer.[46]

With generally good news from the surveys, Callaway had one very troubling piece of news standing in his way. Despite a projected 2-to-1 lead over Arnall during the summer primaries, he would not have the votes to win a November election. Callaway could win a plurality in a six-man race, but he could not defeat a Georgia Democrat in a two-man race. Survey analysis found a GOP victory relied on converting "one-third more Democrats, even if all Independents go [Callaway's] way."[47] It would be a daunting task, but surveys showed women where to target their voter registration efforts. When phone surveyors in Troup County realized there was a likely pocket of support for Callaway among unregistered voters, they went out to register them. The Callaway campaign might use the surveys to set campaign strategy, but on the local level, women used the results to build Republican strength.[48]

Finally, Bo Callaway officially announced his candidacy for governor on July 4, 1966, at the Columbus Fairgrounds.[49] Almost immediately, he hired Lee Ague as women's activities director for his gubernatorial campaign. The new title recognized the work she had already begun, organizing Georgia's women to ensure a Callaway victory. She vowed to channel the "tremendous enthusiasm" of the women volunteers into "votes for Bo Callaway on November 8." She offered a simple mnemonic device for anyone who wanted to learn her strategy: "the five W's—When Women Work We Win."[50]

Ague was so in tune with women's political style that she ran a workshop for the Atlanta Campaign Manager's School, a GOP project for southern states' party leaders. She told attendees that if they would "make women feel wanted, needed," then women would "put aside their household chores—their home & dedicate themselves to your campaign—& many a husband won't have a hot meal for the duration." She reminded candidates and campaign managers that women had many volunteer options, "So if *you* don't get them out of the kitchen for a day or two, the garden club will." She concluded with her assurance that women were excellent campaign workers and even better voters. Part of leading Women for Callaway also meant making sure that Callaway—or other candidates—were equally for women.[51]

As women's activities director, Ague set the schedule for the candidate's wife. Beth and Bo Callaway met as high-school sweethearts before he enrolled at Georgia Tech (to be followed by West Point) and she went to Agnes Scott College, a women's college outside Atlanta. When the gubernatorial campaign began, Beth Callaway balanced the responsibilities of a congressman's wife and a stay-at-home mother to the couple's five children. With mother-of-two Ague controlling the schedule, both women balanced full-time campaigning with full-time mothering.

Recognizing the importance of wives to political efforts, the Republican Congressional Committee (RCC) published a booklet of helpful tips for a candidate's wife. The booklet prioritized fashion, reminding the women to schedule regular beauty appointments into the busy campaign schedule. It also suggested that wives always have an extra pair of hosiery and white gloves. Beyond appearance, the booklet encouraged wives not to speak publicly on the campaign trail. An anonymous incumbent legislator described the wife's role: "Above all, the ladies must be homemakers, wives, and mothers, which exemplify the still remaining concept of the American home and scene." The booklet continued with tips for thank-you notes, coffee etiquette, and ways to encourage one's husband.[52]

In contrast, Lee Ague recognized that wives contributed much more than fashion to a campaign. She wrote her own booklet for the male candidates entitled, *The Women in Your Political Life: A Candidate's Primer*. While the booklet assumed male candidates, Ague reminded the men that they could not run, much less win, elections without womanpower. Unlike the RCC, Ague addressed the male candidates and asserted, "The most important woman on your campaign team is your wife!" Where the RCC booklet encouraged visibility combined with silence, Ague called the candidate's wife "your partner in politics" and said, "If your wife has the inclination or ability to address groups, by all means, encourage her to do so." She reminded the candidates to "consult your wife and listen to her opinions during her campaign." She warned that staffers might try to impress or appease a candidate, but "your wife will be with you—win or lose." She reminded men that the role of the wife was a critical campaign position, often overlooked and always unpaid. She told them voters were always watching: "Your attitude toward your wife in public will be noticed. Something as insignificant as walking ahead of your wife instead of alongside her may cause comment." Ague recommended that a candidate begin every speech and every public appearance with recognition and gratitude for his wife and the mother of his children. Women would notice such seemingly minor touches at public engagements and work that much harder for the candidate. Undecided women would remember a candidate's respect for his wife when they went to the polls.[53]

Beth Callaway aptly performed the duties of a candidate's wife, and Bo, in turn, recognized her contributions. Beth was the honored guest at Two Party Tea Parties all over the state. Women in fledgling GFRW groups from counties of all sizes wrote Ague to schedule a Tea Party with Beth Callaway. One who requested a women's event in Coffee County admitted the area was "down in [Lester] Maddox Country," but promised "a real enthusiastic group of citizens for Callaway." A visit from the Republican wife encouraged the Callaway faithful without inciting the opposition. Seemingly benign women's activities like tea parties provided perfect cover for Beth Callaway to crack open rural areas that would never welcome her husband. Lee Ague and Beth Callaway scheduled up to six coffees per day in an attempt to meet the numerous requests.[54]

In addition to properly recognizing and thanking the candidate's wife, Ague reminded Callaway to turn his attention to the scores of volunteers and hundreds of thousands of women voters. Her booklet aimed to make sure the candidates valued the role of the tea-party hostesses. Ague reminded all Georgia Republican candidates, Bo Callaway included, that the GFRW boasted nearly seventeen hundred members positioned as "the nucleus for a vast source of volunteer workers who will help you 'Find them, Vote Them, and Count Them.'" These women, she stressed, were trained in canvass techniques and brought a strong knowledge of and passion for the Georgia political scene.[55] Rather than challenging white women's roles, the GFRW used their position for political influence. In appreciation, Bo Callaway began his biennial sponsorship of the Bo Callaway Award, presented to the GFRW member "who has done the most to further the Republican Party in Georgia."[56]

In a state dominated by the Democratic Party but also increasingly responsive to the GOP's form of conservatism, the wives of many conservative Democratic candidates offered a kind of loophole, a way for their husbands to get around party rules against endorsing a Republican. Steve Knight of Columbus was a longtime Democratic elected official, serving as city commissioner, mayor, and state senator. His pledge to the Democratic Party required him to support the party's candidates for all offices. His wife, Jane, however, was under no such obligation. In the month before the election, Knight announced that his wife had witnessed the work he had done in various elected posts and that "she feels that all of the ladies of Georgia should help to elect a man ... interested solely in the betterment of Georgia such as Bo Callaway is." Officially, Knight backed Lester Maddox in the governor's race. But the very fact that he made a point of announcing and praising his wife's independence in her decision that "Bo Callaway would be the best man for the job" was not hard to read as an implied endorsement by Knight himself. A wife's endorsement provided the loophole that allowed her husband to send a signal to the electorate without having to endanger the security of his position in the party.[57]

Women related to Beth Callaway as a wife and mother. In the same way, other women could use their influence for Bo. Florence Cauble, active GFRW member and wife of GOP Ninth District chairman John Cauble, sent a letter appealing to doctors' wives saying that they, "as M.D. wives, must become more politically alert and politically active." As spouses of professional men, she continued, "Our positions in our communities give us the influence and responsibility ... to become effective voices for the GOP."[58] Wives of professional men could bring influence, money, and volunteer hours needed to build the Republican Party in towns all over Georgia. Ague's women's campaign focused on stay-at-home women who had flexibility to attend or host daytime tea parties and to volunteer. In the directions for Two Party Tea Parties for Callaway, Ague specified, "We Want Middle income ladies if possible, i.e., no 'Nob Hill' groups exclusively."[59] Social exclusion limited political influence, so Ague encouraged them to cast a wider net.

In addition to hosting Two Party Tea Parties, the volunteers of the GFRW supported Callaway in numerous other ways. The Albany FRW served "over 1,000 plates" at a "Bar-B-Q for Bo" in their city.[60] A Macon woman sold "Go Bo" earrings to make money for her GFRW club and to publicize area women's support of Bo Callaway. She suggested that any club could host "earring coffees" to make and sell them for fifty cents a pair.[61]

In contrast, the Callaway campaign gave limited recognition to working women. In the southwest corner of the state, the Decatur County Republican Party mailed out letters to all the teachers, telling them of Callaway's commitment to use the state's budget surplus to increase teacher salaries and reduce crowded classrooms.[62] However, Congressman Callaway's vote against an increase in the minimum wage made outreach to nonprofessional working women more challenging.

Despite their work, women continually confronted the problem of trying to turn Georgia Democrats into Callaway voters. Barbara King in Waycross railed against the local newspaper with its "putrid Democratic party policy" and support for Democratic candidates even though "they subscribe to an anti-Johnson cartoon series." King did find one reason to hope, however, when she overheard a woman in a downtown Waycross dress shop purchasing a pink mink shoulder shrug "to wear to Bo Callaway's inaugural ball."[63]

Surveyors in other areas had less reason to be optimistic. Whether out of boredom or frustration, some surveyors risked accurate results in order to make a point about the impossibility of converting voters. In the northeast Georgia town of Hartwell, one woman's teenage son conducted some surveys in which he inserted the question, "If Stokely Carmichael, a Democrat, and Bo Callaway, a Republican were on the ballot, who would you vote for?" Exasperated, the woman reported "3 Hart County morons said Stokely Carmichael just because he was designated as a Democrat."[64] The teenager's prank meant to show the steep challenge of swaying loyal Democrats. The question, though, also reveals that the surveyors showed disdain for people who—knowingly or not—preferred an African American candidate over a white man.

While surveys were secretive work—as noted earlier, those conducting the survey didn't reveal that they were also Republican Party activists—the Georgia Federation of Republican Women continued to organize publicly to keep their name and that of the Republican Party at the fore of voters' minds. Mary Malone, a district GFRW officer, celebrated that women in the Second and Eighth Congressional Districts "took on the job," as she reported, "of organizing the first Republican conventions ever held in their precincts and counties." Two Party Tea Parties built the party one person at a time, and these local conventions built it one precinct at a time.[65]

In addition to her official work with Women for Callaway, Ague continued to build the GFRW. In the summer of 1966, Georgia women participated in the WoW—Women on the Warpath campaign, which NFRW literature described as "a housewives' rebellion." The strategy called for "members and committee people [to] go to supermarkets with homemade posters and brooms . . . protesting the Democratic Congress which is responsible for high prices." The brooms symbolized sweeping out Congress the next year.[66] The WoW campaign literature suggested women do their shopping while wearing a feathered headband—an appropriation of Native American imagery common in the day—to promote the idea of the grocery aisle as a "warpath" in the fight against inflation. The newsletter included a pattern of a padlock for women to cut out of yellow construction paper. Each woman would hang the paper padlock from her purse with the handwritten message, "LBJ Keep Out." The grocery aisles became recruitment territory for new GOP voters.[67] In southern Thomas County, Republican women highlighted their crafting and gardening skills with their entry into the town's Rose Festival parade, "Everything's Coming up—Roses and Republicans."[68] This alignment of political activity as a part of a woman's work in the home became a central component of the New Right as the explicit language of family values developed.

Women continued the housewives' revolt with "LBJ supermarkets" at county fairs all over the state. These booths displayed common grocery items with their November 1963 prices and the current August 1966 marked-up costs. Ague stressed that the displays should not blame farmers, but government. Women distributed flyers telling shoppers to "hold down runaway food prices" by "electing a cost conscious Republican Congress."[69] The LBJ supermarket displays reinforced the message the GFRW had emphasized all along—politics was women's work.

In taking the fight against Johnson to the grocery store, the GFRW developed a gendered and partisan approach to Georgia politics. Significantly, they focused on economic programs and inflation. Strategically, they did not mention the Civil Rights Act, the Voting Rights Act, nor any Massive Resistance slogans. White Georgia Democrats already opposed Johnson's progressive civil rights agenda. Through a politics of motherhood, Republican women paved a path for the Georgia GOP to articulate a new language of conservatism in the state.

Georgia Republican women skillfully linked home economics and national politics. NFRW literature suggested taking out Women on the Warpath advertisements in local newspapers, but the upstart Georgia Federation did not have enough money for such extravagance. The Rath Packing Company, however, had enough money for its own large newspaper ads—inadvertently providing Lee Ague with an opportunity for free media coverage. In June 1966, the Rath Company announced that it would help the homemaker fight inflation by giving away a free slice of bacon inside each pound-size package. That advertisement incurred the calculated wrath of Lee Ague, who penned a letter to the company and a press release to media outlets statewide. She chastised the company, saying that the free slice would "feed one-third of one of my two children one meal." Instead, if the company wanted to fight inflation, she suggested that it "include in every pound package . . . Republican literature urging consumers to vote for Republican candidates at all levels of government." In reporting the story, the *Atlanta Constitution* quipped, "The Democrats apparently have not taken a stand on the free slice of bacon."[70]

With her only expense being the cost of mailing press releases, Ague won broad coverage for Republican women and positioned the GOP as the party concerned with families. A GFRW volunteer in rural Georgia wrote Ague that she had read "your article on the 'high bacon.' Good and effective—do some more. The farmers in this area would like a 'fair show' and this sort of article is meaningful to them."[71] This sort of messaging on inflation—and use of the news media to spread it—carried through into the fall, when the Sunday *Atlanta Journal and Atlanta Constitution* featured Ague's campaign against inflation in its women's pages. A photo showed Ague with her grocery cart in the produce aisle as she cradled a head of cabbage. The caption for this image of the trim mother read, "It's not the pounds she counts, it's the $."[72] Ague appeared as a typical Georgia mother and housekeeper, just trying to stretch her husband's salary to feed the family. The article mentioned that she was the GFRW president but emphasized her role as a cost-conscious mother. Such savvy political publicity reinforced the GFRW message that the Republican Party cared about issues that affected families. In time, this Republican women's strategy of framing family concerns as conservative political concerns would revolutionize the party's platform.

While Republican women conducted statewide surveys, Ague planted more local GFRW chapters. She put out a call for suggestions of women who had potential as club-starters, and Ague traveled all over the state following up on those leads. After survey data showed Callaway's numbers lagging in the First and Eighth Districts, she focused her efforts on those counties. In the summer of 1966, she reported twenty new federations organized all around the state, including many in the rural counties Maddox had claimed as "Maddox Country." She organized five new chapters of Women for Callaway in areas that would not yet support a full-fledged Republican organization but that showed strong anti-Maddox sentiment. She put women to work with surveys, Republican pamphlets, and voter education materials. Any county with no GOP women's organization got the notation, "Need Contact" or "Weak. Needs Work." She did not surrender any county or any voter.[73]

As Republican women tended to the grassroots, the two remaining Democratic candidates squared off for a September runoff vote for the Democratic nomination. Ellis Arnall began his runoff campaign as though he had already won it, proclaiming, "I am running against Callaway." Lester Maddox, however, did not accept defeat. Maddox sought to link Arnall to the national policies of the unpopular President Lyndon Johnson, saying that a vote for Arnall was a vote for "a wild socialist who is the granddaddy of forced racial integration." Arnall's moderation of the 1940s was a liability in the context of the Massive Resistance of the 1960s.[74] The Democratic contenders battled on the grounds of civil rights and segregation.

A week before the September 14 runoff, Atlanta's Summerhill community erupted in violence. Atlanta Police shot and killed an African American car theft suspect outside his mother's home. Hours after removing the body, police in full riot gear arrived to monitor the crowd, which had grown in size and in frustration. Mayor Ivan Allen arrived, hoping to prevent further violence. The crowd flipped over one police car and began rocking the car on which Allen stood. Protestors threw bricks and bottles at law enforcement. Police responded with warning shots into the air. Finally, as Allen left the area, he gave the authorization to use tear gas.[75]

The next week, when Georgia Democrats went to the polls, twenty-eight thousand more Georgians cast ballots in the runoff than had done so in the primary. Lester Maddox took just over 54 percent of the vote to become the Democratic candidate who would face Bo Callaway in the November general election. Maddox took 137 of the 159 counties. Arnall had been polling well before the Summerhill protests. However, Arnall's strategy of portraying Maddox as an extremist backfired: after newspaper reports of race riots, many white voters decided an extremist was exactly what they wanted.[76]

Arnall lost for another reason, too. The runoff election included voters who had cast ballots in the Democratic primary as well as those who had not. Many voters who ultimately supported Callaway in the general election voted for Lester Maddox in the Democratic runoff. Maddox, they assumed, would be easier to beat in the general election. Former governor Vandiver, an avowed Arnall foe, admitted to taking this route because he thought Callaway would have an easier time beating "a political clown" than the experienced Arnall.[77] *Atlanta Constitution* editor Ralph McGill estimated that seventy-five thousand Republicans probably cast Maddox ballots following this strategy.[78] The Callaway campaign denied that it encouraged anyone to vote for Maddox—not that anyone had to be encouraged. One woman bragged to Callaway, "'Them lyin' Atlanta Newspapers' are right about one thing. Many of us loyal Republicans did vote for Maddox with the idea that he will be the easier candidate to beat, and we still think so."[79]

The Callaway campaign did not have to explain to Republican voters that Lester Maddox would probably be the easier candidate to beat. They were aware that Lester Maddox was a three-time political loser best known for chasing African American preachers off his property at gunpoint. That stood in contrast to Bo Callaway's record as a West Point graduate, a naval veteran of the Korean War, a sitting congressman, and a trailblazer for a two-party system in Georgia. Callaway was also a member of a well-known Georgia family and son of a wealthy textile manufacturer whose family owned Callaway Gardens, a popular resort and nature center. With such a record, campaign staff and followers felt confident about the chances for the first Republican governor in a century.

Despite the obvious differences between Callaway and Maddox, many moderate voters in Georgia complained that both men stood strongly for segregation. Both men had opposed the Civil Rights Act of 1964 and the Voting Rights Act of 1965. The *Atlanta Constitution* refused to endorse either candidate. Many voters were dissatisfied with the choice and unwilling to give up on a more progressive governor. Historian Kevin Kruse writes, "The rise of southern Republicanism, in the person of Bo Callaway and others like him, was largely due to the white backlash against the Civil Rights Act."[80] However, in 1966, Republican Callaway faced Democrat Lester Maddox, known for his violent opposition to integration. Therefore, in such a contest, with both partisan sides loudly opposing federal intervention and integration, white backlash alone does not explain voter choice. In 1966, white backlash could lead to support for either candidate.

Bo Callaway's campaign relied upon statistical polling and grassroots volunteerism to define the Republican Party brand of conservatism, which included opposition to integration cradled in a pro-business and pro-family message. Georgia Republicans hoped that image would play a greater role in a campaign between two opponents of civil rights legislation. This similarity between the candidates in their stance on civil rights means that the 1966 gubernatorial race is valuable not simply for testing white backlash theories, but for recognizing a significant point in the state's political realignment.[81]

The contributions of women as volunteers demonstrate an important step in the creation of a gendered language of conservatism a decade before the recognized Pro-Family Movement was linked with the Republican Party. Ague's campaign to bring Republican messages to women at the grocery store and in living rooms also brought women's issues of household budgets and parenting school-age children to the attention of the Republican Party. Maddox, as a segregationist firebrand, preached the need to protect white women. In contrast, Ague understood that white women voted to protect their families.

Tift County legislator W. Frank Branch made the pro-Callaway case before a women's group, asking, "Have you ever heard of Bo Callaway chasing a car down the street and waving a pistol at it as Lester Maddox was shown doing in *Life Magazine* last week, to the eternal shame of Georgia?" Branch was a member of Democrats for Callaway, a group established in support of the Republican candidate, but even more in opposition to Lester Maddox. Highlighting the Callaway campaign's main point of difference between the two candidates, Branch reminded the women that Callaway was both experienced and polished. Violent opposition to racism made for good national copy, but bad business relations. Branch continued, "Georgia boys fighting Communist aggression in the jungles of Viet Nam are embarrassed by the thought that Lester Maddox could ever be the Governor of their home state." Callaway, meanwhile, had spent his own money to travel to Vietnam twice while in Congress, educating himself on the heated conflict of the Cold War and shoring up his anticommunist credentials. The Callaway campaign appealed to business sense, family, and pride in making the case for how Callaway's business-friendly, polite conservatism differed from Lester Maddox's "bed sheets, axe handles, and pistols."[82] It boiled down to which white supremacy voters preferred.

Faced with the choice between rabid segregationist Lester Maddox and Republican civil rights critic Bo Callaway, many Georgians sought another option. On October 4, several hundred citizens gathered in a biracial meeting in Atlanta and determined to organize a write-in campaign. They selected Ellis Arnall as their candidate, though Arnall neither formally accepted nor endorsed the movement. The movement, known as Write-In Georgia (WIG), set to work immediately with voter education about Arnall and about the write-in procedures.[83] Importantly, the WIG movement had to make the case for not choosing either of the candidates appearing on the ballot. The literature argued, "You already know about LESTER MADDOX. ... How many days and nights of fighting and bloodshed would his election bring to us all?" The case against Callaway, aside from his Republican affiliation, might not have been as clear to voters. The WIG movement pointed out that "Callaway is a Democrat who turned Republican, a segregationist with money." Further, "Callaway voted *against* Federal Aid to Education, *against* Civil Rights, *against* the minimum wage. With more money than sense, why should he worry about *your* rights, *your* children, *your* future?"[84] This focus on Callaway's wealth made sense, because while many voters opposed Lester Maddox because of his racial radicalism, many also felt they could not support Callaway because of his conservative opposition to working-class initiatives.

The prospect of a three-way race concerned Republicans. Both Arnall and Callaway were professional men and experienced politicians. Arnall might peel away anti-Maddox voters who might otherwise go for Callaway. If no candidate won a majority of votes on November 8, the election would go to the Democratic-controlled General Assembly, where Callaway would certainly lose.

Faced with the horrifying likelihood that a write-in campaign would help elect Lester Maddox, even the African American Republican women's organization, the Metropolitan Club, energized in support of Callaway and hosted a "Two-Party Oriental Tea" to introduce the candidate's platform to voters in the Auburn Avenue neighborhood.[85] Q. V. Williamson, a Republican Atlanta alderman and co-chairman of the Atlanta Negro Voters League, voiced his opposition to the write-in effort. The *Atlanta Daily World*, the African American daily newspaper with a longtime moderate Republican leaning, encouraged its readers not to support the write-in movement because it would be akin to supporting Maddox. Even civil rights opponent Callaway was better than segregationist warrior Lester Maddox, it reasoned.

Other African American leaders in civil rights groups and local politics endorsed the write-in movement rather than choose between two demonstrated

civil rights opponents. A speaker at a Southern Christian Leadership Conference fundraiser for the WIG movement warned, "You cannot pressure us, buy
us or blackmail us into voting for Bo Callaway by giving us as an only alternative Lester Maddox." SCLC organizer Hosea Williams led a campaign to allow
the use of stickers with Arnall's name, charging that denying voters access to
the candidate's name violated the recently passed Voting Rights Act, which
struck down requirements of "any degree of literacy."[86]

Trying to keep up with the constantly changing political scene, the GFRW
conducted three surveys in the final month of the campaign. In mid-October,
they asked voters to choose between Callaway and Maddox. Not two weeks
later, that question included the option of "Other—write in" but did not mention Arnall's name. Most of the questions challenged respondents to consider
the differences between Callaway and Maddox. By showing the two men were
different in more than party, survey questions might push voters toward Callaway and away from the write-in option. Immediately after the runoff, the volunteers asked voters to "describe the quality you dislike most about Lester
Maddox... his appearance, his inexperience, his extremist views, or his irre-
sponsibility?" In the final survey, they asked, "Which candidate for Governor
is most likely to help President Johnson in his race for reelection in 1968—Bo
Callaway or Lester Maddox?" Of course, both candidates had campaigned actively for Goldwater in 1964, but they hoped to associate Democrat Maddox
with the unpopular Johnson.[87]

By the end of the summer, many GFRW women expressed their disgruntlement
with the phone surveys. Some volunteers found that the Friend Company had
supplied inaccurate phone numbers, leaving them to hit the phone books
themselves. In Augusta, the company sent women North Augusta phone numbers, not realizing that it was a separate town in South Carolina. Mrs. Carl
Ponder wrote that of the twenty-four names she received, only ten phone
numbers worked and only four of those she reached would speak to her. Some
complained that each survey took so much time that they just could not get
through their quota in the few days allotted. In Baker County, Gladys Blackett
expressed her concern that the surveys were an imposition on new Republican converts and reminded, "We have a very long road ahead and it is necessary to keep their enthusiasm." Fatigue became a major concern as the women
conducted surveys, tea parties, and voter registration campaigns in addition
to their regular homemaking work.[88] In one rural area, an organizer reported
that canning season cut into women's volunteer time in the late summer.[89]

Young women also joined the Callaway campaign. Recalling the success of the
Goldwater Girls, Ague created the "Go Bo Girls" to fill the same role in the
governor's race. A campaign memo asked members to provide their own uni-

form of a "Navy Blue A-line skirt, Red Belt, Red Scarf or Hat, White Poor Boy Shirt," and white tennis shoes. The campaign provided a straw hat and a "Big 'Go Bo' Button." Campaign staff could contact Ague to request Go Bo Girls for "any appropriate function for the distribution of campaign literature and buttons, and to greet and welcome the people."[90] Like the Goldwater Girls two years earlier, these young white girls served to remind voters of the candidate's strong record of upholding segregation.

When Bo Callaway celebrated the kickoff of his final campaign stretch on September 30, Go Bo Girls filled the route. Early that morning, the uniformed young women visited businesses along Callaway's parade route, handing out flyers and drumming up excitement. Just a few weeks after the violence in the Summerhill neighborhood, scores of young white girls marched through the city's business district in support of law and order and Bo Callaway.[91]

The Callaway kickoff parade began with three antique cars carrying successive banners reading "Goodbye to antique ideas," "Farewell to ancient promises," and "So long to the past." Following the American flag and the state flag with its prominent Confederate emblem, the Go Bo Girls flooded in, representing the future. White girls marched in front of new white convertibles that promised "New Life—New Strength for Georgia." Various state Republican candidates rode in the convertibles, accompanied by Go Bo Girls, with the last carrying Callaway and his large family. The Go Bo Girls who had lined the route fell in and followed the Callaways into Hurt Park, where Bo Callaway spoke to the excited crowd.[92] Ague estimated that "between 25,000 to 40,000 people" saw the candidate either in the park or along the parade route.[93]

That fall, the GFRW took two of the top awards at the National Federation for Republican Women meeting in Washington, D.C. They won a silver tea set for most new clubs in the nation and another prize for most active organization in the southern district. Ague told NFRW president Dorothy Elston that she opened the silver tea set in front of Bo and Beth Callaway, "who were both thrilled at our achievements."[94] Opening the tea set in front of the Callaways reminded the candidate of the work women had contributed to his campaign. While Callaway conscientiously recognized the women's contributions on the state level, Lee Ague ensured that the Georgia party leadership also knew that the national women's leadership commended the local workers.

Ague recognized that the contribution of GFRW volunteers was the type of "endless, unglamorous" campaign work that higher officials often took for granted. She also recognized that it would be detrimental to the campaign if her volunteers ever came to feel that way. Despite the need to keep their GFRW identity hidden for survey work, the women knew that they were building the GOP in Georgia. In case any had not read the *Atlanta Constitution* article that marveled at the Callaway campaign's ability to take the most accurate polls, Ague sent a letter out to every volunteer, writing, "There were many professional firms taking surveys for various political candidates prior to the Primary. We were the only ones who hit home! All of the credit goes to you—the survey worker—for making our accuracy possible!"[95] Ague worried about polls that predicted a plurality rather than a majority for Callaway.[96] She pushed to squeeze all the commitment she could from the GFRW. Volunteer appreciation could go a long way toward keeping her workers in the uphill battle. While the promise of a Republican governor was enough to motivate most volunteers, the Callaway campaign also issued gold eagle pins to any woman who contributed more than one hundred hours' work. Twenty women in southeastern Waycross, Georgia, qualified for a pin by the end of September.[97] Women who volunteered forty hours received a red, white, and blue "Go Bo" pin and a certificate.[98]

By the time November 8 came, women across Georgia had made thousands of phone calls, served numerous cups of tea, registered new Republican voters, and hosted other campaign events. Exhausted, they prepared to reap the rewards of their work with the state's first Republican gubernatorial victory in a century. By the end of Election Day, however, they realized that their work was not yet done.

As feared, the Write-In Georgia movement meant that none of the candidates won a majority. Bo Callaway claimed victory with 46.6 percent of the vote, narrowly beating Maddox, who received 46.3 percent, or three thousand fewer votes. Write-in votes gave Ellis Arnall the 7 percent that prevented a clear victory for either of the other candidates. In the old county-unit system, Maddox would have enjoyed a landslide with 130 of the state's 159 counties. Callaway's strength, unsurprisingly, was in urban and suburban areas, which only gave him twenty-nine counties. In African American districts around Atlanta, Callaway won a majority of the votes, with Arnall coming in a strong second. Lester Maddox polled under three percent in African American precincts.[99] Instead of a runoff, the Georgia Election Code required that the vote go to the state legislature.

Despite being in his own political limbo, Callaway's coattails had helped carry some down-ticket candidates to victory. Two more Republicans from Georgia went to the U.S. Congress: Ben Blackburn won in the Fourth District while Fletcher Thompson took the Fifth, both suburban Atlanta districts. Callaway's own Third District seat, however, returned to Democratic control.[100]

On January 10, 1967, the 259 members of the Georgia House of Representatives and the Georgia State Senate met in a joint session to elect the new governor. After the defeat of a bill to return the decision to the people for a runoff election, the members of this General Assembly elected Lester Maddox as the state's next governor. Lee Ague sat in the gallery and later recalled, "There really weren't many dry eyes up there."[101] The numbers had, of course, always been in Maddox's favor, with 229 of the 259 General Assembly members being in his party. Callaway, however, pulled 38 Democratic votes to join the 28 Republican votes. Only ten members abstained, nine of whom were African Americans from Atlanta districts.[102] Finally, Georgia had its next governor.

Bo Callaway thanked Lee Ague in a handwritten note, saying, "The women were the greatest. Beth and I will always be grateful." He expressed his own "disappointment . . . to lose the office of Governor after winning the popular vote" and expressed his hope for "another day and another race."[103] GFRW membership chairman Katherine Gunnell expressed, "Never have I felt so much frustration and bitterness about the unjust outcome. . . . I think now we must dust ourselves off and start getting ready for the next governor's election and raise our voices for change in the Georgia Constitution."[104]

By the time Ague addressed the NFRW board of directors meeting in late January, she had still not recovered from the General Assembly's vote. "History records that on November 8th, Bo Callaway was elected governor of Georgia," she began. She described the "way our GFRW formed the backbone for the women's effort in the Governor's race." Ague boasted that over eleven hundred women conducted fourteen surveys, interviewing more than twenty-five thousand Georgia voters. The worth of the women's work was "over 15,000 woman hours . . . providing a contribution to the campaign which in monetary value would exceed $60,000." After expressing her anger at the legislators and her pride in the GFRW volunteers, Ague wrapped up: "History records that in 1967 the Georgia Legislature elected a Democrat Governor in spite of the fact that one-half million Georgians had selected Bo Callaway. We will set the record straight in 1970."[105]

Disheartened but vowing to fight on, the GFRW held its awards luncheon in Atlanta in February 1967. Rather than having a head table for the dignitaries, Republican officials and their wives sat at the tables with the women who had volunteered so many hours. Over lunch, the women "had the opportunity to discuss any legislation" and build relationships with state officials. In addition to sitting with legislators, the GFRW volunteers also met women from other local federations, forging ties that strengthened their statewide network. Bo Callaway took the stage as keynote speaker before presenting the first annual Bo Callaway Award to Florence Cauble, treasurer of the GFRW and "a full-time Republican worker." Mary Aven received the award for outstanding service during the 1966 campaign for her efforts in organizing the Seventh District.

GFRW members were boosting themselves up, rededicating themselves to the establishment of a two-party state and Republican victory the next time.[106] After what they saw as the Democratic theft of the governorship by the state legislature, many Republican women committed themselves to changing Georgia's politics altogether.

CHAPTER 3

Fighting Factions

Following Bo Callaway's victory in the popular vote and defeat in the legislative vote for governor in 1966, Republican women took solace in their show of strength in Georgia politics. However, the extended gubernatorial campaign gave them little time for rest before the next battle—this one, within their own ranks. In a matter of months, the GFRW membership would participate in selecting new leaders of both the NFRW and the Georgia Republican Party. While both organizations had previously enjoyed uneventful nominations and elections, the post-Goldwater GOP was a party in search of its future. Women of the GFRW had to choose sides in factional friction between Republicans who wanted to continue a rightward shift and the moderates who sought a retreat to the center. The Republican Party had finally gotten a toehold in Georgia and already consensus began to crumble.

On the heels of a nationwide humiliation in the 1964 presidential election, national Republican leaders struggled over the direction of the party. Conservatives saw reason for hope in the grassroots organization and believed that their wing would only gain momentum. In contrast, moderates worried that extremists had driven the party to a place not only of defeat, but of ridicule. Moderates determined to wrest control back from Goldwater conservatives. The NFRW, with its grassroots power, became a focal point in the national party's tug-of-war.[1] The Georgia Republican Party, emerging as nationally important, also proved to be the focus of a critical contest as the 1968 presidential election loomed.

While the state was undoubtedly conservative, it remained unclear which brand of conservatism Georgia would embrace. Would the state vote Republican again, or had the 1964 victory been due to the one-time charm of a Goldwater candidacy? Could a Callaway machine of Georgia Republicans keep chugging on not just to a plurality, but to a majority? Would the state vote for the most extreme candidate opposing civil rights, regardless of party affiliation? These questions occupied and eventually split the Georgia Federation of Republican Women over the course of 1967 and 1968.

The struggle within the GFRW played out as a microcosm of the national party's internal battle, with those seeking a return to moderation pitted against those wanting to continue down a rightward path. The 1967 NFRW presidential election was a choice between the staunch conservatism of National First Vice President Phyllis Schlafly and the more moderate stance of California Republican leader Gladys O'Donnell. Though the NFRW was, at heart, a grassroots organization, the contest over its leadership would determine the types of educational materials and training sessions that half a million women would receive over the following years. Meanwhile, as one of the fastest-growing state federations, the GFRW could exert influence on a national party level.

Outgoing NFRW president Dorothy Elston had endorsed Barry Goldwater's candidacy in 1964, but his embarrassing loss pushed her back to the center. When the NFRW membership elected Elston in 1963, they also unanimously chose Illinois FRW leader Phyllis Schlafly as first vice president.[2] Unlike Elston and many other Republican leaders, Schlafly staunchly opposed any nods to moderation, even in the name of party unity. In contrast with GOP leadership after 1964, Schlafly believed the GOP should pull the country rightward rather than making a retreat to the center.

The election for NFRW president had previously been a formality in which the board of directors submitted a slate of candidates that the general membership unanimously and graciously approved. Historian Catherine Rymph writes, "At times, dissenting voices grumbled about the official slate, but such dissent was handled quietly."[3] In 1967, displeasure over the official ballot made it into newspapers from the national level all the way into Georgia dailies.[4] The grumbling echoed in living rooms where local federations held their meetings.

Despite her personal support of O'Donnell, outgoing GFRW president Lee Ague tried to put the organization's interests first. With the hope of maintaining calm and unity, she extended invitations to both O'Donnell and Schlafly to appear at the state convention in Atlanta on April 20, 1967.[5] Local federations and individual members had no obligation to remain neutral in the O'Donnell-Schlafly race. Most chose to stand firmly with Schlafly. As the NFRW competition developed, Georgia women's involvement increased, and the publicized factionalism threatened both the group and the friendships of women in it.

As early as 1965, Dorothy Elston had voiced concern over Phyllis Schlafly's rise in the NFRW. In 1964, Schlafly authored the wildly popular critique of national Republican leadership, *A Choice Not an Echo*, in which she condemned party "kingmakers" who selected the GOP candidate each year and then trotted him out to the voters. Arizonan Goldwater, she insisted, was the *people's* "choice," and conservatives refused to "echo" the selection of the Republican leadership. Schlafly's book asserted the role of grassroots workers and urged precinct voters to stand up, even to the national leadership of their own party. Now, with the NFRW leadership at stake, she and her dedicated followers again charged the "kingmakers" with interfering with the choice of the people. In Schlafly's language, she provided a "choice" whereas Gladys O'Donnell was an "echo" of establishment Republicans.[6]

Schlafly's *A Choice Not an Echo* listed her own party credentials as having been a party volunteer for two decades. She reported that she had experience with motivating clubwomen, encouraging "little clubs [to] build stronger Republican organizations, inject enthusiasm, inspire and persuade women to work for the Party, and solve problems of many kinds."[7] Even when the kingmakers put forth a candidate she did not prefer, Schlafly had worked for the party. She argued that she had earned the right to advocate for her conservative candidate in 1964. She did not stop after Goldwater's loss. Rather, she continued visiting clubs in Illinois and around the nation, inspiring and persuading women to support the GOP. By 1967, Schlafly was one of the most popular—and most polarizing—Republican leaders.

Elston and others who advocated party unity over conservatism threw their support behind Californian Gladys O'Donnell. Though O'Donnell had never held an executive position in the national organization, she had led the large California federation and served as a California delegate to three previous RNC conventions. Though she endorsed Goldwater in 1964, O'Donnell sponsored a 1965 California FRW board resolution opposing political extremism. An NFRW brochure described O'Donnell's philosophy as "one which embraces the conservative and moderate points of view," even as she understood the "danger and futility of extremism."[8]

In March 1967, the federation nominating committee put Gladys O'Donnell's name on the official ballot. In the two months before the national convention held on May 5–6, the NFRW split into irreconcilable factions. Not one to roll over in defeat, Phyllis Schlafly insisted that, as first vice president of the NFRW, she had the experience to lead the organization. Moreover, custom dictated that the first vice president assume leadership. The nominating committee had improperly passed over Schlafly, she argued, in offering the presidency to O'Donnell. On April 5, Schlafly launched a campaign to challenge the NFRW nominating committee's candidate, announcing her own candidacy in a joint press conference with Maureen Reagan Sills, the twenty-six-year-old president of the Orange County (Calif.) FRW and daughter of California governor Ronald Reagan.[9] This time, Schlafly employed her grassroots organization skills for her own benefit.

Caught in the middle of a battle between two staunch supporters, Barry Goldwater expressed his frustration to Dorothy Elston over party disunity and refused to endorse either woman. Goldwater praised both O'Donnell and Schlafly for their longtime service to the Republican Party. He assured Elston and, by extension, all NFRW members, "I will look forward to working with and supporting whomever the members of the Federation, in their wisdom, shall choose as their President."[10]

Schlafly's networks reached deep into local federations, including those in Georgia. Representing one of the few states that had voted for Goldwater in 1964, the Georgia federation leaned toward the more conservative candidate. Schlafly's close friend and GFRW officer Kathryn Dunaway immediately began organizing Georgia for Schlafly. Dunaway had several copies of *A Choice, Not an Echo*, which she offered to interested women as she set about organizing Georgia in support of Schlafly's campaign.[11]

In her service as an NFRW officer, Schlafly encouraged women to educate themselves, read "pro-American books," and practice public speaking on political issues. Conveniently, Schlafly published books that fit that description. She rallied women around her motto, "Every member a leader."[12] This message of empowerment and education spread to Georgia, where several local clubs implemented Schlafly's teachings. In May 1965, the president of Troup County FRW in west Georgia used the club newsletter to encourage members to pick up Schlafly's latest book on national defense, *The Gravediggers*.[13]

Another local federation focused on the civility and health of the state federation. When a copy of Goldwater's letter praising both NFRW candidates reached the members of southern Georgia's Lowndes County FRW, the women studied it with great interest. After verifying the letter with Goldwater's personal secretary, the chapter's officers penned a letter to GFRW members expressing their concern that "the 'Rockerfeller [*sic*] forces'" were not powerful enough to put forth a liberal presidential candidate, but that they could "maneuver conservatives into fighting one another." The women reminded readers that the Georgia federation had "tripled in size and can now speak in a loud voice instead of a whisper." The Valdosta women warned that "[the Democrats] won't be able to stop us, but we can, if we split our ranks."[14]

Savannah federation member Rosalind K. Frame brushed aside arguments for unity and made her case for Schlafly in a letter to GFRW members, urging them "to vote for Phyllis Schlafly for president, in order to overcome the [Nelson] Rockefeller influences in Georgia." Frame had seen Schlafly give a talk to a military audience and marveled at her commitment to anti-communism and national security, "presented," as Frame wrote, "in a masculine manner by a lady who is feminine." Frame's contention that Schlafly provided the as-

sertiveness and knowledge necessary to fight the Cold War without sacrificing one iota of American womanhood echoed a rallying point of the extreme
right.[15] In years to come, Schlafly would train many other women in how to
fight hard while maintaining their femininity.

On April 20, just a couple of weeks before the NFRW convention, the Georgia Republican women met in Atlanta for their biennial convention. They
boasted, "A Republican State in '68—from the Precinct to the Presidency."
Ague rotated off as GFRW president and First Vice President Bootsie Calhoun
of Augusta assumed the top post. Unlike the national organization, the Georgia nominations proceeded smoothly, with each officer moving up one post.[16]

Upon leaving her position as GFRW chair, Lee Ague assumed the role of
state finance chairman for the Republican Party of Georgia. After successfully
leading the Goldwater canvass and tripling the size of the GFRW, Ague was
now part of the state party leadership, alongside the men. State finance chair
was not traditionally a woman's role, meaning Ague had brought her "womanpower" to new levels.[17] In this position, she simultaneously challenged the
Democratic hold on Georgia and the men's hold on the state GOP leadership.

With an early convention and a large membership, GFRW became a battle-
ground for Gladys O'Donnell and Phyllis Schlafly, who both agreed to speak,
though not debate, at the state meeting. O'Donnell, listed in the program as
the "National Nominee for President," spoke to the morning session. In the afternoon, Kathryn Dunaway introduced her friend Phyllis Schlafly to speak to
the Georgia women. The GFRW program recognized Schlafly as an NFRW officer, but not as a candidate for federation president.[18]

The appearance of O'Donnell and Schlafly at the Georgia convention confirmed the state's growing influence in the national organization. By-laws of
the NFRW apportioned delegate votes among the states based on the number
of clubs with dues paid in full by March 6. Thanks to the grassroots organizing
of the previous few years, Georgia boasted the largest number of delegation
votes among all southern states, even outdistancing border states with a longer Republican tradition. With ninety-four delegate votes, Georgia had more
clout than Florida with eighty-seven and Maryland with seventy-four. Ninety-
four votes from a state that had yet to elect a Republican to statewide office
reflected Georgia women's grassroots efforts of the past years.[19]

As the solid Goldwater region, the Deep South favored Schlafly. However,
she needed to take Georgia, Florida, and Maryland votes along with Texas, Alabama, and South Carolina just to equal moderate New York's four hundred delegate votes, which would likely go to O'Donnell.[20] A union of South and West,
though, could threaten the East Coast hold on the NFRW. Schlafly and her supporters suspected it was this possibility of an alliance of South and West that

led the NFRW board to move the meeting from Los Angeles to Washington, D.C., where more East Coast Republican women might attend, tossing more support to O'Donnell.[21]

Kathryn Dunaway organized Georgia for Schlafly. Aware of the friendship between the two women, local federations wrote Dunaway to express their admiration for Schlafly and request campaign materials. Even neighboring Alabama federations proclaimed their support of Schlafly. Dunaway shared a pamphlet of pro-Schlafly songs like, "We've all come over / To the Four Leaf Clover / That *Some* overlooked before." "The Battle Hymn of the Republican Women" called the troops into combat for moral government: "We are called to save our country / Lest God let the Enemy sword / Strike 'cause reform is late."[22]

Although she tried to appear neutral during the state convention, Lee Ague personally supported O'Donnell. After the state meeting, O'Donnell wrote Ague expressing appreciation for her "understanding and adroit management of a sticky situation" in planning and moderating the convention. Shirking off neutrality after the Georgia meeting, Ague agreed to work for O'Donnell from the floor of the NFRW convention. After all, Ague owed her leadership position in Georgia to the intervention of Elston and the NFRW board in 1965, when they recognized Ague's faction as the official GFRW.[23] In supporting O'Donnell in 1967, Ague firmly placed herself on the side of the friends who had supported her so much in growing the women's federation in Georgia. O'Donnell asked Ague to forward "the list of your delegates, with an indication of their sentiment, at the earliest possible date." O'Donnell hoped Ague would help line up sympathetic delegates who could ensure Schlafly's defeat.[24]

The candidates' ideas about the future direction of the NFRW were not the only difference between them. Literature from both NFRW candidates focused on motherhood, age, and women's experiences. A widow, the sixty-three-year-old O'Donnell had already raised her children. O'Donnell supporters believed the empty nest allowed her more freedom to commit to Washington, D.C., where the organization would benefit from her proximity to legislators and party leaders. Traditionally, NFRW presidents did move to the nation's capital for the duration of their term. However, Phyllis Schlafly pointed out that moving was not a requirement. Schlafly, at age forty-two, regularly spoke of her six young children. One pro-Schlafly article framed women's successful political action in maternalist terms: "[A mother] realizes that not only the home but also the community and the country must be kept strong and sound for the child." Schlafly predicted that a younger president would "double the membership of the Federation," since, as she said, "our great potential growth is young women. To attract young women we have to have youth in leadership."[25] Whenever possible, Schlafly stressed that her husband supported her candidacy and did not see it as being in conflict with her dedication to her family. Her husband Fred even joined her campaign, distributing literature that, according to one reporter covering the campaign, featured "violent protests about the 'unfair and divisive tactics' being employed by Mrs. O'Donnell."[26]

Days before the convention, O'Donnell and Schlafly finally met face-to-face at the nonpartisan Women's National Press Club. A *Washington Post* reporter wrote that the "White gloves were off" as the two sparred over questions of GOP direction, allegations of unethical campaigning, the role of women in politics, and American policy in Vietnam. The two candidates were not even scheduled to speak at the NFRW convention, so this would be their only debate. National press covered the showdown between the two women as foreshadowing the future of the Republican Party. Their one debate took place not in front of potential voting delegates, but in front of the press and notable women in Washington, including Margaret McNamara, wife of the secretary of defense, and Louella Dirksen, wife of the senate minority leader, who listened but did not talk with the candidates.[27]

When the NFRW finally convened in Washington, D.C., on May 5–6, 1967, over three thousand women attended.[28] While some Georgia women paid their own way, many clubs applied their well-honed fundraising skills to the goal of sponsoring a delegate's trip. The Metropolitan Club, for example, held a "fashion tea" and sold candy to raise the necessary funds.[29] Other women had first-class transportation to the event. Roscoe Pickett Jr., a candidate for Georgia GOP national committeeman, flew two planeloads of women to the convention using his personal plane and a chartered plane to make sure that Georgia's Schlafly delegates could vote. Pickett was in a tight race for committeeman with Georgia's most prominent Republican, Bo Callaway. Pickett understood the contributions women made to the state GOP just as much as he knew the sway women might have over delegate votes for the committeeman position. Callaway remained neutral, not lending his substantial financial or political support to either side. Ague threw her support in the committeeman race to Callaway.[30]

At the NFRW convention, Schlafly boosters recognized one another by the eagle pins they wore. Schlafly biographer Donald T. Critchlow explains that the pins referred to Isaiah 40:31: "But they that wait upon the Lord shall renew their strength; they shall mount up with wings as eagles; they shall run, and not be weary; and they shall walk, and not faint." Other supporters wore ribbons that played on the title from a popular song, "P.S. I Love You."[31] Schlafly warned followers to be aware of any possible election fraud or any efforts to silence the conservative wing. Previously trained as poll watchers for local precincts, the women now turned their eyes on their own group.

On Friday night, both the O'Donnell wing and the Schlafly supporters held receptions. The NFRW sponsored receptions for the official nominees for various positions, including the one for O'Donnell. Californians for Schlafly sponsored the reception for her supporters and boasted fifteen hundred partygoers. In contrast to the official reception's bar with alcohol served, the Schlafly event served fruit punch and cookies. Among the special guests at the Schlafly reception were Republican legacy figures Maureen Reagan Sills and Edith Kermit Roosevelt, granddaughter of Theodore Roosevelt. Perhaps the most prominent southern Republican of the time, Senator Strom Thurmond of South Carolina, arrived to support Schlafly.[32]

Voting commenced the next day. Pro-Schlafly delegates complained about last-minute changes to the credentials process that created obstacles when they went to register. Some charged that busloads of unregistered delegates from Rockefeller-friendly New York and New Jersey had cast ballots. Despite all the charges and delays, the vote proceeded. Gladys O'Donnell won the election with 1,910 votes to Schlafly's 1,494.[33] Despite a 12 percent difference, the outsider candidate had presented a serious challenge to the GOP establishment.

Having primed her followers to suspect fraud, Schlafly played hardball after her defeat. Upon the announcement of her loss, Schlafly and hundreds of her supporters—including Kathryn Dunaway—walked out of the convention hall. A Baltimore newspaper reported that Schlafly had already applied for a legal charter for a new group, the American Federation of Republican Women, but Maureen Reagan Sills had convinced Schlafly to wait to announce the rival group. Minutes after their convention exit, the adamantly pro-Schlafly Sills encouraged the crowd to "go home and think it over."[34] Knowing her father was a possible presidential nominee the next year, Sills understood that the women's organization was critical for campaign organization. For the benefit of her father, Sills needed the Schlafly energy to stay within the party structure.

When Schlafly finally spoke, she did not introduce a new women's organization, but neither did she back down. Instead, she praised her loyal delegates for maintaining integrity, implying they were the exception in doing so. She echoed Reagan Sills's call to pause before a next step. Schlafly reassured her supporters, "You believe in the same things I believe in, and we have just begun to fight. . . . I will do anything you want me to do."[35]

Within a month, Schlafly wrote her delegates that she planned to stay in the NFRW and work to change the organization from inside. She reminded the women that "each individual club in the federation is autonomous," and, as such, they did not have to follow O'Donnell's leadership. Schlafly asserted, "Your club has every right to accept or ignore the direction, the literature, or the speakers sent out from the *top*."[36] She positioned herself not only as the persecuted conservative, but also as the champion of the local grassroots women. She deftly defined the national Republican leadership as part of an elitist plot within an honest conservative movement. She positioned herself as having followed Goldwater in her fate: national party leaders had been queen makers, elevating O'Donnell above the people's choice of Schlafly.

According to Schlafly, moderates in the national power structure had not only purged those who believed in taking the party further right, but had also neglected to listen to the local-level party workers. Individual clubs, she reminded, elected their own leaders and could put conservatives in those roles. By digging in at the grassroots, she braced her followers to pull the party rightward.

Kathryn Dunaway assumed her role as second vice president of the GFRW, placing her in line to lead the state federation in four years. She committed to following Schlafly in tugging local clubs further right. Dunaway had volunteered to monitor fraud at the NFRW convention and repeated her suspicion that "the election was improper and illegal." She worried that the growing distrust of national leadership at the local level resulted in "a feeling of apathy and uselessness, which has affected the activities and memberships of the Ga. Fed of Rep. Women this summer." She met with Annette McEachin in the Fourth District and Marjean Birt in the Fifth so that they could "revive interest and confidence" well before the critical 1968 campaigns. Hoping for some news to encourage conservatives, Dunaway reported that more local federations had paid their dues and applied for reinstatement. Perhaps next time, the conservatives would win.[37]

Of course, Schlafly may have conceded the election, but she did not relinquish her influence in the NFRW. Not even three months after her defeat, Schlafly sent a letter to her supporters in the NFRW announcing the formation of the Eagle Trust Fund to educate women about issues important to conservatism. Those who donated would receive her new newsletter, *The Phyllis Schlafly Report*, a four-page information sheet educating subscribers about the conservative viewpoint on important national issues. Kathryn Dunaway, of course, sent in her subscription immediately so as not to miss a single issue. The first issue in August 1967 examined the history of the Panama Canal, its position in current Cold War foreign policy, and the dangers of ceding control of the canal back to Panama. In preparation for upcoming campaigns, the October 1967 *Phyllis Schlafly Report* centered on the question, "Is Your Congressman in the Republican Mainstream?" Because she perceived a purge of the extreme right after 1964's losses, Schlafly argued that electing Republicans was no longer enough. Women needed to elect *conservative* Republicans.[38] Kathryn Dunaway did her part in delivering Schlafly's message to Georgia women.

In appreciation of Dunaway's support and hoping to encourage conservatives in Georgia, Phyllis Schlafly visited the state in autumn 1967. During the Atlanta leg of the trip, Dunaway hosted Schlafly in her home. This time, rather than speaking to the GFRW, Dunaway arranged for Schlafly to address her chapter of the Daughters of the American Revolution. Roscoe Pickett Jr. again lent his plane and the two women visited several Georgia towns. They kicked off the tour at a reception in Schlafly's honor in coastal Savannah. The president of the Tift County FRW traveled nearly two hundred miles to attend. On the western border of the state, the Columbus Area FRW hosted a dinner in Schlafly's honor and arranged radio and television interviews. Schlafly thanked Dunaway for joining her "to hear the same speech several more times! This was truly dedication above and beyond the call of even your famous southern hospitality!" She ended with thanks "for your constant and loyal support."[39] Over the next decade, Dunaway's loyalty to Schlafly would elevate Georgia's conservative women to being valued members of conservative movements beyond the GOP. Their travels around Georgia laid the foundation for their future work organizing against the Equal Rights Amendment from the local to the national levels.

On the other side of the fight, Lee Ague received a letter of appreciation from Gladys O'Donnell, who wrote, "In the aftermath of the explosive and traumatic convention, I search for words to express my gratitude to you who contributed so nobly . . . and who stood so valiantly during the ordeal." The new NFRW president asked for support in "repairing our damaged image by going resolutely forward with sincerity and quiet determination." During the months after the convention, O'Donnell encouraged state leaders to help local clubs smooth over any differences, recognizing that "the great majority of Republican women represent the finest in American womanhood."[40] She did not articulate what she thought of the minority.

Despite the calls to heal, members had a difficult time coming together. Women tried to unite within the local and state chapters. For a while, the two factions did bind together, but efforts at unity soon failed. Over time, factions only hardened, each claiming the mantle of conservative womanhood. Ague and new GFRW president Bootsie Calhoun tried to hold the state federation together and grow it during the 1968 campaigns, but the extreme right wing only grew more frustrated.

In July 1967, the Georgia GOP and the GFRW suffered a great blow when Lee Ague developed a blood clot in her leg and moved to Florida to recover. Preparing for the 1968 elections, several state candidates agonized over the loss of the woman who had led Georgia to victory for Goldwater and a plurality for Bo Callaway. Callaway campaign chairman G. Paul Jones and first vice chairman Frank Troutman, among many others, wished Ague a speedy recovery.

Most began with expressions of concern for her health, but all noted deep concern for the Georgia Republican Party.[41]

Ague had trained a cadre of women in savvy grassroots organizing tactics. For years, her political strategy empowered and educated the local-level volunteers. Volunteer labor helped win the state for Goldwater in 1964 and for Callaway in 1966, and they all begrudged the legislature for denying them victory. For their part, the local chapters of the GFRW knew exactly how to organize campaigns due to Ague's effective grassroots training. Some chapters worked on the off-year local elections while most chapters worked on voter registration and education, setting out to sign up newcomers and convert natives. All chapters tried to heal after the wounds of the NFRW convention. Everyone was working to help position the party in anticipation of the 1968 presidential elections.

Republican women continued to work for electoral success at the state and local levels across Georgia. The GFRW temporarily put aside differences to return to voter registration and education as well as recruitment of new members. In 1968, Lee Ague missed a GFRW meeting for the first time in four years. At the February board meeting, Kathryn Dunaway, now second vice president, challenged, "May I remind you that women can and will make the difference in '68 and thereafter." Focusing on Republican victory at all levels, Dunaway gave up her disappointment in the NFRW election and committed herself to helping secure wins for the GOP. In the suburban Fourth and Fifth Districts around Atlanta, Dunaway planned workshops to train and retrain precinct workers for the 1968 campaigns. She became certified as a precinct chairman, a job that would utilize her well-developed eye for monitoring elections.[42]

Women at all levels of the GFRW tried to heed leaders' calls to cast aside differences for the sake of victory in 1968. They kicked into gear using strategies learned in previous campaigns—local fundraising, voter education, and voter registration drives. Social events built enthusiasm and educated attendees on the latest Republican talking points. State membership chairman Marjean Birt encouraged local federations to concentrate on recruitment and retention, saying, "Remember to Re-member! Don't let one member slip from you by neglect." Modeling her advice on Ague's earlier recruitment programs, Birt suggested each chapter member invite one new person to the next meeting, with each officer recruiting two women. When new people moved to town, Birt suggested a GFRW welcome: "find out if they would be interested in joining your Federation by tactfully mentioning the two party system." As an incentive, the state GOP offered "two free tickets from one of the local airlines during the Republican National Convention in Miami" to the club with the greatest growth.[43] Birt continued to reinforce strategy, language, and incentive to grow the Republican Party in every district.

Around the state, local women set to work identifying Republican voters and recruiting new members. The Third District FRW coordinator celebrated the "over 150 enthusiastic Republicans" at her workshop in southwestern Americus. In the Fourth District, leaders reported a successful booth at the suburban Atlanta DeKalb County Fair and celebrated the theme "A Republican Revival in Georgia!" Troup County FRW hosted a public screening of a Ronald Reagan film in anticipation of the 1968 primaries. In Cherokee County, the federation placed the book *The Republican Party* in the local library and ran an ad in the local paper asking, "Are You Republican and Don't Know It?" Hall County FRW members prepared Christmas care packages for soldiers in Vietnam in addition to their usual work of fundraising and publishing a club newsletter.[44]

Some clubs were able to report local off-year electoral successes. In 1967, GFRW president Bootsie Calhoun's home club in Augusta celebrated a "66 2/3% membership increase" over the previous year and reported 111 active members. However, their biggest news was that the Republican candidate had won the sheriff's race, with "a loud wail of woe from the Democrats." They attributed part of the momentum to an October visit from former First Lady Mamie Eisenhower. In the wake of the NFRW split, Eisenhower "gave us extra inspiration for closer unity and harder work."[45] Even Bootsie Calhoun herself had won elected office, gathering the highest number of votes out of a field of sixteen candidates running for the Augusta Board of Education.[46] As candidates on the local level, Georgia women were moving from supporting to starring roles. Calhoun called women "the Strong Right Arm of the Republican Effort in Georgia" and demonstrated her own electoral star power.[47]

Bibb County FRW celebrated, "Macon [the Bibb County seat] now has the second Republican Mayor in the state, Ronnie Thompson, and three Republican City Aldermen." They also managed to establish a county Republican Party headquarters, staffed completely with volunteers.[48] The election of the city's top official and a strong GOP slate of aldermen affirmed the years of grassroots work the women had invested in phone calls and bake sales. The women knew the Republican Party was now a permanent presence in Bibb County. Significantly, all of this local-level organizing and winning occurred before any coordinated southern strategy from the national Republican Party.

Despite their promises to move past the NFRW election, some GFRW infighting seeped into the Georgia Republican Party. Even a contest for National GOP committeeman became a showdown between the right and the far right as Bo Callaway and Roscoe Pickett Jr. battled for the position. Callaway was a recent but successful Republican convert. He had ridden Goldwater's coattails into the U.S. House of Representatives in 1964 and mounted a serious contest for the governorship in 1966. His opponent, Roscoe Pickett Jr., had credentials rare in Georgia, hailing from a longtime white Republican family. His father had run and lost as the Republican gubernatorial candidate in 1916. Plus, Pickett was the incumbent committeeman.[49] Though Callaway and Pickett were only battling for a party position, it was the first time two Republicans had faced off in the state.

A national committeeman's primary task was organizing the state for the presidential nominee. Therefore, committeemen usually waited to endorse a candidate until the party actually had a candidate. Roscoe Pickett bucked tradition, declaring his support for conservative favorite, California governor Ronald Reagan. Honoring custom, Bo Callaway refused to endorse any likely candidate—Reagan, Vice President Richard Nixon, Michigan governor George Romney—nor anyone else. Thus, in the Georgia race, Pickett became the preferred candidate of staunch conservatives, while Callaway remained the choice of slightly more moderate conservatives. True moderates did not have much place in the Georgia GOP.[50]

Quickly, the GFRW fractured once again. Fresh from her disappointment as a Schlafly supporter, Rosalind Frame distributed a letter in which she charged that Callaway would not support Reagan. She revived old GFRW fights, attacking the absent "Lee Lieberman Ague" for having "voted 37 times for Mrs. O'Donnell." In using Ague's maiden name, Frame strove to whip up anti-Semitism to sway Georgians away from moderation. Lucille Bedford of Tucker reprimanded Frame for her tone, saying that "the technique of character assassination you are using against our Georgia state Republican leaders must not be used," as it would divide Republicans.[51]

In the end, Bo Callaway defeated Roscoe Pickett Jr. to become national committeeman. Longtime GFRW activist Florence Cauble became national committeewoman. Callaway and Cauble would direct Georgia through the Nixon campaign and then would direct Georgia through a Nixon presidency. But the Georgia Republican consensus that had supported both Goldwater and Callaway had cracked.

Once elected, Bo Callaway and Florence Cauble faced the daunting task of organizing Georgia for the 1968 presidential race, which increasingly resembled the 1966 gubernatorial race, with a Democrat, a Republican, and a third-party George Wallace all campaigning for the White House. Georgia Republicans knew to worry. In 1966, they had put up their most experienced, most recognized Republican and had still lost to a Democrat who embraced white supremacy.

In the 1964 presidential election, fiscal and racial conservatism had mingled. In that race, Lester Maddox had led the Democrats for Goldwater movement. After Goldwater suggested that Maddox go "back to serving hot dogs" after the 1966 gubernatorial race, Maddox refused to support the national Republican Party again. In 1968, segregationist Maddox looked to Alabama and threw his support behind fellow segregationist governor George Wallace. By May 1968—one month after Martin Luther King Jr.'s funeral in Atlanta—Governor Maddox unabashedly wore a Wallace for President button.[52] Maddox went a step further with his venom toward the GOP when he reminded voters that it was a Republican president who appointed Chief Justice Earl Warren and who gave the order that "invaded Little Rock."[53] Like many segregationist southerners, Maddox believed both parties had abandoned him.

Recognizing Georgia's emerging place in the national GOP, two Republican leaders visited the state in the fall of 1967. Michigan governor George Romney included Atlanta on his tour of nineteen urban areas, touring "Atlanta Negro slums" before holding a strategy session over dinner with state GOP leaders. Stealing some of Romney's thunder, Bo Callaway scheduled a press conference on the same day at the same hotel to announce that Illinois senator Everett Dirksen would be the featured speaker at a state party fundraiser the next month. Romney, still unannounced as a presidential candidate, was far more moderate than Dirksen, who was favored by the conservative wing. Dirksen's October visit brought out almost twelve hundred Georgia Republicans who paid one hundred dollars each to attend a dinner event. The Illinois conservative hoped to excite core party activists to work for Republican victory in 1968.[54] For its part, the GFRW continued to support all Republican candidates, allowing individual members to support the candidate of their choice. They did expect, though, that members would eventually rally behind the nominee.

All the national Republican candidates sought to reap the rewards of years of women's grassroots organizing. Two Party Tea Parties had already introduced the GOP to the region, so candidates only had to introduce themselves. Whoever won the nomination would also win the network of trained volunteers, ready to mobilize voters and monitor polls. Republicans of both wings had begun to focus on the South and its shifting political preferences. With twelve electoral votes, Georgia had the most pull of any of the Deep South states that had gone for Goldwater in 1964. By 1968, many Republican presidential hopefuls—including Romney, Dirksen, Reagan, and Wallace—had developed a southern strategy to woo Georgia voters. All of their campaigns grafted on to the existing Republican structures these women had built over the last five years.

Republican political strategist Kevin Phillips outlined the southern strategy in his book about the 1968 campaign, explaining that they had decided to go for the "outer south" states that had trended for Republicans in elections prior to 1964. The Nixon camp wrote off the five Deep South states that went for Goldwater—including Georgia—as Wallace territory. Campaign managers assumed that after the 1965 Voting Rights Act, African American voters would vote for the Democratic candidate, while Deep South white voters would vote for the rabidly segregationist George Wallace. As African American voting increased, Phillips saw more white southerners moving to the GOP, going as far as to say, "Maintenance of Negro voting rights is essential to the GOP. Unless Negroes continue to displace white Democratic organizations, the latter may remain viable as spokesmen for Deep Southern conservatism." Analyzing voting patterns over the past century, Phillips also observed, "The opinion-molding upper-middle classes of the urban Deep South are already trending heavily Republican." Predicting the future of the Republican Party, he wrote, "the Republican Party cannot go to the Deep South, but . . . the Deep South must soon go to the national GOP."[55]

Had Phillips looked carefully, he would have seen that the process was already well underway. Indeed, most interpretations of Nixon's southern strategy view it as going after disgruntled white southern voters, frustrated with the encroachment of the civil rights movement into their lives. Yet as scholar Dan T. Carter notes, Goldwater's Deep South victory lifted several southern Republicans even before any such strategy existed.[56]

So why could Phillips not see these processes already underway well before 1968? Phillips completely neglected to recognize the importance of gender as a framework and a force in Republican politics. His understanding of political work was too narrow. Had he looked closely at existing party structures in the South, he could not have missed the grassroots organizations of thousands of women. Even Democratic-leaning southern newspapers featured Republican women at supermarkets and county fairs, promoting the Republican platform in the language of American motherhood. Like many strategists and scholars before and since, Phillips did not recognize the hard political work of tea parties, bake sales, and staffing county fair booths. Uniforms of Victory Girls and Go Bo Girls were at least as political as white collared shirts, red ties, and flag pins. Ignoring women's work may lure one into believing the southern strategy was a new idea, but centering women reveals that the paid professionals arrived late on the scene.

Historian Matthew D. Lassiter argues that Nixon's focus shifted from the overtly racist, anti–civil rights legislation politics that had won for Goldwater, toward a "suburban strategy." Lassiter explains the shift in economic terms, with the GOP emphasizing "the middle-class corporate economy" rather than pursuing "the working-class politics of racial backlash."[57] Infusing a gendered analysis into our parsing of the southern strategy reveals that the GOP did not have to choose between middle class and working class. Language of family values crossed class lines while obscuring, but not obviating, racial politics. The model voter in a suburban strategy was not the father in the station wagon but the mother at the grocery store, stretching the budget to feed the children.

Richard Nixon must also have understood that he could not completely write off the Deep South. When he sought to select a southern organizer for his campaign, he narrowed in on one of the leading men of southern suburban politics; Bo Callaway joined the Nixon campaign as its southern campaign director.[58] Callaway had networks across the South and the valuable experience of running against a racist southern demagogue. A *New York Times* article explained that Callaway's 1966 gubernatorial campaign taught him to "never underestimate the politician whose basic appeal is to the underdog, the redneck, the fundamentalist, and the kook."[59] In fighting George Wallace for southern white votes, Nixon needed an advisor with just that experience.

Bo Callaway also understood the value of women in the campaign organization. Despite the internal rifts of the previous year's NFRW elections, the women of the Georgia Federation again vowed to put party loyalty above party ideology. In doing so, they chose the national Republican conservatism over the southern racial conservatism of George Wallace. Dee Hardin headed up Georgia's Women for Nixon organization. Hardin had long been involved in the Tucker FRW in suburban DeKalb County. She coordinated with local chapters as well as the NFRW leadership to mobilize women for the Republican candidate.[60]

The national party also increasingly recognized the value of women to the GOP strategy. Assistant RNC chairman Mary Brooks ensured women would have equal representation on convention committees at the 1968 Miami meeting. Any state that did not send four women as delegates would be penalized with a loss of representation on major committees. Because each state had at least eight nominating delegates, this ensured increased representation of women. Brooks said the rule was a means of "recognizing the steadily increasing participation and influence of women in the Republican Party." After the NFRW conflicts the previous year had garnered such negative press, the presence of women as leaders encouraged the message of unity. Additionally, the women leaders within the national Republican Party understood the value in positioning their party as attractive to the burgeoning women's equality movements.[61]

The national GOP also highlighted racial minorities at the Miami convention. A few well-placed African Americans allowed the conventioneers to address law-and-order and education issues with an appearance of inclusivity. The RNC welcomed Massachusetts senator Edward Brooke as the convention emcee.[62] Brooke won election to the Senate in 1966, becoming the first African American senator since Reconstruction. Representing Georgia, Metropolitan

Club president Evelyn Frazier attended as an alternate delegate. While at the RNC national convention in Miami, Frazier reported that "in a turn of fate" she "became a voting delegate." Frazier and her husband owned and operated Frazier's Café Society, a social club and restaurant in the city's famous Sweet Auburn neighborhood. In selecting Frazier as an alternate delegate, the Georgia GOP was trying to attract middle-class African American voters.[63]

Despite rising to a national position, Callaway continued to return to Georgia to support the women who had worked for him. Together, they all tried to apply the lessons they had learned against Maddox to a fight against Wallace. After the Miami convention, Bo Callaway shared his lessons in political rhetoric in a workshop for the Hall County FRW. They learned to "emphasize the importance of trying to overcome the specious arguments of George Wallace." Callaway stressed that the women approach the Wallace supporter "courteously and positively." The newsletter reported that whenever the members welcomed a new person to town—some of whom may be moving from Alabama—they should remember these tips. Additionally, the Hall County newsletter reminded women, "Your job is not to persuade Republicans, but to influence and convert Democrats and independents."[64] In order to win, they had to grow beyond their own club boundaries.

GFRW women again went to work, supporting Republican candidates from Nixon down to the local level and welcoming new Republican voters. In 1968, they also educated voters on the differences between Nixon and Wallace. In East Point, south of Atlanta, the GFRW chapter worked for the election of a Republican mayor and four councilmen. Coweta County's FRW opened a local party headquarters on October 1 so that forty-nine women volunteers could support Nixon-Agnew and other GOP names on the ballot. The Cobb County chapter sponsored a float in Atlanta's "Salute to America" parade in addition to continued fundraising and volunteer work.[65] Wherever they lived, Republican women worked to keep the GOP in voters' minds.

Statewide, women volunteered as precinct workers for Georgia's first-ever Republican primary on September 11. Groups all over Georgia held fundraisers, selling elephant pins, elephant clips, and other themed jewelry as well as GOP toothbrushes. They cleaned out their houses and raised money at Republican rummage sales. In Clarke County, women donated stuffed elephants for charity Christmas stockings and contributed "3 books from the Mamie Eisenhower Library list to . . . the two local high schools and the public library." Women focused on all registered voters as potential Nixon voters even as they made sure that the GOP brand reached to future voters as well.[66]

Rural Georgia, once nicknamed Maddox Country, became Wallace Country. GFRW chapters in those areas had a more challenging fight to keep the GOP viable in voters' minds. Houston County women volunteered at two offices to cover their area for the GOP ticket. Neighboring Peach County reported a gain of three members, no small task in rural Georgia that year. Central Georgia's Bibb County women boasted that they contributed labor to their county GOP's monthly newsletter.[67] Women's volunteer labor supported the GOP all over the state. With no coordinator in the First Congressional District in the southeastern corner of the state, Bessie M. Militades in the Tenth District volunteered to step in until the GFRW reestablished a presence there. She promised, "We will work diligently until all 20 counties have been organized." However, describing the reality of the situation, she said, "Our greatest problem is the apathy of the voters, unless the magic name 'Wallace' is mentioned. . . . The rural areas are overwhelmingly for Wallace."[68] Still, they organized, remembering Ague's 1964 lesson that even a few voters might make the difference in the state's electoral votes.

In the district including Augusta, Athens, and some rural counties, the GFRW chair reported, "George Wallace thinks he'll carry the 10th District, but we have 300 women working to make sure that won't happen." Actually, she suspected, "We probably have a larger number than that," but too many women hesitated to form official FRW chapters. Just as Ague before her converted Women for Callaway chapters into GFRW groups, she settled on planting Women for Nixon chapters, which she would focus on making permanent federation chapters after members caught the political fever. With the clock ticking, the women took any support offered. To target rural areas, Tenth District chapters also hosted a speaking tour by Macon's Republican mayor Ronnie Thompson, who brought the Republican message along with his country music show.[69]

Cobb County's federation newsletter explained that neither party could dismiss Wallace, describing him as "an extremely clever, perceptive politician." The March 1968 newsletter predicted that "he has, at best, only a slim chance at winning the Presidency" but a greater chance of dividing the conservative vote, especially in southern states. In June, they reprinted a letter from Cobb County soldier Mike McKenzie, then stationed in Vietnam. McKenzie expressed shame at southern conservatives who had supported Goldwater but then left the GOP for Maddox and Wallace. "Perhaps with the candidacy of Wallace," he hoped, "some of the very conservative/racist group will leave our ranks for good." The CCFRW president assured him, however, that a condition of membership in the federation was pledged support for the Republican candidate and that the women would work hard to defeat Wallace and keep his influence out of their chapter.[70]

In the end, Georgia's electoral votes did go to George Wallace, even though Wallace failed to win a majority of the state's popular vote. The American Independent candidate pulled 42.8 percent of the popular vote, with Nixon coming in second at 30.4 percent. Democratic candidate Hubert Humphrey had 26.7 percent. Wallace won in rural counties, with Nixon taking the majority in the suburban Atlanta counties of Cobb and DeKalb, both of which had strong GFRW organizations. Women for Nixon coordinator Dee Hardin celebrated that her home county DeKalb came through. In the Tenth District, Clarke and Richmond Counties—home of Athens and Augusta, respectively—were the only two of the district's nineteen counties to vote for Nixon. Henceforth, the women of Richmond County would brag that their county went Republican in 1954 and "it has gone Republican ever since, [and was] even one of the counties in Georgia to resist George Wallace in 1968 and go for Nixon." Additionally, five rural counties on the northern border with Tennessee landed in the Nixon column.[71]

Despite losing the state's electoral votes to Wallace, once the general election had been held the women could celebrate the fact that the nation again had a Republican president. Even more promising for them, Georgia had failed to vote Democratic in two consecutive presidential elections. Moreover, the Fourth and Fifth Districts reelected Republicans Ben Blackburn and Fletcher Thompson, and Georgia now boasted its first second-term Republican congressmen in a century. Newly inaugurated GFRW president Virginia Estes wrote, "Even though we didn't carry the state for Nixon, we have held our Party together, and have increased within the Women's Federation."[72] Again, GFRW members committed picked themselves up, brushed themselves off, and looked to the next election.

Some GFRW members, though, picked themselves up and out of party politics. By the end of 1968, despite good intentions on both sides of the O'Donnell-Schlafly feud, the Georgia Federation of Republican Women could not maintain unity. The National Federation, also unable to heal, dropped from a half million members to fewer than 250,000. Many resigned from clubs in Georgia. In the spring of 1969, the GFRW reported only fifty-three local clubs, a decrease since the rapid growth of 1964. Despite the loss of chapters, the state organization still boasted 1,740 members, an increase in total membership.[73]

Less than two months before the November election, several prominent women resigned their membership in the GFRW. Among the most significant were President Bootsie Calhoun and First Vice President Kathryn Dunaway. The committee chairs of publicity, finance, protocol, and legislative affairs also stepped down from their posts.[74] The women did not state their reason for resigning at that time, although some may well have supported Wallace. In coming years Dunaway would establish the Georgia chapters of Phyllis Schlafly's STOP ERA and Eagle Forum, working for even more conservative causes and candidates.[75]

Whether or not the women remained in the GFRW, most remained dedicated to conservatism in Georgia. The moderates who remained in the party continued working to build the state GOP, including pushing for women in appointed and elected offices. Those of the far right that left the GFRW remained Republican voters but worked for a more extreme conservatism. Working as outsiders, mostly under the leadership of Phyllis Schlafly, these women battled not only moderate Republicans but also second-wave feminism. Over the next decade, they would codify the gendered language of conservatism, a language that provided a path to Republican dominance in the southern states and the rise of family-values language in national conservative movements.

Left to right: Cobb County FRW officers Clara Curtis and Lee Ague, dressed in their Victory Girl uniforms, accept the Exemplary Award for the club's activities from NFRW president Dorothy Elston at the 1964 national meeting. GFRW president Rita Creson looks on. (Lee Ague Miller Papers, Special Collections and Archives, Georgia State University Libraries, Atlanta, Ga.)

National Federation of Republican Women meetings encouraged women to build networks across state lines. Here, southern state federation presidents pose at the 1965 NFRW Board of Directors meeting at the New York World's Fair, October 1965. *Left to right:* Hon. Mary Grizzle (president, Florida FRW); Mrs. Frank Smith (president, North Carolina FRW); Hon. Mary Brooks (assistant the chairman of the RNC); Mrs. Lee Ague (president, Georgia FRW); Mrs. Jim Reynolds (president, Virginia FRW). (Lee Ague Miller Papers, Special Collections and Archives, Women's Collections, Georgia State University Libraries, Atlanta, Ga.)

The Metropolitan Republican Women's Club float at the 1971 WSB Salute to America Independence Day Parade proceeds down Peachtree Street. "Miss Patriotism" and "Honorary Queen" Evelyn Frazier sits upon the heart-shaped throne at the back of the float. Accompanying her are young women representing the historic reforms of the Republican Party, including "Miss Emancipation Proclamation Queen," "Miss Thirteenth Amendment Queen," "Miss Fourteenth Amendment Queen," "Miss Good Citizenship Queen," "Miss Civil Rights Queen," and "Miss Welfare Reform Queen." Club member and local florist Irene Hendrix pulled the float with her blue station wagon. (Evelyn J. Frazier Papers, Archives Division, Auburn Avenue Research Library on African American Culture and History, Fulton County Library System)

Members of the Metropolitan Republican Women's Club at Frazier's Café Society. Club president Evelyn Frazier stands center at the podium. Club member Ruth Duncan is to her left. A Nixon poster hangs on the wall behind them. No date. (Evelyn J. Frazier Papers, Archives Division, Auburn Avenue Research Library on African American Culture and History, Fulton County Library System)

STOP ERA volunteers on the floor of the Georgia legislature. Kathryn Dunaway stands in the front center, holding her pocketbook. (Kathryn Fink Dunaway Papers, Stuart A. Rose Manuscript, Archives, and Rare Book Library, Emory University, Atlanta, Ga.)

By the end of the 1970s, Georgia STOP ERA had begun a tradition of serving a Valentine's Day luncheon to state legislators. In 1979, Kathryn Dunaway reported they had served five hundred lunches in that year alone. The women also delivered bread, cakes, and other home-baked goods as part of their message of the importance of women's work in the home. In this photo, Georgia STOP ERA cochairman Lee Wysong stands second from the right. (Kathryn Fink Dunaway Papers, Stuart A. Rose Manuscript, Archives, and Rare Book Library, Emory University, Atlanta, Ga.)

Speaker of the Georgia House of Representatives Tom Murphy was one of the staunchest STOP ERA allies. *Left to right:* Unidentified, STOP ERA founder Phyllis Schlafly, Speaker Tom Murphy, unidentified, Georgia STOP ERA chair Kathryn Dunaway. Undated. (Kathryn Fink Dunaway Papers, Stuart A. Rose Manuscript, Archives, and Rare Book Library, Emory University, Atlanta, Ga.)

Kathryn Dunaway presents Speaker of the Georgia State House Tom Murphy with a STOP ERA valentine at the Georgia State Capitol in an undated photo. (Kathryn Fink Dunaway Papers, Stuart A. Rose Manuscript, Archives, and Rare Book Library, Emory University, Atlanta, Ga.)

Eliza Paschall Morrison was a civil rights leader in Atlanta. She founded the Atlanta chapter of the National Organization for Women (NOW) in 1970. In 1978, she came out in opposition to the Equal Rights Amendment and worked with Kathryn Dunaway and Lee Wysong on STOP ERA. In 1984–85, Paschall served as associate director of the Office of Public Liaison in the Reagan White House. (Photo courtesy of Suzanne Stephenson)

CHAPTER 4

Thousands of Mothers
Make a Movement

In his first inaugural address, Richard Nixon challenged American citizens to take action in their communities to tackle the nation's troubles. "To match the magnitude of our tasks," he said, "We need the energies of our people—enlisted not only in grand enterprises, but more importantly in those small, splendid efforts that make headlines in the neighborhood newspaper instead of the national journal." Just as women were ahead of Nixon in targeting the South for GOP expansion, Republican women already had a record of making local news headlines with their volunteer efforts. Nixon's message resonated so much with Republican women's work that the NFRW reprinted it on the front page of the federation newsletter with a reminder for members to continue in their dedication. Elly Peterson, assistant to the RNC chair and one of the highest-ranking women in the party, explained that women became the party's ambassadors to their towns: "When you step into community affairs at the leadership (or followship, for that matter) level, you are indicating to everyone that this is the Republican way of life."[1] By the end of 1969, Georgia women's GOP volunteer work featured not only in their local newspapers, but in neighborhood newspapers across America. Georgia's white Republican women developed and piloted an anti-busing program that provided the GOP a veneer of family values to mask massive-resistance politics. African American Republican women, meanwhile, maintained a presence in the party, working tirelessly to be a bridge between the African American community and the Republican Party.

In 1968, Nixon lost southern states, including Georgia, to third-party candidate and famed segregationist Alabama governor George Wallace. Still, top party officials targeted the region for Republican growth. South Carolinian Harry Dent joined the White House Counsel's Office where he became Nixon's southern advocate in the White House. In February 1969, Dent identified the major issues for Republican expansion into the South. Two dealt with the textile industry and one encouraged more appointments of southerners to federal positions. Dent also advocated more focus on "law and order." The number one issue, though, that would win the South for the GOP was "school guidelines."[2] To shape and amplify the president's strategy on education and, especially, busing, Dent turned to the NFRW, the party's volunteer base of mothers, school volunteers, teachers, and PTA members.

Central to the anti-busing strategy and volunteerism of the NFRW was Lee Ague, now Lee Miller. She had divorced Bob Ague and married Gene Miller, a car dealer in Columbus, Georgia. The two had met on Bo Callaway's gubernatorial campaign when Lee was women's activities director and Gene was finance chairman. Gene Miller visited her in Florida "and asked my father for my hand." With her health restored and her divorce final, Lee and her children settled with Gene in Columbus, the county seat of Muscogee County, 120 miles southwest from her previous Cobb County home.[3] With school-aged children, the Millers' political interests focused on the school board and the rising debates over desegregation and busing.

Lee Miller's own belief about political action complemented Nixon's inaugural address. Reflecting on her Republican volunteerism, Miller recalled, "I've always said that politics is local. Politics is where you live, where you shop, where you vote, where you work." In discussing her move to Columbus, she added, "Politics is local. Education is local." Despite first enrolling the children in public schools, they soon moved them to a private school. Yet both Lee and Gene Miller remained active in the growing battles over busing and school choice. The work began locally in Columbus, but Lee Miller's anti-busing crusade would grow statewide and nationwide until her activism became a model for Richard Nixon's volunteerism program and amplified the voice of the base he called the "silent majority."[4]

Republican leaders realized the power of busing to unite white parents across the nation—and Lee Miller realized it was an issue that could unite southern and northern parents. At the 1968 RNC convention, southern delegates had questioned Nixon about his position on school busing. Nixon replied, "There is a problem in the North, too. . . . I don't believe you should use the South as the whipping boy, or the North as the whipping boy."[5] Nixon wanted to bring the South into the national party and one of his strategies would be to act as if the entire country, not simply the South, had a racial problem. As Lee Miller strategized her anti-busing campaign in Georgia, she, too, shunned any idea of southern exceptionalism. She framed busing opposition in terms of parenthood, especially motherhood, using language of personal responsibility and motherhood. Miller argued that parents simply cared about the education of their own children, not about decades of racial segregation. Nixon assured southerners he did not believe any judge "is as qualified as your local school board."[6] Miller's and Nixon's language overlapped not simply because they were both reciting GOP lines, but because Lee Miller had spearheaded a national campaign to discover the language white parents already used in talking about education.

In the spring of 1969, NFRW president Gladys O'Donnell appointed Lee Miller to chair the newly created NFRW Educational Advisory Committee. Miller's charge included researching education issues and advising the national organization on policy. O'Donnell linked the new committee to Nixon's call to community service: "With the establishment of this committee, we begin at the heart of the problem: the home and the neighborhood schools."[7] She did not claim to be working on federal education policy, though she certainly hoped Republican women would influence it.

As director of the Educational Advisory Committee, Lee Miller reunited with her GFRW friends to develop a plan to tackle busing, support the president, and recruit for the Republican Party—and do it all without sacrificing any of their femininity. Miller, along with GFRW president Virginia Estes, Women For Nixon coordinator Dee Hardin, and Clarke County FRW president Bette Bannister, developed Operation Lend-An-Ear (OLAE) to collect people's opinions about public schools. Implementing a structure that had worked so well for phone surveys for Bo Callaway in 1966, the women assigned an OLAE coordinator in each of the state's ten congressional districts. District leaders appointed county chairs who coordinated women at the local level. Within a week of Miller's appointment as Educational Advisory Committee chair, Georgia's Operation Lend-An-Ear project kicked off at the country club in Columbus.[8]

Georgia was the pilot program, but the goal was to take OLAE nationwide and gather five million Americans' opinions on education. Initially, it collected mothers' opinions, but quickly spread to include fathers, teachers, and anyone else who mailed in a response. Within a week of the kickoff, the survey appeared in several statewide papers. Readers simply had to clip it out, complete it, and mail it to Mrs. Gene Miller in Columbus, Georgia. Where she had been Lee Ague previously, she now identified by her new husband's name, reinforcing her connections to marriage and motherhood. The ads clearly stated that the project was "sponsored by the Educational Advisory Committee of the National Federation of Republican Women and staffed by volunteers with no expense to the taxpayer." They were promoting the GOP as friendly to both education and taxpayers.[9]

OLAE surveys consisted of three short, open-ended questions:

1. What in your opinion are the three most important problems in education today?
2. Why do you consider each of these to be important problems?
3. What do you believe should be done to remedy these problems?

Instead of imposing prewritten choices, the open-ended questions allowed respondents to address any concerns they had with the schools, even as it gave the GFRW greater flexibility in interpreting and communicating the response. Though they did not ask a respondent's race, they did record profession and residence. Finally, to capture potential Republican converts, the survey asked if the person would like to know the final results of the full survey; if so, they should include their name and address. Operation Lend-An-Ear was as much about expanding the Republican Party base as it was about listening to citizen concerns about education.[10]

OLAE workers had little trouble securing publicity for their mission. Miller boasted that they had "hit the front page of the *Atlanta Journal*, the Sunday Magazine section of the *Columbus Ledger* and even received a beautiful write-up from the *Albany Herald*, which is owned by the Chairman of the Democrat Party of Georgia." In addition to the newspapers, she appeared on television "both as part of the women's news and the hard news."[11]

Beyond the media outlets, women blanketed communities with the surveys. State OLAE coordinator Bette Bannister shared successful strategies from local members such as working through churches, day camps, their local PTA, and other community volunteer organizations where parents might gather in the summer months. Dentists and doctors might allow surveys in their waiting rooms, and women could stop by to pick up the completed questionnaires at the end of business.[12] Placement in the newspapers the women read and the businesses the women frequented could also skew the results to reach more white parents.

Lee Miller was not exaggerating when she told NFRW members that the Education Advisory Committee planned to show their results to the White House. In a letter from June 1969, White House special counsel and former South Carolina GOP chair Harry S. Dent wrote to thank Miller for her presentation on Operation Lend-An-Ear and added, "We are very interested in the implementation and the results of your program, and hope you will keep us posted."[13] Only Georgia had even begun such surveys, and Miller was already in regular communication with White House advisors.

As responses came in, results showed that many Georgians blamed troubles in education on the counterculture that had seeped into—or, at least, awareness of which had seeped into—even remote parts of Georgia by 1969. A woman from Brooks County expressed frustration with drugs in the schools that led to "unrest and rioting." A salesman from the same county complained of a general lack of discipline and poor teacher quality. He believed that the key to solving the problem was to "give educators the school" and "gov. furnish the money."[14] These south Georgia respondents lived in the heart of what had been Maddox Country in 1966 and George Wallace's 1968 stronghold. The Republican Party had made few electoral gains there, but the OLAE surveys paved a road into territory that otherwise proved resistant to the GOP.

Lee Miller, Dee Hardin, Bette Bannister, and Virginia Estes had found a model that worked. They could address southern racial problems and the hot-button issue of school desegregation without adopting the racially charged language of southern Democrats like Lester Maddox or George Wallace. Rather, they sounded like concerned mothers who directed parental concern into political action. Of course, people completing the surveys could vent in racist language, but the women simply recorded just another voice against forced busing, sanitizing the language of Massive Resistance with the aura of motherhood. Miller reported that the project blanketed "millions of Georgians with the message: Republican women care about schools and you."[15]

The Georgia pilot program excited women across the state and even resulted in non-Republican volunteers. The president of the Georgia Women's Clubs said that their members would love to participate, saying "ours is a non-partisan, though not non-political organization . . . but we are on the side of better education." Miller welcomed their participation and hoped that at least a few of the women might become active Republicans. She hoped more would become GOP voters.[16]

Operation Lend-An-Ear fit well into the Nixon administration's goals for citizen engagement. Put another way, Nixon's goals for national volunteerism meshed well with Miller's plan. In the spring of 1969, Gene and Lee Miller as well as Dee Hardin were part of a "relaxed crowd" that also included White House deputy council staffer Joel Fisher. This group worked casually with "shoes off" on goals and standards for a Voluntary Action Program, a national call for volunteer work. In drafts, the program name changed from "I Care About Others" to the more active "Be A Doer" and finally settled on "Voluntary Action Program." The primary goal of the program was to inspire community involvement, but a close secondary goal was to tell Americans "that they now have a President [Nixon] who really and truly does *care* and *cares* without regard to political party membership or affiliation, creed or color. *President Nixon cares about people.*" Of course, a "By-product or side effects objective" was "to very quietly and yet assiduously work toward broadening the GOP base." This effort, the program planners asserted, should be "not especially from the National Party down but actually from the grassroots level up." While the planning document is not credited to any one author, the emphasis on the efficacy of the grassroots for party building certainly reflects Miller's lifelong beliefs.[17]

Miller kept a copy of a confidential White House memo regarding the administration's Voluntary Action Programs that encouraged volunteer projects that "should be geared to work in conjunction with the Republican National Committee." The memo stressed that "the President wishes to spotlight these programs in terms of individuals. That means people caring at the local level."

The OLAE surveys about local schools emphasized the validity of every individual's opinion. Additionally, the surveys fit the administration's goal of appearing nonpartisan while simultaneously promoting the Republican Party. The focus on a contentious issue like education all but guaranteed coverage in local media, meeting the goal Nixon set out in his inaugural address to "make headlines in the neighborhood newspaper." By lending a friendly ear to people's school concerns, local Republicans hoped to earn a "far more favorable recognition for the Party than could otherwise be normally obtained." Additionally, the memo predicted that the GOP would benefit from converting survey volunteers into campaign volunteers by the next election. Individual participants would "realize that it is the Republicans who share their commitment to social improvement." OLAE certainly fit all of the standards for a Voluntary Action Program.[18]

The concern for "social improvement" through individual action corresponded with other administration emphases on the power of the silent majority. The administration criticized what it saw as federal overreach, specifically from the Supreme Court, to address the disgruntlement of the silent majority. Many of these issues directly related to schools. In its 1962 *Engel v. Vitale* decision, the court declared mandatory prayer in public schools a violation of the First Amendment. By the launch of OLAE, more school cases were working their way through the federal courts. In the 1969 case *Alexander v. Holmes County Board of Education*, the justices ordered an end to dual school systems by race and the immediate unification of such systems. In 1971, the Court handed down yet another ruling relating to school desegregation when it decided in *Swann v. Charlotte-Mecklenburg (N.C.) Board of Education* that the busing of students from one school district to another was an acceptable means of desegregating the school system.[19]

Miller's home-grown anti-busing campaign offers a way to understand how grassroots politics shaped the Republican southern strategy. In summer 1969, Republican strategist Kevin Phillips published *The Emerging Republican Majority*, identifying the South as the future strength of the GOP. Phillips believed that the 1968 electoral success of George Wallace indicated a pattern of conservative Democrats' movement out of their party and predicted movement "towards the GOP." More specifically, Phillips targeted the rapidly growing suburban Sunbelt populations.[20] However, if one reexamines the strategy as a grassroots movement from the local level up, then a larger context of southern realignment emerges. Led by Lee Ague Miller, Georgia women learned to look beyond one election cycle as a signal of the effectiveness of their work. They had celebrated a statewide victory for Goldwater in 1964, but then had a crushing defeat in the 1966 gubernatorial race. In 1968, the women saw their state again support a southern segregationist rather than a conservative Republican with a national appeal. Where Phillips saw the South as emerging into Republican politics, the women fiercely believed that they had already shifted into the middle stages of a Republican turn in southern states. Republican women were implementing a strategy before Nixon even hired a strategist.

OLAE gave the Georgia GOP a means to push beyond its suburban strongholds into rural counties. With the demise of the county-unit voting system, the suburban areas had gained strength, but the women knew that party growth had to happen vote-by-vote in every region. Georgia would never be a Republican state without rural voters. Busing was the ideal issue to make that push into rural areas that had supported Lester Maddox, George Wallace, and other Democratic segregationists.

Lee Miller and Bette Bannister had access to high-ranking state and local GOP officials but operated outside of top-down party channels. Working through the NFRW and established grassroots networks of the Georgia federation, Miller and Bannister had autonomy to develop OLAE as they wanted. The program implemented what historian Michelle Nickerson labeled "housewife populism," accumulating the political capital associated with motherhood and "ordinariness, anonymity, and community."[21] The potential of OLAE lay in its blandness: this was just mothers discussing their children's schooling. It was not one mother's campaign, but many mothers' concerns. On their own, each voice would be ordinary and anonymous. The power of the program was in the community. One complaining mother was a nuisance; thousands were a movement. Miller and Bannister did not have to get approval from campaign managers or candidates, nor did they have to run the ideas through leadership of the state or national GOP. They did not pay consultants or survey firms, but instead used their experience as women, mothers, and political volunteers over the past decade to develop three simple, open-ended questions that would give respondents the sense that someone cared about their opinions. Where men in national party leadership were only just seeing the potential of the region, women who had been volunteering in local party work for over a decade realized the seeds they had planted in 1964 had begun to ripen.

Lee Miller eloquently combined all of these social concerns in her winning speech for the Dixie Region Convention of Toastmistress International. Her April 1969 speech mourned a dying America, while expressing hope that women would bring the nation back from the brink. "When God was taken from the schools, America died a little bit," she began. Miller was only getting started on the long list of her constitutional disappointments. "When little children are senselessly bused to schools one hour from home . . . when laws are twisted to protect the guilty instead of the innocent . . . when promoters of drugs, pornography, and riots are allowed to roam the nation unchecked," she continued, "America dies a little bit." Of course, a winning speech does not end in despair, and Miller saw the hope of America in the nation's women, who "are writing an end to the indifference which allowed the country to reach its present state."[22]

Miller proposed a women's movement for conservatives when she concluded, "In homes across the nation when husbands ask, 'And what did you do today, Darling?' instead of describing the battle of the broken dishwashers, [the women] say, 'I am learning the ways of politics and I am mastering them.'" While she criticized courts and legislatures, the savvy attorney and organizer directed more blame on individual citizens. Without explicitly saying that men had made the mess, she did say that only women had the ability to clean it up. Because she had a nonpartisan audience, she made the charge to American women rather than specifically to Republican women.[23] Had anyone spoken to her after the judges placed the tiara on her head, she probably would have directed them to the Republican Party.

Miller put her message into practice in her leadership of the NFRW Educational Advisory Committee. In her report to the NFRW that autumn, Miller boasted of the positive effect Operation Lend-An-Ear had had on her state's GOP: "The word Republican was used and heard by more people in Georgia during an off-election year than ever before." Even in the summer heat when children were out of school, "the Republican Women of Georgia proved conclusively that citizens were anxious to discuss educational problems." The pilot program had the effect not only of getting the GOP name out more broadly, but also of attracting new volunteers. "New leadership emerged. New faces appeared," Miller boasted. "Responsibilities were assumed and met by federation members who had been somewhat reluctant volunteers in the past."[24]

In addition to bragging about how OLAE built their volunteer base, Miller outlined the findings for the Republican women gathered at the convention. "What did we find in Georgia?" Broadly, the Georgia team had discovered "a concern for the education of the individual child." She stressed the importance of local control and the belief that unique needs of individual children could not be addressed through national educational policies. "Specific areas of concern," she continued, "included lack of qualified teachers, inadequate teachers' salaries, overcrowded classrooms, inordinate pupil-teacher ratios, lack of discipline, the need for neighborhood schools with more local control and the need for more freedom of choice."[25]

On that same trip to Washington, Miller "squeezed in a brief visit with Strom Thurmond," who "was quite enthusiastic . . . and suggested that we deliver the final results directly into the hands of President Nixon."[26] Nixon advisor Harry Dent had told her the same thing in June. Southerners Dent and Thurmond looked forward to the results of the survey on education, which they certainly knew would tackle the hot-button issue of school desegregation. OLAE, implemented by Republican women, let the silent majority Nixon praised in his campaign know that they did not have to be silent anymore. It was a curated listening program and one that would yield results useful to the Republican agenda. OLAE in fact enabled the southern strategy by providing a way for the Republican administration to address southern racial concerns through a national message of family responsibility and neighborhood schools. They learned to soften racist appeals with a maternal language emphasizing protection of home and children.

National interest in OLAE confirmed Miller's belief that she had tapped into an American problem, not simply a regional concern. Through her NFRW network, she expanded the program to any state that appointed an OLAE chair. Mothers across the country expressed interest in conducting local surveys. When New York's Republican senator Jacob Javits inquired about the work of the NFRW Educational Advisory Committee, Lee Miller gladly referred him to his state's OLAE coordinator, Mrs. Marion Granowitz in New York City. Miller added, "I am sure that any assistance you can render to her will be appreciated."[27]

Women in other states jumped on board. With a goal of having a first round of national surveys completed and analyzed by January 1970, the information gathered through OLAE would be valuable for the midterm elections. The surveys collected not only individual voter information, but also let candidates know the language voters used in addressing educational concerns. NFRW first vice president Constance Armitage complimented Miller's leadership of the Educational Advisory Committee and added, "the information which you are garnering should be an invaluable guide both in campaigning and in education reform."[28]

Georgia women eagerly shared their successful strategies with women in other states as OLAE spread. The key to success, especially in Democratic states, Miller said, was "stressing all of the time that this was a non-partisan, community involvement program with the Republican women acting only as the vehicle." By framing the program as nonpartisan, the Republican women would have more paths open up to them. She suggested that federations save money by asking a local businessman or vocational school to donate printing services.[29] In keeping their activity level high but their political identity lowkey, Republican women reached broader audiences and won more goodwill for the project than they would have if they had led with the party's name.

Part of piloting the program included sharing successful strategies with women across state lines. Georgia women found success in asking mayors to declare Operation Lend-An-Ear Days in their towns. Because the Democratic mayor in Athens, Georgia, had been the first in the state to do so, Miller reminded women in other states not to let partisanship stand in the way. Once one mayor backed the program, the women could approach other mayors throughout the state to follow that example. In Georgia, that strategy "had 100% success." Some states, Miller added, might even ask the governor to make a statewide OLAE proclamation. However, she did make the point, "We didn't go near Lester Maddox."[30] Involving Lester Maddox in a school desegregation question could too easily muddy their efforts at conveying middle-class respectability through association with southern segregationist demagoguery. Besides, Miller and the GFRW had not forgotten how Maddox had won the governorship from their own Bo Callaway. The women would not start helping Lester Maddox now.

Lee Miller vigorously promoted the Operation Lend-An-Ear program in the national media. She discussed it on the *Today* show in November 1969. After the segment aired, some people mailed their OLAE responses to the *Today* show, which then forwarded them to Miller.[31] As OLAE responses flooded in from across the nation, they revealed little regional difference in the concerns. In particular, it seemed that nobody anywhere supported integration of schools by means of busing. The concerns covered a wide range, from teacher quality to student-teacher ratios to vocational education and special-needs children. Of course, none of the surveys recorded the race of the respondents.

Thirty-one surveys came from Stevens Point, Wisconsin, where one parent identified "bussing [*sic*] children long distances" as a top concern and suggested "less transferring from school to school and from neighborhood to other neighborhoods. Social problems cannot be solved by sacrificing little children's needs." If children had to transfer, though, she suggested allowing their "familiar teachers" to accompany them. Another mother identified her main concern as too much pressure for all students to go to college and the corresponding lack of vocational-technical education.[32] The seventeen surveys collected by a volunteer in the southern California town of Calabasas revealed different concerns but similar frustration with local schools. The respondents complained about crowded classrooms, drugs in schools, and low-quality teachers. Some of the responses called for more federal funding for education, particularly minority education, even if it meant less funding for defense. However, even in this school system, respondents pleaded to "retain neighborhood schools" and that no child be bused without a parent's permission.[33]

In April 1970, Lee Miller and Gladys O'Donnell visited the White House to present their report. They met with deputy counsel Harry Dent, who promised to pass it along to the president. Reporting back to the NFRW, Miller told the women that the returned OLAE questionnaires stressed "the need to eliminate excessive Federal Control." Specifically, their report told the White House that Americans "were concerned about the need for qualified teachers and relevant curriculum ... the return of Bible reading and prayer to the schools, the urgent need for education and action regarding the drug menace, the importance of discipline, the need for vocational and technical schools ... an emphasis on citizenship and patriotism as subjects," and greater parental involvement.[34]

In her report for the NFRW and the White House, Miller underscored the virtually nationwide anti-busing sentiment: "You wanted neighborhood schools. You objected to the loss of parental choice in the school your child attended. You rejected forced busing and judicial ratios. You said the additional cost of buying and running buses was prohibitive." In nearly every way possible, Miller made the point that parents, "irrespective of color," opposed busing of school children for the purpose of integration.[35] To address these problems, the NFRW report proposed three actions. First, of course, was "to eliminate forced busing to achieve integration." The report did not suggest what other means might be taken to implement the Supreme Court's decision. The second recommendation, closely related to the first, was "to reinforce local control of busing." Finally, the report proposed that the White House establish a cabinet-level Department of Education, separate from Housing, Education, and Welfare.[36] The lack of information on the race of respondents elevated the sense that the survey was capturing average American voices, but also effectively silenced minorities while amplifying Nixon's silent majority.

OLAE offered Miller and her fellow Republicans a means to maintain white supremacy without ever mentioning race. Lester Maddox, George Wallace, and the southern Democrats' version of racial conservatism relied heavily on language of fear, violence, and slurs. Those men hollered about race and performed rabid racism for the cameras. OLAE, in contrast, highlighted school conditions, motherhood, discipline—codes for race, but never race itself. In smoothing the path to the national GOP, Miller turned in an American report, piloted by Georgia women but representing everyone. She could not have distanced the project more from the ugly past of southern segregationists and Massive Resistance campaigns.

Basking in national success, Georgia Republican women felt hope at home because for the first time, the state GOP was strong enough that it had to run a Republican gubernatorial primary. The GFRW did not allow chapters to endorse any candidate before the general election campaign, so the women could work for either man. Once television newsman Hal Suit defeated Ed Bentley in the primary, the GFRW set to work on Suit's campaign against State Senator Jimmy Carter in the general election. In the race for lieutenant governor, the Georgia GOP faced an old foe as Governor Lester Maddox, barred by law from a second term, ran for the second seat.[37]

Hal Suit's campaign reflected the findings of the GFRW's Operation Lend-An-Ear. After a meeting with President Nixon, Suit reinforced the message that Nixon cared about education: "[Nixon] asked me what I said about schools,"

Suit told Georgia voters. "I said you don't solve problems in the streets. I am a believer in the judicial process." However, since the judicial process had desegregated the schools and ruled in favor of busing, Suit added, "I'm a firm believer in neighborhood schools." Echoing other findings from the OLAE report, Suit proposed more funding for teacher pay and vocational education.[38]

The 1970 campaigns saw a rise in African American participation in both parties. Unlike the 1966 gubernatorial race, the 1970 general election saw major party candidates vying for the votes of African Americans. When Hal Suit opened an office in West Atlanta, "In the heart of the Black Neighborhood," he won front page praise from the city's African American newspaper. Republican Suit and Democrat Carter appeared together before the Hungry Club, a political and social club of Atlanta African Americans. Both candidates promised to appoint African Americans to positions in their administration.[39]

Hal Suit accepted an invitation to address the African American Metropolitan Republican Women's Club at their fall banquet. In her introductory remarks, Metropolitan Club president Evelyn Frazier introduced Suit along with the other candidates, including the club's own Mabel Sanford Lewis, who had recently resigned her position at the *Atlanta Daily World* to run for the Georgia House of Representatives.[40]

On Election Day, both Hal Suit and Mabel Sanford Lewis lost in their bids for office. State Senator Jimmy Carter won the gubernatorial race. Lester Maddox won for lieutenant governor. Lewis lost her race to an African American Democrat. In total, a record eleven African Americans, all Democrats, won election to the state legislature. Civil rights activist Andrew Young lost his congressional bid to unseat incumbent Republican Fletcher Thompson, who represented a part of Atlanta and its suburbs.[41]

Predicting in 1969 that the South would be a key part of the GOP's future, Republican strategist Kevin Phillips argued that the new Republican coalition "includes very few Negroes—they have become almost entirely Democratic and exert very little influence on the GOP." Rather than fight the trend, he advised that Republicans should give up the African American vote to the Democratic Party and focus instead on white suburban voters. Phillips's version of the southern strategy relied on Wallace voters from 1968 switching to the Republican Party. However, in order to push those voters to the GOP, he argued that "abandonment of civil rights enforcement would be self-defeating. Maintenance of Negro voting rights in Dixie, far from being contrary to GOP interests, is essential if southern conservatives are to be pressured into switching to the Republican Party."[42] Phillips assumed that increasing numbers of registered African American voters would support the Democratic Party, leading Wallace voters to turn to the GOP. Rather than supporting voting rights as a means of holding on to the historic Republican loyalists within the African

American community, Phillips counted on the racism of southern white voters to grow the party.

In Atlanta, Evelyn Frazier and the members of the Metropolitan Club refused to accept that message. The African American women who had joined the party of their grandfathers and who chartered one of the earliest GFRW clubs tenaciously clung to the GOP. Evelyn Frazier joined the National Black Silent Majority Committee, which asserted that "progressive, upstanding but silent citizens—by the millions—are being shouted down by a handful of militants who do not represent us."[43] Historian Leah Wright Rigueur called the group "dogmatic in its embrace of conservatism, adhering to an anticommunist, antiwelfare, antibusing, anticrime agenda." Members of the committee defined themselves as professional and working-class Americans, seeking to represent "the voice of patriotism and responsibility" and "demand[ing] the rightful share of national attention due us as the majority within the black community." In appropriating Nixon's "silent majority" language, the members of Black Silent Majority firmly asserted both African American and Republican identity. Their material called upon African Americans to "urge blacks to participate in the electoral process and to develop a strong two-party system within black voting districts."[44]

As an organized Republican group for African American women in the Nixon era, the Metropolitan Club was a rarity. In 1970, Mrs. Jessie Hargro Kelly moved from Atlanta to Columbia, Maryland, but sent her dues back to Atlanta "until I can contact some of the local Negro Republicans here." She kept herself busy with church work until she could find a new political home for her partisan energies.[45] As the leaders of the national GOP listened to policy advisors like Kevin Phillips and catered to the conservative wing of the party, longtime African American Republicans struggled to maintain a place in the party. Their forebears had turned to the GOP decades earlier as the party of civil rights; now they hoped to encourage the party's civil rights commitments while also demonstrating the power of the African American electorate. Mrs. Kelly felt adrift in Maryland without the anchor of the Metropolitan Club connecting her with her conservative African American women's community.

The Atlanta Black Silent Majority Committee formed in 1971 with numerous anti-crime initiatives and youth activities. In both the Black Silent Majority and the Metropolitan Club, some members, like Frazier, became critical conduits between the Republican Party and the African American community. Counter to the southern strategy proposal, the Metropolitan Club women asserted that African Americans were not going to skulk away from the party. Indeed, they developed youth programs to raise the next generation of conservative African American voters. The Metropolitan Club sponsored a float in WSB's Salute to America July 4 parade. The money the women raised went to the Foster Parents Club and the Carrie Steele-Pitts Home, a historic home for orphaned African American children in Atlanta. They chose the theme "Let Your Light So Shine With 'Queen' Charity for All" and featured young African American women of Atlanta as queens representing the rich heritage of the Republican Party. Club president Evelyn Frazier was featured as "Miss Patriotism" and the "Honorary Queen," accompanied by her court consisting of "Miss Emancipation Proclamation Queen," "Miss Thirteenth Amendment Queen," "Miss Fourteenth Amendment Queen," "Miss Good Citizenship Queen," "Miss Civil Rights Queen," and "Miss Welfare Reform Queen."[46] The titles reminded parade-watchers of the party's past work for African Americans even as the queens themselves represented what Frazier hoped would be the future of the GOP. The African American queens in flowing white gowns joined the city's patriotic celebration, following other floats featuring Atlanta mayor Sam Massell, U.S. senators Herman Talmadge and David Gambrell, Governor Jimmy Carter, Lt. Governor Lester Maddox, and Vice Mayor Maynard Jackson, the only elected African American in the group. Evangelist Billy Graham served as grand marshal. No Democratic club had a float in the parade, while the Republicans featured two: the Fulton County Young Republicans float preceded the Metropolitan Club queens by a few city blocks. Later, the American Party of Georgia, a remnant of Wallace's 1968 campaign, followed down Peachtree Street. Nonpolitical parade participants included the Atlanta Braves' Wives and team mascot Chief Noc-A-Homa, select Atlanta churches, a unicycle show, and the Georgia Confederettes baton twirling team.[47] The parade was an opportunity to publicize the Metropolitan Club and its charity work before a much wider audience, including the extensive WSB television viewership. The African American Republican women on the float may have been silent, but they were visible.

In November 1971, the featured guest at the Metropolitan Club's awards banquet was Melvin Evans, the recently elected Republican governor of the Virgin Islands. With such a prominent guest, Frazier hoped again to increase the profile of the only African American women's Republican club in the state. Frazier read President Nixon's greeting to the club and Governor Evans. When Evans delivered his address, he reinforced the message the Metropolitan Club had been trying to deliver to Atlanta's African American community. "Nothing is more dangerous," he said, "than for most of the Negroes to belong to one party." Metropolitan Club member Marguerite Mathis delivered the response to the keynote address, assuring Evans that the women "would accept the challenge to build a strong Republican Party in Atlanta."[48]

After Governor Evans's address, the women handed out awards to recognize the work of Georgians who sought to maintain a two-party system in both the state and the African American community. GFRW leader and Georgia GOP national committeewoman Florence Cauble, in a show of support from the state party, presented the Metropolitan Atlanta Republican Women Charter Member Award. C. A. Scott, publisher of the *Atlanta Daily World*, won the Public Relations Service Award. Evelyn Frazier presented the governor of the Virgin Islands with an award for "outstanding service to the nation."[49]

In her own correspondence, Evelyn Frazier personalized the message of the Black Silent Majority. She told Democrats that African Americans needed to be in the two-party system and she told Republicans to pay attention to African American communities. In 1972, civil rights activist Andrew Young defeated incumbent Republican congressman Fletcher Thompson. Democrat Young was the first African American elected from Georgia to Congress since Reconstruction. In her congratulatory letter, Frazier admitted, "We did not vote for you," and explained that "a representative number of blacks need to belong to the two-party system."[50] It was reminiscent of her letter to Thompson two years earlier, reminding the Republican to serve the African American community.

Just weeks later, in a letter congratulating President Nixon on his reelection, Frazier introduced herself as "president of the only black Republican Women's Club in the State of Georgia." She expressed her hope "that you will include some of the few black minority who worked so hard for your election the past four years when it was so unpopular for us." Evelyn Frazier believed Republican implementation of strong civil rights programs would empower African American communities, inspiring African American voters to return to the GOP. She urged Nixon to "revise your methods for assisting the black minority and other poor persons in the South."[51] In January, Luther and Evelyn Frazier attended Nixon's inauguration along with several other longtime African American Republicans from Atlanta.[52]

Even without a strong Republican presence in elected offices, Georgia's women managed to lead the party from the outside. Without paid positions or even a budget, the volunteers of the GFRW developed and implemented Operation Lend-An-Ear, a program with nationwide reach. Lee Miller, Bette Bannister, and others operated within the gendered space of motherhood and schools to influence White House education policy.

Elsewhere, other conservative women were finding their own platforms for advancing the politics of motherhood. The women who followed Phyllis Schlafly out of the NFRW in 1967 were beginning to follow her back into state houses and onto debate stages. Just as Lee Miller made Georgia a critical state for busing politics, so did Kathryn Dunaway and Lee Wysong build up the state as a critical line of defense against the Equal Rights Amendment. Though their friendships had faded, the Republican women of anti-busing and the conservative women of STOP ERA together built a powerful gendered conservatism, rooted in motherhood and as Georgian as peach pie.

CHAPTER 5

The Cause of
American Womanhood

In March 1973, Lee Miller and seven friends visited Washington for a Republican women's luncheon with Second Lady Judy Agnew. Miller left a message with Jill Ruckelshaus, director of the White House Office of Women's Programs, asking Ruckelshaus to stop by and meet the group "because of the support it will give ERA in Georgia."[1] Lee Miller was just about to launch her anti-busing work, and this is the only mention of her work with GFRW on the Equal Rights Amendment. The NFRW had endorsed the ERA and Ruckelshaus supported it from within the White House. Busing was Miller's battle, and she did not split her focus to include the ERA.

However, Miller's former GFRW colleague Kathryn Dunaway was just getting started on what would be a decade of grassroots work to make sure the ERA never passed in Georgia, nor, she hoped, nationwide. For Dunaway, the early 1970s involved shoring up the Schlafly supporters in Georgia and searching for the movement that would keep them united after leaving the GFRW. Schlafly and Dunaway soon had their movement and would spend the next decade battling the ERA. As Miller used gendered language to battle busing, Dunaway used a language of family values to fight feminism. After Dunaway and Miller led the competing Georgia factions out of the O'Donnell-Schlafly showdown, their paths do not appear to have crossed again.

Both houses of Congress passed the Equal Rights Amendment by late March 1972. The amendment moved on to state legislatures with great momentum and high expectation for quick ratification. The legislation allowed seven years for three-fourths of the states to ratify the ERA, but hardly anyone expected it would take that long. Hawaii ratified the amendment only thirty-two minutes after the U.S. Senate's passage of the bill. Eight states ratified it within the first week, none with significant opposition.[2] Georgia's legislative session had ended for the year by the time ERA passed in Congress, but amendment supporters had begun to organize. It was only two years before that the state legislature had symbolically ratified the Nineteenth Amendment granting women the right to vote, and Georgia ERA advocates did not want to be fifty years behind again.[3]

NFRW leadership enthusiastically endorsed the amendment. President Gladys O'Donnell actively worked for the ERA and encouraged all state chapters to do the same. She warned, "We cannot let the Democrats win the most powerful force in the electorate—the women."[4] Providing statistics on sex discrimination in professions ranging from bartenders to bureaucrats, O'Donnell concluded that the NFRW should not only endorse the ERA, but also try to elect more Republican women. She blamed the amendment's failures on radical feminists for "burning bras and smoking cigars" and creating "a picture of trying to destroy marriage, home life and motherhood." O'Donnell urged the women of the NFRW to write their congressmen in support of equal rights and reminded them, "The women are going to remember the lawmaker who refuses to give them equality." She chose the theme "WOMANPOWER '72" for the next election cycle. Her letter to state chapter leaders meant to educate and enrage women about existing discrimination and imprint a Republican face on the fight for the ERA.[5]

The credit—or blame, depending on one's point of view—for defeating the ERA in Georgia largely goes to Kathryn Dunaway, the former GFRW officer and Phyllis Schlafly booster. Having sided with O'Donnell and the NFRW establishment, Lee Miller rose in the ranks of GOP women's leadership, shaping the organizational strategy opposing busing. Meanwhile, Kathryn Dunaway followed Phyllis Schlafly in her next steps of conservative women's organizing.

After Schlafly lost the NFRW presidential election in 1967, she established the Eagle Trust Fund, which she called "a conservative war chest." Anyone who paid the five-dollar subscription rate received the monthly *Phyllis Schlafly Report*.[6] A monthly newsletter allowed Schlafly to communicate directly and regularly with her supporters. The text ran in blue ink on white paper to make mimeographing easy for quick sharing. Hers was not a think tank, but a movement. Walking out of the NFRW gave Schlafly the freedom to criticize both parties and to advocate for a stronger conservatism than either party had theretofore embraced. That those walking out with her had been trained by local Republican women's organizations gave her the advantage of experienced volunteers. Schlafly described her followers as the "grassroots" of American women and claimed subscribers among conservatives from both political parties, diverse religious faiths, and every region of the nation.[7]

In Georgia, Kathryn Dunaway became, in Phyllis Schlafly's words, "my first and my best state chairman" of STOP ERA.[8] Schlafly built a national network that relied on strong state and local organizing. Georgia women took Schlafly's anti-ERA message and applied their tried-and-true techniques of tea parties and phone trees to fighting the ERA. Phyllis Schlafly enjoyed strong support among Georgia conservative women. Georgia delegates had voted overwhelmingly for Schlafly in the 1967 NFRW election and many continued backing her even after the convention debacle. With their organizing skills and dedication to Schlafly, Dunaway's STOP ERA organization held off the amendment for a decade, rarely allowing it even to come to a floor vote in the state legislature.

Phyllis Schlafly dedicated the entire February 1972 issue of her eponymous newsletter to the issue of the Equal Rights Amendment. The issue reached subscribers one month before the ERA's final passage out of the Senate. Though she had failed to stop it in Congress, that issue of Schlafly's newsletter laid the foundation for the next decade of anti-ERA organizing nationwide. She argued that the family, not the individual, was the basic unit in American society. In her view, family was the grounds for the difference between men and women, as she pointed out that "women have babies and men don't. If you don't like this fundamental difference, you will have to take up your complaint with God." Because woman gave birth to the children, man balanced the burden by providing "his share by physical protection and financial support." The institution of the family unit, Schlafly argued, was "the greatest single achievement in the entire history of women's rights."[9] The family reflected God's plan. In this passage, Schlafly provided an important link between Judeo-Christian belief and conservative political rhetoric. This language became the basis of the emerging political discourse regarding family values.

After Schlafly asserted that, "of all the classes of people who ever lived, the American woman is the most privileged," she continued to describe the threat of the Equal Rights Amendment to that status. She pointedly asked readers, "Why should we lower ourselves to 'equal rights' when we already have the status of special privilege?" Respect for the family and for the stay-at-home mother was a tradition that "dates from the Christian Age of Chivalry." Without basis, Schlafly criticized other societies, "such as the African and the American Indian, [where] the men strut around wearing feathers and beads and hunting and fishing." Women in these societies, she maintained, "do all the hard, tiresome drudgery including the tilling of the soil (if any is done), the hewing of wood, the making of fires, the carrying of water, as well as the cooking, sewing and caring for babies." She stressed that such labor for women "is not the American way." In her analysis, the nonwhite societies did not have Christian traditions that respected Mary as the mother of Jesus, and thus did not have the same ingrained respect for women. In her view, the most endangered American families were two-parent, Christian, and white.[10]

Schlafly then turned to those who disagreed with her. She warned that pro-ERA forces were composed of "radicals." She described contributors to the new *Ms. Magazine* as "anti-family, anti-children, and pro-abortion" and its contents "a series of sharp-tongued, high-pitched whining complaints by unmarried women." A key difference between pro-ERA women and Schlafly's readers was marital status and motherhood—or, at least, the hope for marriage and family. Schlafly assumed her readers shared her idea of American womanhood as involving marriage, motherhood, and class status allowing them not to work outside the home. Even when a woman worked for a wage, her ultimate goal must be marriage, children, and freedom from paid labor. Most of Schlafly's text addressed middle- and upper-class women who did not have to work for a wage. Her historical and contemporary examples failed to recognize the historical work of women in farm labor and industry. She likewise neglected to acknowledge the paid work of women, especially women of color, as domestic laborers and paid caretakers of children.[11]

Schlafly's concluding argument echoed Richard Nixon's famed 1959 Kitchen Debate with Nikita Khrushchev: the free enterprise system liberated women more than any law ever could. According to Schlafly, the heroes of women's liberation were Thomas Edison, who introduced electricity, and Clarence Birdseye, who developed the frozen-food industry. Because of these advances, women in America had free time to spend with children, volunteer, or even pursue full- or part-time work if they pleased.[12]

She positioned women as soldiers on a Cold War battlefield. In communist countries, she wrote, women suffered the "slavery of standing in line for daily food." Ever the Cold Warrior, Schlafly warned that the Soviet Union did in fact ensure its own version of equal rights for women. In practice, this meant that the "Russian woman is *obliged* to put her baby in a state-operated nursery or kindergarten so she can join the labor force.... 'Equal rights' in Russia means that the women do the heavy, dirty work American women do not do." Schlafly's anti-ERA movement, then, was a gendered army fighting the Cold War.[13]

By making gender rights a Cold War contest, Schlafly spoke to readers who, like her, had been actively concerned about national defense for two decades. Schlafly, like her followers, was never solely a housewife. Before she married Fred Schlafly, Schlafly was one of thousands of American women working in wartime factories. Before marrying John Dunaway, Kathryn Dunaway worked at Sears, Roebuck in Atlanta while her husband attended Emory Law School.[14] Marriage elevated both women's social status, but those years of working for an hourly wage reminded them of what they had to lose. As married women, both Schlafly and Dunaway continued to work, though no longer for a wage. They became adept political strategists and volunteers who battled communism, liberalism, and moderation. These seasoned conservatives now committed to stopping the amendment they believed endangered the American family.

The February 1972 *Phyllis Schlafly Report* issue became a foundational document for the anti-ERA movement. Schlafly biographer Carol Felsenthal marveled that the issue "became a collector's item among feminists—like the first issue of *Playboy*." Feminists, according to Felsenthal, thought the anti-ERA newsletter was amusing—until they realized that women and state legislators not only read it, but believed it.[15]

Over the course of the next decade, Schlafly dedicated many more monthly reports to the defeat of the ERA. Feminists soon understood Schlafly was no laughing matter, though most pro-ERA groups failed to comprehend the strength of their opposition. From the original three thousand subscribers in 1967, the *Phyllis Schlafly Report* circulation swelled to eleven thousand readers by the end of 1975.[16] These numbers represent only the subscriptions to the newsletter. Because Schlafly encouraged readers to copy and share the report, the actual number of readers would likely be several times larger than the subscription rates.

Phyllis Schlafly established her anti-ERA organization in the fall of 1972. She called the movement Stop Taking Our Privileges Equal Rights Amendment, yielding the acronym STOP ERA. Immediately, Schlafly selected her old friend Kathryn Dunaway to lead STOP ERA in Georgia.[17] In turn, Kathryn Dunaway invited Lee Wysong, a reliable Daughters of the American Revolution and GFRW friend and proven conservative, to be her co-chairman.[18] Dunaway had been friends with Schlafly for at least eight years, and with Wysong even longer. Wysong recalled that after she and Dunaway had accepted the leadership position, "From then on, everything was STOP ERA in our lives."[19]

Though born in Louisiana, Lee Wysong grew up in Atlanta. She attended John Birch Society meetings with her husband Charles, who had been invited by the head of his department at Georgia Tech. The meetings interested Lee very much, and she remembered, "I don't know if they ever asked [husband Charles] to join or not, but he didn't and I did." Her membership in the intensely conservative organization sparked her dedication to fighting communism. When they realized a local department store was selling imported goods from communist nations, two carloads of Birchers, including Wysong, went to the downtown Atlanta Davison's store and slipped "these little cards, like calling cards, that just said, 'Davison's is selling communist goods,'" into pockets of the imported items. Through the Birch Society, Wysong also developed an antipathy to the United Nations. A lifelong Catholic, she later took a strong anti-abortion stance.[20]

Kathryn Dunaway and Lee Wysong had been friends so long that, in her interview, Wysong could not remember where they met. She did remember clearly that they shared a commitment to anti-communism and other conservative matters. Unlike Dunaway, Wysong was not a housewife. She helped her husband run their family business manufacturing industrial ceramics. However, her STOP ERA work came first. As head of the company, she had the freedom to take days off as needed to fight the amendment.[21]

Both Kathryn Dunaway and Lee Wysong were passionate about defeating the Equal Rights Amendment, and they split duties according to their strengths. The two women's styles complemented each other. Wysong remembered Dunaway as "a high-strung woman, smart as she could be, but quite high-strung." Thus, Dunaway handled the strategy, organizing, and media relations while the more laid-back Wysong represented the organization in debates. Dunaway feared losing her temper and damaging relations with potential volunteers or losing her ladylike image.[22] Late in the ERA fight, a reporter from the *Atlanta Journal* observed that, when asked about a specific bill before the state legislature, "[Dunaway's] ladylike demeanor is eclipsed, for the moment, by anger."[23]

Kathryn Dunaway and Lee Wysong quickly replicated the organizational structure they had learned in conducting GFRW surveys and campaigns. From their trusted networks, they chose one chairman for each congressional district of Georgia. This network allowed for quick dissemination of materials. Schlafly telephoned only Dunaway. Following that call, Dunaway and Wysong split the calls to the ten chairmen in each of the congressional districts. Then the information sped through the phone wires to the county and local levels. Working in reverse, a matter of five or six phone calls could get critical information to Dunaway or even Schlafly for inclusion in state or national STOP ERA newsletters.

The STOP ERA structure that flowed from Phyllis Schlafly to the local level meant that each legislator heard opposition to the ERA from his or her own constituents. Georgia legislators, for instance, heard Schlafly's arguments being made in familiar southern accents by local voters. Schlafly generated the message and trusted local women to carry it to power. Even within the state, rather than Atlanta-based Dunaway and Wysong contacting legislators, they relied on women all over Georgia to contact their representatives and senators. Thus, letters opposing the constitutional amendment came from within a legislator's district, reinforcing the idea of the ERA as a local issue. Ratification would change small-town life—girls would play on the local high school football teams and neighbors' daughters would be drafted into military service. Local organization meant that legislators had to face STOP ERA activists at church and in their neighborhood.

That Schlafly appointed a Georgia chair so early is indicative not only of her great friendship with Kathryn Dunaway, but also the significance of Georgia to the STOP ERA movement. As a state yet to ratify the ERA and one with a long record of opposition to civil rights legislation, Georgia proved to be an important front line over the course of the battle. Because its legislative sessions were among the earliest in the country, Georgia could set a precedent for other states. Lee Wysong explained, "We were one of the first ones because . . . our legislature was in session from January to early March. So, we were the first ones who would have voted on it." The STOP ERA women knew the importance of the legislative calendar and, Wysong recalled, "We were just frantic because we felt if Georgia went, if Georgia fell, then these other states that had withheld their vote—at least one of them would go and that would put them over the top!"[24] Their most effective strategy was to keep ratification off the legislative calendar completely in order to prevent any publicity for the measure.

Even though Democratic governor Jimmy Carter supported the ERA, he could not push it through the state legislature. Indeed, the ERA came up only once for a floor vote during his term. A few years later, even with the power of the White House behind him and a dire need for a domestic policy victory, President Carter could not get his home state's legislature to budge.[25] Dunaway and Wysong deployed the political power of women as lobbyists, campaign workers, and mothers against the ERA anytime they saw even a glimmer of hope for ratification in Georgia.

Dunaway and Wysong faced a tough challenge. In the spring of 1973, the ERA appeared unstoppable. Thirty states ratified the ERA in the first year. Only eight state legislatures had to ratify within six years for the amendment to pass. In addition, many national organizations supported the amendment. Pro-ERA groups included the National Organization for Women (NOW), the American Association of University Women, the League of Women Voters, the Young Women's Christian Association, and, of course, the NFRW. Both the Democratic and Republican Party platforms endorsed the amendment.

The STOP ERA movement framed its outsider status as a benefit, especially for southern conservatives. In the South, working outside national party platforms had become a way of life. Though remaining registered Democrats, many southern conservatives had not felt at home in the national Democratic Party for years. In 1968, Georgia's electoral votes went to the outsider George Wallace for president. In 1972, when there was no third-party challenger, the state voted Republican. The STOP ERA women used the familiar status of political outsider—belonging to neither party—to their advantage as the battle dragged on.

In contrast, Georgia's ERA advocates remained more centralized in Atlanta. Its supporters wholeheartedly believed their state would pass the amendment and were eager to be one of the necessary thirty-eight states to ratify. In 1973, Georgia feminists did not worry that the amendment would fail nationwide. Their concern was that eight other states would pass it first, leaving them on the sidelines in passing progressive initiatives. They saw the possibility of taking Georgia out of its reactionary political traditions and into the mainstream on a civil rights initiative. Mamie K. Taylor, chair of the Georgia Commission on the Status of Women ERA Steering Committee, emphasized that Georgia needed to lead on the ERA. With so much momentum behind the amendment, she wanted Georgia to be one of the crucial states to ratify the amendment rather than just going along years after passage, as the state had done with the women's suffrage amendment.[26]

The Georgia Commission on the Status of Women (CSW) was determined that its state would lead on the ERA. Since 1967, by which time every state had a Commission on the Status of Women, following Dwight Eisenhower's establishment of the Presidential Commission on the Status of Women in 1958, each governor had appointed members to research and report on the situation and needs of women within their state. The slate of women Governor Jimmy Carter appointed to the Georgia CSW did not reflect ideological or geographic diversity, mimicking trends in other state women's commissions. Most members were from the Atlanta region and all supported the ERA.[27] Following Schlafly's lead, as a sign of disdain, the STOP ERA membership used the acronym SOW, rather than the official CSW, when they discussed the commissions.[28]

The CSW members decided it would act as an ERA Task Force until the amendment passed, "presumably in January 1973," and they appointed eight women to serve on the ERA Steering Committee. One of the Steering Committee's first actions was mailing a questionnaire to all representatives and senators asking for a commitment of support for the ERA. Steering Committee chairwoman Mamie K. Taylor reported that 65 percent of legislators responded, but added that many legislators resented being asked to sign any commitment form. While commissioners sometimes traveled to speak, they did not actively recruit local women to write letters. Rather, CSW members managed the pro-ERA message and movement from the top down. Because they expected quick passage, they saw no need and no time to build local support. They miscalculated. Since most CSW members were from the Atlanta area, members divvied up the legislators so they would not overlook any of the rural district representatives.[29]

Another blunder on the part of ERA proponents concerned identification of the opposition. The CSW's research led them to believe that the greatest opposition came from the John Birch Society. For the time being, the CSW remained unaware of, or at least unbothered by, the local women all over Georgia under Schlafly's direction who were fighting the ERA from within the legislators' home districts.[30] By the next legislative session, the CSW members would be well aware of the conservative grassroots movement that operated in every district of the state.

CSW and STOP ERA disagreed fundamentally over what they expected the amendment would do. Both sides linked their position with current events to prove the amendment's relevance to voters' lives. ERA advocates targeted the plethora of laws that restricted women's social and economic equality. For example, banks limited women's access to credit and loans, and often required a male co-signer. Supporters believed the ERA would make such practices unconstitutional. One of the most persuasive points for the ERA was the wage gap that revealed that women earned sixty-four cents for every dollar a man received.[31] The ERA presumably would prohibit differential wages based solely on the sex of the worker as well as ending sex discrimination in hiring and promotion.

STOP ERA, in contrast, argued that the ERA would negatively affect families in the workplace. Schlafly addressed public fears of a declining economy. She blamed the 8.9 percent unemployment rate on federal legislation requiring equal opportunity and equal pay. Men could not find jobs, she argued, because women had left the home and flooded the workplace. With more people seeking jobs, wages decreased and men could no longer earn enough to support a family. Protective labor legislation kept women safe and men employed. If a woman could not meet the physical demands of a job, then she might harm herself and bring down the productivity of the entire company. Schlafly decried the new system of "reverse discrimination" that gave preference to women and minorities in hiring.[32]

While STOP ERA proponents warned that the amendment endangered the wage-earning man, they also predicted grave dangers to the stay-at-home housewife. Schlafly's newsletter claimed that even the most personal aspects of a woman's life would not be safe from the federal government under the ERA. She conjectured that husbands would have to pay "at least $960 per year" in additional taxes in order to keep Social Security benefits for a housewife. That would be taken out of the family income, leaving more American families to get by on less. Even more dire, Schlafly warned that a man would no longer have the legal responsibility to support his wife and children, "the most important of all women's rights." In the case of a divorce, the mother could lose custody of her children because she did not have an income, she predicted. Daughters would also not be safe in schools, where the ERA would make separate bathrooms unconstitutional.[33] Later, Dunaway drove the point home for white southerners when she said, "After the Civil Rights Act, there were no more 'black' and 'white' bathrooms." The ERA would do the same to men's and women's (and girls' and boys') rooms.[34]

The ERA's potential negative impact on the military also became a primary talking point for STOP ERA. The military draft lottery did not end until late 1972, so the fear of drafting women was very real for citizens who watched the Vietnam War on television every night. Schlafly's newsletter, the source of talking points for STOP ERA activists nationwide, seized on the fear of daughters in the draft.[35] She reminded readers that Senator Sam Ervin (D–N.C.) had proposed an amendment to the ERA that would have exempted women from the military draft, but ERA proponents fought it and the Senate defeated it.

Even some ERA advocates conceded that women would be drafted, and then would have to face combat. In a debate with Schlafly, U.S. Rep. Patricia Schroeder (D–Colo.) downplayed the threat of conscription by saying, "The draft is going out. . . . We are entering a new phase because of technology. . . . It is more a push-button type of war."[36] Schlafly and STOP ERA were not appeased.

Because the issue of the draft spoke convincingly to young women and their parents, among others, it became a central recruiting message for ERA opposition groups. In Texas, Lottie Beth Hobbs formed Women Who Want to be Women (WWWW), which also dedicated itself to the battle against the ERA. Many women joined more than one group, or at least shared literature and strategies across organizations. The Atlanta branch of WWWW distributed a pink information sheet that cautioned that the ERA would require "all women [to] register at age eighteen, subject to all military duties including combat." In addition to playing on public disdain for the draft, they cautioned that it would break up families, since "whichever parent was called first might be eligible for service. . . . Do you want this for your daughters?" It went on to warn soldiers' wives that the ERA would mean "your husband will be sharing sleeping quarters, restrooms, showers, and/or foxholes with women."[37] If the horror of drafted daughters was not enough to convince women, the fear of cheating husbands might do the trick.

Further, ERA opponents cautioned that the amendment would result in the legalization of homosexual marriage and greater rights for gay and lesbian Americans. Schlafly warned her supporters not to be deceived by a "live-and-let-live attitude." She informed readers, "[Homosexuals] want the right to teach in schools. . . . They want the right to 'marry' and thereby qualify for joint income tax and homestead benefits enjoyed by husbands and wives. They want the right to adopt children." If the amendment outlawed consideration of sex, then the sex of individuals presenting themselves for marriage could not matter under the law. The implementation of gender-neutral language jeopardized the family unit. Because the family was the most basic unit of society, then all of America was under threat. Schlafly maintained the right of parents "to have their children taught by teachers who respect the moral law." Connecting the issue to the recent kidnapping of Patty Hearst, she warned that parents had greater right to control their child's education than, "say, the two college-educated lesbian members of the Symbionese Liberation Army."[38] This extreme example played on parents' fears of losing a child, whether to the military, homosexuality, or terrorism.

Ultimately, STOP ERA's greatest weapon against the ERA was fear of the unknown. Schlafly repeatedly warned that the effects of the amendment could not be predicted with any certainty. Linking the ERA to the morass in Vietnam, she quoted a Yale Medical School professor who asked, "Is the Equal Rights

Amendment to be the Tonkin Gulf Resolution of the American social structure?" The Gulf of Tonkin resolution gave unprecedented war powers to the executive branch and was a critical factor in the escalation of U.S. military action in Vietnam. Schlafly warned her readers that the ERA would result in federal intervention and chaos in the American family.[39] Even more dire, it would be federal courts that interpreted the meaning of a new amendment. Southern white citizens, including state legislators, had developed a distrust of the federal courts, which STOP ERA organizers targeted to their advantage. Federal courts had ruled against segregation and school prayer. Most recently, the Supreme Court had ruled in favor of legal access to abortion. The ERA would make American families susceptible to the whims of the courts and legislatures.

With Schlafly's newsletters in hand, STOP ERA state leaders set about organizing the grassroots. In Georgia, Lee Wysong and Kathryn Dunaway spread Schlafly's message among their target audiences of local women and state legislators. The ERA never even made it out of committee in the 1973 Georgia legislative session. When the amendment was introduced to the floor of the Georgia House, Speaker George Smith immediately referred it to the House Special Judiciary Committee. During a two-week recess, Governor Carter warned the amendment's advocates on the CSW that constituent letters to legislators ran "nine to one *against* ratification."[40] Suddenly, passage did not look so certain.

The Special Judiciary Committee held public hearings on the Equal Rights Amendment in February 1973. Each side had one hour and forty-five minutes to present arguments. The *Atlanta Journal* reported that amendment supporters "appeared generally younger than the opponents." Pro-ERA speakers used their advantage of opening the debate to refute popular scare tactics of the anti-ERA group. The Georgia state coordinator for NOW apologized to representatives "that our time should be taken on such a non-issue as public restrooms since the Constitution provides the right to privacy." Speakers from the state League of Women Voters and Church Women United testified that existing rape laws would remain under the ERA and that the personal relations of husbands and wives would not be affected.[41]

The anti-ERA side then took the stand. STOP ERA had only been organized for a few months and it did not have the control over the opposition message that it would develop in later years. Dunaway selected some but not all of the opposition speakers. In later years, she would have final approval over who took the podium. Giving heft to these first hearings in a crucial state, Phyllis Schlafly flew in to testify about the amendment's danger to women. Mrs. Russell Kelly of Moultrie, Georgia, told representatives that American women did not need the protections of a constitutional amendment "because we are protected by our men." Other opponents speaking to the Special Judiciary Committee, according to the newspaper, "included quite a few older women from church groups and conservative organizations."[42]

However, not all the speakers delivered the approved STOP ERA message. Chairman of the National States' Rights Committee J. B. Stoner testified. He had run for Georgia governor in 1970, losing badly in the Democratic primary to Jimmy Carter. In 1972, he lost in the primary for U.S. Senate to Sam Nunn. Stoner proudly admitted to being a white supremacist and warned that the ERA would force women into military service and lead to "race mixing in the barracks" and that it would "legalize prostitution."[43] In an article written for the National States Rights Party newsletter, Stoner expounded on his reasons for opposing the amendment. Running the article with photos of Gloria Steinem, Bella Abzug, and Betty Friedan, he called it "that evil amendment that is sponsored by Jews, lesbians, and other assorted enemies of White womanhood."[44] Reacting to Stoner's racist testimony, one opponent worried, "I wish he would leave. He hurts us, bad."[45] As a regular loser in state politics, Stoner may have brought celebrity, but did not bring respect or constituents to the opposition.

Stoner's language echoed previous decades' white Massive Resistance campaigns and did not reflect the new, more moderate language celebrating American home and family. While far from progressive, STOP ERA tried to keep their arguments from being utterly regressive. By the 1970s, blatantly racial appeals in politics had given way to a more coded language. ERA opponents never specified that the American family they wanted to protect was white, but they never had to. They tied the ERA to current events regarding the economy, abortion, or military service. Members of STOP ERA might have opposed integration, but they did not publicly link the ERA with civil rights or integration. Rather, the STOP ERA women sent out what political scientists Angie Maxwell and Todd Shields called "the anti-feminism rallying cry [which] became as successful as the well-known dog whistles of race and religion."[46]

Schlafly and her legions of local followers redirected southern conservatism away from its overtly segregationist past. Instead, they embraced a gendered language of conservatism, emphasizing the protection of families, the rights of any woman to stay at home, and concern for children. That minorities might have been shut out from this middle-class vision of a family was not STOP ERA's concern.

Within a few years, Dunaway distributed a "Check List for Witnesses to Speak against ERA" and explained, "It is important to schedule a variety of witnesses with a good distribution of age, religion, color, economic group, organizational affiliations, political party, and geographic section of the state." She sought diverse women, including women lawyers, "Representatives of various religious faiths," teachers, a "draft-age girl," a "senior woman who was a suf-fragette," female veterans, union workers, and a "Black woman or minister or representative of NAACP or Urban League."[47] While the record does not show how many of the types she was able to check off her list, Dunaway recognized the value of at least appearing to represent diverse women to legislators and to the public.

While linked issues of race and sex may have been behind some legislators' and constituents' opposition to the amendment, the organization typically re-frained from blatant racism for the remainder of the decade. The women in STOP ERA usually focused on the language of home, family, and motherhood. While they sounded the occasional dog whistle of segregation, those not steeped in southern culture could miss the call. By shunning overtly racist lan-guage, the women also hoped to appeal to socially conservative African Amer-ican women, pastors, legislators, and voters who were exercising recently won voting power all over the state. Grassroots STOP ERA organizers crafted a new conservative language that softened racist messages while still advocating states' rights and a traditional white, middle-class family. This language later became recognized as the family-values politics of the New Right.[48]

Georgia's STOP ERA prevailed in this early round. Despite the nearly four hours of hearings, the ERA did not leave the Special Judiciary Committee in 1973. Leg-islators held it over until the next session, when they would once again debate the ERA. Proponents and opponents had nine months to organize and lobby. Other states' STOP ERA groups had not been as successful. Eight other state legislatures ratified the amendment that year. At the end of 1973, the Equal Rights Amendment was only eight states away from passage. However, Ne-braska legislators voted to rescind their initial ratification, a vote that, accord-ing to Schlafly, "blew the steam out of the momentum for ratification."[49] This vote opened a new topic of debate: Once passed, could a state rescind its rat-ification?[50] For Georgia STOP ERA, the answer was simple; it was best not to pass the amendment at all.

Kathryn Dunaway, Lee Wysong, and other women of STOP ERA spent the remainder of 1973 developing and implementing strategy to defeat the amend-ment. They educated themselves and friends with the *Phyllis Schlafly Re-port*; at least eight of the year's monthly issues focused on specific arguments against the ERA. In May, Schlafly argued that the amendment would consoli-date federal power, a strong argument in the South. She specifically cited the Fourteenth Amendment, which "opened the door to endless litigation and ex-tensions of federal power never dreamed by its authors."[51] She did not need to mention race specifically in order for readers to understand that most civil rights cases had been decided on the basis of that amendment. If the Four-teenth Amendment had opened up the judicial path for such drastic upheavals of society, what unexpected changes would the Equal Rights Amendment bring?

Back on the ground in Georgia, Dunaway and Wysong assessed the battle ahead. They asked Georgia STOP ERA district leaders to gauge the level of support for the ERA among legislators in their regions. An organizer from Sandersville reported to Dunaway, "We have heard from twenty of the men.... Eight are against, five definitely for and seven undecided.... Hope you all get a better response than we did."[52] Margaret Scharmitzky of Thomasville left a Schlafly article for her representative but did not press him for an opinion. A few weeks later, Scharmitzky happily reported that the representative had come out in opposition to the ERA.[53] Also in south Georgia, Erin Sherman reported the Valdosta STOP ERA was working hard to defeat the amendment. They collected signatures on petitions, warning voters about the dangers of the amendment and demanding that legislators vote against it. After passing out "What ERA Means" flyers, Sherman felt sure that their legislators would be flooded with letters from concerned voters.[54] Women across Georgia reported to Dunaway and Wysong, who in turn kept track of the legislators for and against so they could organize for the vote that would come in 1974. The model of local canvassing and central data collection replicated the structure Dunaway and Wysong had learned as volunteers for Barry Goldwater in 1964 and Bo Callaway in 1966.

In addition to their efforts to reach legislators, STOP ERA workers endeavored to recruit ministers to their side. Most churches already had women's organizations that could easily set aside one meeting to address the threat of the Equal Rights Amendment. Schlafly encouraged state chairmen to reach out to churches in 1974, reminding readers that "the church women of all faiths are our biggest reservoir of potential allies." She included a letter that Illinois STOP ERA used and encouraged chairmen to copy the text onto their own state's letterhead. Each district chairman should get one hundred copies to send to local churches. In this project, Schlafly shared the idea and the text from her friends at her home state's STOP ERA, but relied on state chairmen to implement the plan. At the local level, each district chairman used her own community expertise to select the churches most likely to yield results.[55] Deploying women's church auxiliaries as political forces laid valuable groundwork for the connection of evangelical religion and politics later in the decade. By 1979, male Christian leaders like Jerry Falwell and Pat Robertson proclaimed a "New Christian Right" that mobilized voters on moral issues, but women's groups like STOP ERA had already begun to define and defend American family values.[56]

One of the most powerful issues for STOP ERA, and later for the New Christian Right, was abortion. In January 1973 the Supreme Court ruled on the Texas case *Roe v. Wade* and its companion case out of Georgia, *Doe v. Bolton*, declaring abortion a legal procedure. ERA opponents latched on to the decision as another reason to defeat the amendment—and another way to recruit conservative women to fight the amendment. Schlafly's December 1974 newsletter explained the link between the ERA and abortion. She charged that feminists wanted to legalize abortion in order to diminish the "greatest 'inequality' between men and women ... women get pregnant and men do not."[57] She provided her interpretation of the findings of the Rockefeller Commission on population growth, which warned of increased population and diminishing resources. Schlafly argued, without context, that the Rockefeller Commission supported the ERA in the hopes that more women would enter the workforce rather than have babies. Abortion, she claimed, would speed the goal of zero population growth.[58] Schlafly viewed abortion rights not just as violating the life of a fetus, but also as negating the natural difference between men and women.

Over the next years, the pro-life movement and the anti-ERA movement reinforced one another. STOP ERA women used the issue of abortion to recruit more religious conservatives to fight the amendment. Kathryn Dunaway distributed copies of an undated Eagle Forum pamphlet titled *The Abortion Connection* showing two threads—one labeled "abortion" and the other "Equal Rights Amendment"—intertwined, forming one rope. The pamphlet quoted Senator Sam J. Ervin, saying, "I think there is no doubt of the fact that the ERA would give every woman a constitutional right to have an abortion at will." Many abortion opponents believed that a more conservative future Supreme Court might reconsider and overturn *Roe*, but they had to keep the ERA out of the Constitution until that day. Finally, the pamphlet warned that "the same people support abortion and ERA ... almost always."[59] If feminists linked the two issues, then conservatives had to fight them equally. The brochure's naming of prominent Jewish feminists Bella Abzug and Gloria Steinem signaled the difference between abortion and ERA advocates and Sunbelt evangelicals and Catholic conservatives. The women at Georgia's grassroots level certainly got the message. One STOP ERA worker mailed Dunaway information on abortion and fetal research, while promising that ERA material would soon follow. The women began fighting both battles in the name of the American family.[60]

In the early years of the 1970s, Phyllis Schlafly and her followers had to find their footing outside of party politics and the structure of the NFRW. The NFRW exodus provided Schlafly with enough supporters to make a movement if she could articulate the message. Resistance to the Equal Rights Amendment, specifically, and anti-feminism, generally, shaped a movement that united women who were no longer partisan, but ever more conservative. The model of STOP ERA relied on top-down communication from Schlafly, but bottom-up organizing from the local level.

In Georgia, Kathryn Dunaway and Lee Wysong recruited, organized, and educated a strong STOP ERA faction. In 1973, the ERA had not even come out of committee, but Dunaway and Wysong already had women deployed at the local level, warning legislators and community leaders of the dangers of the ERA. With Schlafly's newsletters, they had the message. With Dunaway's organization, they had their strategy. When the amendment finally came to a floor vote in the state legislature, Georgia STOP ERA was prepared to face the moment.

CHAPTER 6

Breadmaker Politics

When the ERA finally went to the full Georgia House in late January 1974, Kathryn Dunaway was ready to lead her first major operation. The day of the floor vote, STOP ERA volunteers gave every legislator a loaf of freshly baked bread bearing the note, "From the breadmaker to the breadwinner."[1] The gift, along with a few gently spoken words against the amendment, spoke volumes to the largely male legislature. The "breadwinner," assumed to be male, made both money and laws to support the housewife and children. The "breadmaker," assumed to be female, stayed home to raise the children and maintain the household. The gift of fresh bread reinforced the idea that homemakers nourished the family.

Legislators did not know, however, that all their lobbying efforts took up Dunaway's and her volunteers' own baking time, nor that the bread scheme was a national strategy. Privately, she thanked Chester Gray of Mom's Bakery in Atlanta "for the donation of the many small loaves of your delicious bread."[2] The women had been too busy organizing to take time for baking. The legislators also did not know that Arizona and Missouri STOP ERA had already had success with their "bread project" that "put the libbers on the defensive." Phyllis Schlafly shared the bread idea in a letter to state chairmen.[3] Georgia women did not need to bake the bread or even think up the bread tactic.

Over the next decade, STOP ERA women continued to fight feminism with femininity. The national network, funneling strategies through state- and lower-level organizations, structured the content and the delivery of the message. Throughout the next decade, they waged war wherever they saw a threat and they made sure to do it all in a dress and with perfectly coiffed hair. The national STOP ERA network freed women from the need to develop strategy and allowed them to implement proven methods to get their message across to legislators. The bread project proved so successful that the women made lobbying with baked goods a tradition. One year, they gave legislators cakes with the accompanying poem, "You can have your cake / And eat it, too. / STOP ERA, and / See Us Through."[4]

As the decade wore on, the STOP ERA women began sponsoring an annual Valentine's Day meal for all the legislators. The flavorful meals reinforced their message of representing home and housewives while providing STOP ERA volunteers valuable face time with the legislators whose meals they served. Lee Wysong explained the tradition as "just a gesture to let them know we liked them and to stay in their good graces and maybe convert some of those who had been on the other side—and, apparently, we did!"[5] When Dunaway's adult son Marshall remembered accompanying his mother to the legislature during one visit, he marveled, "She would walk into their [legislative] offices ... unannounced, take the cake [in] back, put it on their desk while they were talking with whoever—the governor or whoever—and she might say a few little selected words to them ... and leave." The morning began with a strategy session among the STOP ERA women, where, as Marshall Dunaway remembered, "They would decide who would go to which office[, saying,] 'He likes this kind of cake, so you take this one to him.'"[6]

In 1979 alone, Kathryn Dunaway reported that STOP ERA volunteers "served 500 lunches at the Capitol. . . . We had so many women up there you couldn't get around."[7] The luncheons and cake drop-offs provided the women valuable opportunities for personal interaction with legislators without the formality of a meeting. They carried the message of femininity and family, hoping that the way to a man's vote was through his stomach.

Georgia's first lady, Rosalynn Carter, recalled visiting the Capitol the day before the ERA vote. She wore an "I'm for ERA" button as she walked through the halls to meet her husband. Carter remembered the corridors being packed with anti-ERA demonstrators wearing red STOP ERA buttons and carrying stop signs emblazoned with the words. "They were camped all over the capitol, lobbying legislators very effectively," she wrote. "I was booed all the way in, and ... booed all the way out." Significantly, Carter did not mention any noteworthy presence of pro-ERA demonstrators.[8]

Before the 1974 floor vote, ERA opponents made their presence known to every sense—the sight of signs, the sound of boos, the touch of handshakes, and the smell and taste of fresh bread. Instead of taking to the streets, the women used friendly, individualized tactics, reinforcing ideas of a woman's role in the home. The first lady, the CSW, and other pro-ERA groups finally recognized the force of their well-organized opponents.

The legislators debated ratification of the amendment for four hours on January 30, 1974, before ultimately defeating it in a 104–70 vote. In his speech opposing passage, Rep. W. W. Larsen of Dublin asked, "Where would we have been when we were attacked at Pearl Harbor if we had to line up men and women equally?" Rep. Dorsey Matthews of Moultrie warned that the amendment "stinks of communism." Thus, echoing the message of STOP ERA, the legislators opposed the amendment based on a perceived threat to national security. The only two women in the legislative body voted for the amendment.[9] CSW chairwoman Jeanne Cahill called the vote "a slap in the face of equality and justice" but reminded ERA supporters that, "in a state that took 138 years to ratify the first ten amendments . . . 70 votes for equality is rather impressive."[10]

Meanwhile, Kathryn Dunaway celebrated momentarily before regrouping for the 1975 session. She wrote that the vote allowed her to "breathe a little more freely for a few days," but that she had to get back to work "countering their [pro-ERA groups'] false claims, and educating the public and lawmakers day and night."[11] Wysong and Dunaway wrote to the legislators who supported the ERA to express regret "that we were unable to convince you of the dangers of the so-called Equal Rights Amendment. However, We won, You won, the Women of Georgia won." They offered the legislators information on the ERA in case they wanted to reconsider their votes before the next session.[12] Dunaway wrote thank-you notes to every representative who voted against the ERA and encouraged local women to do the same.[13] STOP ERA's strategy included outreach to both constituents and legislators because the desired outcome was not limited to defeat of the ERA. Dunaway realized the ERA was only one issue, and she wanted to keep her relationships open for any future conservative campaigns.

Across Georgia, people began recognizing Kathryn Dunaway as the point person for the ERA opposition. Several women wrote her to express gratitude for her leadership in defeating the amendment. One supporter appreciated Dunaway's work "for all of us happy housewives" and specifically mentioned that "your manner was ladylike."[14] Another wrote to say "how much we appreciate your long and great fight to down the ERA."[15] From East Point, Louise Younger also expressed her appreciation and predicted, "I feel that victory in Georgia spells doom for the ERA as a national issue. Let us hope it will soon be dead."[16] A Stone Mountain woman asked for information on "what we women can do to stop the Equal Rights Amendment."[17] Atlantan Lena Fay Parish had already called her representative and senator but wanted to know what more she could do.[18] Supporter Angelynn McGuff expressed her goal to put "500 (!) What ERA Means Quotes sheets" in mailboxes around her Stone Mountain community.[19] Many women enclosed checks to help with victory celebrations or future STOP ERA work. The *Atlanta Journal* even forwarded a letter to Dunaway from a Lawrenceville reader who said she had been "thinking that all those out fighting [ERA], both pro and con, were a bunch of kooks. But . . . you think and reason just like I do. And WE are certainly sane, aren't we?"[20] Dunaway added each correspondent to her network.

In June 1974, Phyllis Schlafly rewarded Kathryn Dunaway's success in person at an Atlanta Victory Luncheon to raise funds for further Georgia STOP ERA work. For ten dollars, Georgians could hear Schlafly in person and learn more strategies for defeating the ERA.[21] Even with a comfortable margin of victory, Dunaway continued to recruit more women, train those already on board, and press legislators to oppose ERA. Because every Georgia House seat was up for election that fall, Dunaway directed the women at the local level to meet personally with every candidate, regardless of party affiliation or previous voting record. Before the election, the women should ascertain each candidate's position on the ERA so the group would know whom to endorse.

Wysong mailed letters on Georgia STOP ERA letterhead to each new candidate before Election Day to remind him that women in his district and throughout Georgia wanted the defeat of the amendment. The letter opened with the foreboding line, "As the November election approaches, we note that you have opposition in your bid for a seat in the Georgia senate."[22] Incumbents might know STOP ERA and would have already received a letter of regret or thanks from the leaders for their 1974 vote. New candidates did not have a record on the ERA and needed to be reached early. Candidate Leonard Brown of Calhoun replied enthusiastically, "I not only will vote against the Equal Rights Amendment, but I will also take a last ditch stand in opposition." He cited the ERA as the primary reason he entered the race before asking for help from STOP ERA in spreading word of his candidacy throughout the district.[23] Unopposed ERA supporters received a letter of "congratulations on your reelection" from Wysong. She added, "[We] wonder if there has been any change in your views."[24] Local women followed up with a personal visit either at the candidate's local office or at a campaign stop.

After the election, Dunaway directed women to develop relationships with the winners, regardless of party affiliation, and to "convince the undecided—and especially the newly elected members—of the evils of this amendment."[25] Dunaway began compiling advice and information in a Georgia STOP ERA voting guide. Between Election Day and the vote on the ERA, Dunaway asked women to recruit friends to write legislators. Sen. Ebb Duncan of Carrollton divided his numerous letters into three piles—letters from outside his district, pro-ERA letters from his district, and anti-ERA letters from his district. Revealing the effectiveness of STOP ERA's grassroots emphasis, the letters from Duncan's district ran 8-to-1 against the ERA. Sen. Lee Robinson of Macon reported that his letters were 9-to-1 against the amendment.[26]

Even though Georgia remained unratified, the amendment made progress nationwide. Three states ratified the ERA in 1974, making Dunaway even more determined to hold Georgia. Only five more states had to ratify for the amendment to pass, and Dunaway and her volunteers focused on making sure Georgia was not one of them. In just two years, Dunaway and Wysong, using Schlafly's resources, had built a successful network of conservative women across Georgia. Over the remainder of the decade, they continued to build their movement in women's kitchens as well as across state lines.

"Only the permanent legalization of abortion and homosexuality could provide the motivating force for the campaign for the ERA," the STOP ERA editorial blasted on a local Atlanta television station. Its author, Kathryn Dunaway, asserted that women already had legal assurances of equality in education, employment, and credit.[27] Airing in the days just before the General Assembly convened, the announcement reviewed a brief history of laws that already guaranteed women's economic equality before shifting to the threats to society if the ERA passed. Three issues—the ERA, abortion, and homosexual rights—formed a foundation for social conservatism and ignited the political activism of socially conservative voters across the nation and in Georgia. This gendered conservatism provided a new constellation of issues that enabled southerners to identify with their peers around the nation. With gender and the developing rhetoric of family values, the South could not only join but lead national conservative movements.

The 1975 Georgia General Assembly session brought another defeat for the ERA, this time by a 33–22 vote in the senate. The debate lasted only one hour. Sen. Hugh Gillis of Soperton celebrated, "We have the most beautiful and gracious ladies in the South.... Let's show the nation that we respect our ladies." The Georgia Senate's sole woman, Virginia Shapard of Griffin, retorted, "Passage of the ERA will not make a woman a lady, nor will it prevent her from being one." Gillis's rhetorical choice of "ladies" conjured up an image of a woman who was well-mannered, demure, and fragile—and, in this context, most likely a white woman with elevated class status. Shapard's sharp reply acknowledged that the ERA did not have the power either to bestow or revoke the status of being a lady.[28]

Fred Schlafly, Phyllis's husband, wrote Kathryn Dunaway to thank her for her phone call telling them of the critical senate vote and to congratulate her for "slowing down" the national ERA momentum with her work in Georgia.[29] Dunaway and other ERA opponents were so effective in slowing down the amendment in Georgia that it did not reach the floor of either house again for five years. Yet the amendment progressed nationwide. North Dakota ratified it on February 3, 1975, cutting the number of needed states to four.[30]

Kathryn Dunaway never slowed down even when the amendment was tabled. In October 1975, she led a Georgia group to Schlafly's Eagle Council meeting, where women from across the nation strategized in workshops on media and legislative preparation. Schlafly planned a "mock ERA hearing to practice testimony before a state legislature." They already had their talking points from the newsletter, but the mock settings provided volunteers space to perfect their presentations. The women practiced among themselves in order to stave off any fear in front of legislators or pro-ERA groups. As part of the learning process, STOP ERA women evaluated one another on their public-speaking performance. Eagle Council attendees thought Kathryn Dunaway had "lots of enthusiasm" but needed to project her soft voice. Her eye contact was good, though one person thought she moved her head too much. The ninety-six evaluations all agreed she looked respectable, but one person criticized her for wearing black instead of a color.[31] They examined every detail of their peers' presentations in preparation for unsympathetic audiences. They critiqued vocal tone, clothing, posture, and grammar so that their colleagues would be prepared and confident in any meeting with legislators or in a debate with a pro-ERA woman.

After the national meeting, Dunaway dispensed the media tips she had learned to other Georgia women to prepare them for outreach opportunities. In a handout sharing some of the lessons learned at the Eagle Council, Dunaway nodded to Schlafly's past bestseller promoting Barry Goldwater when she told women to "Be a Voice, Not an Echo."[32] She told them to be prepared with facts, to avoid losing their temper, and to maintain good posture. As soon as they scheduled a television appearance, women needed to "Reduce. Go on diet. TV adds 10 lbs." Beyond that, women should sit up straight, cover their knees, cross their legs at the ankles, and wear solid, bright colors. All STOP ERA women should wear skirts while women over forty should not show any part of their neck. Jewelry needed to be minimal, and as for "hair, not too much." Finally, women needed to "Look happy. Smile (not forced)."[33] The STOP ERA strategy went beyond the message to include its presentation. Their message threatened the ERA and their appearance would not unnerve men.

The women of STOP ERA did not simply target legislators. They understood that they needed to convince the rest of Georgia of the amendment's potential impact on their lives. Just as they had spent countless hours at Republican booths during county fairs, STOP ERA volunteers set up booths at women's events to educate women across Georgia about the looming dangers of the Equal Rights Amendment. They participated in numerous shopping mall information fairs, such as an exhibition sponsored by the Women's Chamber of Commerce at Lenox Mall in Atlanta in the fall of 1975. With various women's groups setting up around the shopping corridors, event planners separated STOP ERA and NOW with one of the mall's large planters. Within a few steps, shoppers could hear both sides of the issue.[34]

Georgia STOP ERA provided an outline for an anti-ERA speech to ease any volunteers' anxieties about public speaking. Lee Wysong headed the STOP ERA speakers bureau and matched up volunteers with engagements all over the state. Volunteers could select from Schlafly's long list of opposition points those they found most compelling for their audience. The first point was that "ERA is a fraud. It is *unnecessary, undesirable, and uncertain.*" Other points addressed the draft, alimony, federal power, homosexuality, and abortion. Wysong suggested speakers tell their audiences about ERA endorsements from the Southern Christian Leadership Conference, Young Socialist Alliance, Socialist Workers Party, and Atlanta Lesbian Feminist Alliance.[35] Wysong understood that white veterans of Massive Resistance to school desegregation would not want to ally themselves with the SCLC. While some voters may not have developed an opinion on the ERA, they would not want to be on the same side as the civil rights organization. The inclusion of the Atlanta Lesbian Feminist Alliance signaled another step toward a gendered conservatism of family values and opposition to homosexual rights. By presenting a heteronormative family—father, mother, and children—as traditional and anything else as radical, STOP ERA blazed the trail for the conservative Christianity that would develop by the decade's end. STOP ERA women presented communism, civil rights, and homosexuality as imminent dangers to conservative Georgia families.

Kathryn Dunaway's STOP ERA commitment influenced her other civic volunteerism. The Sandy Springs Women's Club proposed Dunaway as Georgia's 1976 nominee for the American Mothers Committee's Mother of the Year Award. Criteria for the award included "characteristics highly regarded in mothers such as love, courage, cheerfulness, patience . . . and homemaking skill" as well as active participation in "community, state, national, and/or international activities."[36] With her record of linking political activism to her motherly duties, Kathryn Dunaway certainly qualified. Her application included descriptions of her volunteer work ranging from her twenty years with the PTA to her Goldwater volunteerism and her leadership of STOP ERA. Speaker of the Georgia House Tom Murphy praised her in a letter of recommendation, writing, "Mrs. Dunaway not only has opinions. She acts." Murphy had only been speaker of the house for two years and did not represent Dunaway's suburban Atlanta district, yet his support signified how successfully she lobbied legislators.[37]

As a finalist in the Mother of the Year contest, Dunaway had to speak before the selection committee. To begin, she described her duties as a mother of three, grandmother of five, and former Boy Scouts and Blue Birds leader—casting herself as a trailblazer: Georgia's first "temporary female Boy Scoutmaster." She had even scared off a bear, "with my only weapon a flashlight."

Her weapons against the ERA were more substantial, and the danger was just as significant, she told her audience. The legislation threatened the family, "which has been the strength and foundation of all nations since God instituted the family." Dunaway closed her speech by stating, "May this blight never come to our great nation, and may our womanhood and motherhood continue to be revered and our families preserved."[38] Though she did not become the Georgia Mother of the Year, she did seize the opportunity of an audience of women to deliver her anti-ERA message.

With the state legislature out of session, Dunaway took a brief break from STOP ERA in the fall of 1975 to serve as chair of Constitution Week for the Cherokee chapter of the Daughters of the American Revolution (DAR). She adapted her media training from the Eagle Council for this job and reported the successes of Constitution Week with the same detail she had provided in STOP ERA reports to Schlafly: "47 7/8 inches of coverage, 4 articles, 1 picture, 1 editorial," in addition to "4 hours of radio, 40 spot announcements . . . 3 minutes on TV." Thirty-six churches and sixteen area schools received information on the DAR celebration of the Constitution's anniversary.[39] Her volunteer work for the patriotic and socially conservative DAR, she hoped, would reinforce her anti-ERA work. The networks for DAR and STOP ERA overlapped, and she hoped her work would strengthen both groups. After that week, Kathryn Dunaway went back to ensuring that the ERA would not join the Constitution she had just honored.

In 1976, STOP ERA women again contacted every Georgia legislator to confirm their positions on the ERA. In her interview, Lee Wysong explained the strategy: "We didn't want any of them to think they were insignificant, no matter whether they were right or wrong. . . . I think that made them feel good and it gave them a good feeling about us."[40] They delivered handwritten notes before the session to ask elected officials to defeat the amendment and protect the ladies of Georgia. Many legislators responded to the tactic. Chuck Edwards of Cobb County reassured them that he had voted against the ERA in the past and would do so again if he won reelection. Wysong wrote to Dunaway that Democrat Edwards's opponent was the Republican Johnny Isakson, who "is also against ERA and sounds like a good candidate."[41] Representative Wade Hoyt told them, "I do *not* favor the Constitutional amendment known as ERA," and offered his wife's help to fight the amendment.[42] Once Wysong had commitments from each legislator, she let district leaders know which campaigns women should work for. STOP ERA leaders became gatekeepers for conservative women's volunteer hours on local campaigns all across the state.

When she was not lobbying candidates, Kathryn Dunaway worked in other ways to rouse interest in STOP ERA. Just before the 1976 election, Dunaway presented the anti-ERA case to a political science class at Georgia State University.

The professor acknowledged, "you may have sensed that some of the students did not agree with your views," but thanked her for visiting the class. In addition to presenting the opposition side, Dunaway was seizing an opportunity to attract young, draft-age voters to the STOP ERA cause.[43]

Perhaps the most critical constituency she recruited, though, was evangelical pastors. Dunaway targeted well-known ministers from around the state to testify before the 1977 Georgia Senate Judiciary Committee about the dangers of the ERA. In letters to Dr. Charles Stanley of First Baptist Church of Atlanta, Rev. Herschel Turner of Emanuel Baptist Church, and Dr. Curtis Hutson from Forest Hills Baptist Church, Dunaway thanked the pastors for their opposition to the ERA and explained, "Our great concern is the effect of the long-range goal of our opposition to destroy the sanctity of the family and dignity of the home." She described the uphill battle STOP ERA faced: "This year our efforts have been made with the power of some in highest offices against us. However, with God's blessing in providing friends such as you, our work has indeed been successful." She closed with a plea for "continued prayers" and assured the men that STOP ERA women would "carry on in those things we feel are pleasing to Him."[44] She invited congregations to join "Prayer Vigil and Fast . . . for defeat of the Equal Rights Amendment and the preservation of family life in the United States."[45] Just as Dunaway recognized the value of legislators to the cause, she also recognized the value of sharing the STOP ERA message with ministers. Though several evangelical churches restricted women from the pulpit, Dunaway ensured that the STOP ERA message reached the worshippers.

Certainly, southerners had combined religion and politics for generations. However, Dunaway's connection of the ERA, home, and conservative religious beliefs connected women's conservatism to the growing religious right. Dunaway and Wysong modified the organization chart used by the GFRW during the Goldwater campaign with the addition of local STOP ERA prayer coordinators throughout the state.[46]

Dunaway and Wysong positioned STOP ERA as David to the Goliaths of the national Democratic and Republican parties. Their group of women volunteers regularly defeated the powerful, professional strategists of national politics and better-funded feminist organizations. In 1975, they declared victory, even though "Mrs. Betty Ford called the Republican members of the Georgia Senate in an effort to get ERA passed." Two years later, they faced an even bigger Goliath when Georgian Jimmy Carter occupied the White House. By 1977, Dunaway and Wysong offered a list of their powerful Georgia pro-ERA foes: "Jimmy Carter and his wife, the Carter daughter-in-law [Judy], wives of our U.S. Senators, Gov. and Mrs. George Busbee, and Lt. Gov. and Mrs. Zell Miller." However, once again, the state representatives "did not buckle under" and "remembered by whom they were elected."[47] In case a legislator forgot, he would soon receive a handwritten note from an anti-ERA constituent. The David and Goliath metaphor spoke to followers who might have felt overwhelmed at the challenge, reminding them that they had the power of a thank-you note or a baked good ready to bring to the battle.

As the anti-amendment movement matured, the women laid a firm foundation for future family-values conservative movements. Using symbols of motherhood and home—bread, cake, luncheons—women reinforced their message of traditional families, with men as the head of the family, but mothers nestled as the heart. STOP ERA forces had moved from a narrow campaign against the Equal Rights Amendment to a full-blown political ideology with the protection of women and the family at its center. While centering mothers, the STOP ERA message signaled to civil rights opponents and conservative Christians. As the women passed out their homemade bread to legislators, they may as well have been offering communion to new converts to a family-values conservatism. Building on their experience in the previous decade of growing the Georgia Republican Party, they understood how to shape a race-neutral message that still implied white supremacy. They continued, even perfected, their grassroots political organization and now put it to use outside party politics to defeat the ERA and promote family-values policies. In time, their focus on protecting the family from federal intrusion became a powerful tool that made gender central to conservative politics and gave the entire nation a way to link social and cultural issues to politics.

   In the coming years, members of STOP ERA continued to position themselves as under-resourced but determined Davids up against the powerful Goliaths of feminism and the federal government. It turned out their message was their slingshot: the language of motherhood and the protection of women felled the Equal Rights Amendment in years to come. What is more, their message of moral femininity blazed the path that conservative men would follow into positions of political leadership and national influence.

CHAPTER 7

The End of an ERA

Determined to pass the ERA by the 1979 deadline, the National Organization for Women and other pro-ERA groups organized a boycott of all unratified states starting in 1977. The movement for the boycott developed gradually, but by the end of 1977 almost fifty national groups agreed not to hold conventions in major cities like Chicago, Las Vegas, Miami, New Orleans, and Atlanta. Participating organizations encouraged members not to vacation in any state that had not passed the ERA. Katie Harris, president of Atlanta NOW, admitted that the boycott created "a rather touchy problem in Atlanta." She worried that the boycott punished the city, even though "the local legislators and the Mayor are for the E.R.A.," but did nothing to "the rural reps who control the Legislature [and] who are against the E.R.A."[1] Atlanta lost the business of the American Psychological Association, the American Home Economics Association, and the National Education Association, among others.[2]

Unfazed, Kathryn Dunaway responded to the boycott by asking all STOP ERA friends to visit Georgia. Speaking to a group of Atlanta broadcasters, she challenged, "Will Atlanta, Georgia and other states sacrifice their womanhood for a few more greedy dollars? Or are we willing to advertise our city as the most beautiful, the most hospitable city in America filled with exciting historical and fun areas?"[3] Her calls for conservatives to visit were not enough, however, and by November 1978 the estimated losses of convention revenue to Atlanta were $21.3 million.[4]

The boycott is one example of the outside pressure that Kathryn Dunaway and Lee Wysong learned to position themselves as confronting. They framed ERA proponents as outside agitators, an ominous label from the days of white resistance to civil rights. Over the next few years, STOP ERA continued to position themselves as the voice of Georgia women and Georgia families, seeking to prevent any outside influence that might disrupt the status quo. The pressure on Georgia to ratify grew with native son Jimmy Carter in the White

House. Dunaway and Wysong lost a few small battles—like spinning the boy-cott or, later, fighting the national women's conference. However, they did win the war when the ERA failed to get the final three states by the deadline. The women focused so much on defeating the ERA that they did not notice the men adapting their own family-values language to build the new religious right, one with the women scribbled in the margins rather than at the center.

One women's gathering could not boycott Atlanta. The Georgia state meeting for the observance of International Women's Year was held in May 1977, the third of fifty such state meetings. After the UN's World Conference on Women, held in June 1975 in Mexico City, American women determined to continue the work for women's equality at home. President Gerald Ford signed an or-der declaring 1977 as International Women's Year (IWY) in the United States, budgeting $5 million to fund fifty state meetings and one national meeting to make recommendations for achieving women's full equality in the United States. Despite its international-sounding name, the U.S. Commission on IWY focused on American women's issues. Historian Marjorie Spruill identified many members who encouraged Ford's commission as comprised largely of "moderate Republican feminists" who sought to "retrofit laws and policies to make American society more equal and open to women."[5] The U.S. IWY com-mittee included a separate commission devoted solely to passage of the Equal Rights Amendment.[6] As American women brought the feminist work home, they retained the International Women's Year name, though they focused on national and state laws that had been holding American women back.

The National Commission on the Observance of International Women's Year included thirty-five feminist delegates who scandalized ERA opponents. Congress appointed bipartisan and pro-ERA representatives from each house: Senator Charles Percy (R–Ill.), Senator Birch Bayh (D–Ind., also sponsor of the ERA), Rep. Bella Abzug (D–N.Y.), and Rep. Margaret Heckler (R–Mass.). Other members of the committee included academics, journalists, and celebrities.[7] Phyllis Schlafly was not invited, nor were any other ERA opponents. As a final affront, the national commission proclaimed ratification of the ERA its "high-est priority."[8] Spinning the losses to their advantage, STOP ERA forces again ad-opted the position of the underdog, relying on the funding and goodwill of pri-vate citizens to battle big government.

As part of their strategy to reach new audiences, women of the Eagle Fo-rum, STOP ERA, Women Who Want to be Women, the DAR, and other conser-vative groups first fought on the financial front, opposing the apportionment of five million dollars of government funding for programs related to the 1977 International Women's Year meetings in the states, rather than immediately focusing on its goals. With Schlafly's newsletter providing the facts and fig-ures, Kathryn Dunaway set about organizing Georgia STOP ERA opposition to

IWY meetings and any federal funding for them. She sent a letter of protest to Georgia's U.S. senator Sam Nunn, who replied that he had favored only three million dollars. In a letter that did little to appease Dunaway, Nunn explained that the five million was a compromise from the ten million that Bella Abzug had written into the initial bill to fund the conferences.[9] Nunn could not have responded in a more inflammatory way to the woman who had worked for years building a political movement rich in volunteer commitment but poor in finances.

Operating through her former GOP networks, Dunaway was able to have a resolution introduced at the Georgia Republican Party Convention to request that the president and congress "immediately cease funding and abolish the International Women's Year Commission."[10] In the end, the five million dollars stayed in the budget and became a rallying point for conservatives. Georgia's share of the national IWY funds totaled $66,252. Schlafly encouraged state STOP ERA organizations to hold garage sales, bake sales, and craft bazaars to raise the equivalent of five percent of their state's federal IWY allocation, and use the proceeds in the local fight against the IWY.[11] They would make up for the other 95 percent with volunteer commitment and a fierce national network.

Again, national and state STOP ERA worked closely, with each state sharing strategies to subvert the IWY meetings. An Illinois group went to court, seeking to end all IWY meetings, but the federal court threw out their lawsuit, saying the commission appeared to be operating within its federal mandate.[12] Though the meetings could not be stopped, they could be thwarted. As one of the earliest states—and the first among the states yet to ratify the ERA—to hold its IWY meeting, Georgia drew attention from both sides, particularly since it was the home state of President Jimmy Carter and First Lady Rosalynn Carter, who had both endorsed the amendment.

Kathryn Dunaway was the sole conservative among the thirty-seven appointees on the Georgia Coordinating Committee on the Observance of International Women's Year. The other members would soon realize that Dunaway had the experience and power to represent a movement. On the committee's letterhead, she was the only member to identify by her husband's name, as "Mrs. John Dunaway," making a statement against feminism every time a letter went out.[13] By the end of her time on the committee, the thirty-seven members remained the same, but she was no longer alone in her opposition. Partly through befriending Dunaway, another member of the committee switched to the anti-ERA side.

Phyllis Schlafly recruited many of her top-level Eagle Forum and STOP ERA officers to coordinate the International Women's Year Citizen's Review Committee (IWY CRC). Illinois Eagle Forum director Rosemary Thomson stepped in to lead the national IWY CRC. Kathryn Dunaway's record of stopping Georgia ratification of the ERA so effectively earned her a spot among the national coordinators. Coming from an early IWY state, Dunaway used her experience in Georgia to train other conservative women in how to plan their own David-like strategies against the Goliath of federal funding and feminist messages.

In preparation for the work of the Georgia IWY CRC, Dunaway trained anti-feminists to spot violations of the ban on lobbying written into the IWY funding and to report high pressure tactics by pro-ERA and pro-abortion attendees. Since Georgia was only the third state meeting held and the first in an unratified state, the IWY CRC observers felt a strong responsibility to record violations in order to prepare other states' conservatives for their own meetings. Dunaway would also use her Georgia experience to warn and to train anti-feminists in other states prior to their own meetings.[14]

Before Georgia's IWY meeting in May 1977, Dunaway focused on recruiting and training "responsible, freedom-loving, Christian women" to hold the line for the traditional family. Highlighting the traditional place of women, the state commission chose Mother's Day weekend for the Georgia meeting. Dunaway commiserated that the event would take mothers away from their families, but reminded them their sacrifice would benefit all families.[15]

Dunaway invited Phyllis Schlafly to Atlanta where they co-hosted a training at the First Baptist Church.[16] Dunaway received reports from national IWY CRC leaders and Vermont's state CRC after their state held the first meeting in the nation. Georgia conservatives studied Vermont's plan while developing their IWY southern strategy. At least two women would attend each workshop of the state IWY meeting, with one responsible for raising the conservative view during the discussion period. Just as Dunaway had practiced public speaking at national Eagle Forum meetings, she now gave women an opportunity to practice before sending them in to IWY events. The women rehearsed speaking to unfriendly audiences, played by their STOP ERA peers, who relished taking on the role of disruptive, boisterous feminists. Knowing they would be outnumbered, Dunaway told the women to use the "Buddy System for support" so that no woman would be the only conservative in the room. She also encouraged attendees to document every session with tape recorders.[17] At the end of the meeting, she wanted evidence for legislators and anyone else who would listen that federal money had supported partisan causes and feminist indoctrination.

After a week of women's arts, fashion shows, and exhibits, the Georgia IWY officially kicked off on May 6–7, 1977, with over twelve hundred women in attendance. Bella Abzug, who President Carter had chosen to head the National Commission on the Observance of International Women's Year, blasted through stereotypes to open the event. "The pedestals have crashed," she announced to the southern women. Abzug celebrated the new southern women who, unrestrained by the pedestal, dreamed of careers. She focused her talk on white southern women, saying their foremothers "were locked into a system that degraded them as it did the slaves."[18] Already a nemesis of conservative women, Abzug only fueled the STOP ERA fire.

After training and strategizing, Dunaway's troops were ready to go to battle at the IWY meeting. Each of the IWY CRC delegates came prepared with three workshop-observation forms in order to record events, discrepancies, and unfair practices in sessions. The women watched for "anything calling for more government control," "violations of *Robert's Rules of Order*," "anything which will take rights away from people under the guise of 'doing good,'" and "half-truths or twisted truths." Dunaway reminded her workers, "Do not be intimidated. . . . Maintain your dignity at all times—even if you are treated rudely. A soft voice and a smile work miracles."[19]

At the meeting, IWY CRC members tried to get workshops they did not like canceled and disrupted the other workshops as much as possible. When their attempts to interfere did not work, the IWY CRC members used the power of the ballot. Each workshop ended with a vote on recommendations for inclusion in the final proposal. The Georgia IWY CRC warned that "affirmative votes on these questions will add support to the IWY program." Therefore, the IWY CRC told its delegates to vote "(A) Strongly Disagree, (B) Disagree, or (C) Neutral" on all issues.[20] Dunaway planned every detail, from note-taking strategies to voting. She considered numerous scenarios in which a housewife attending her first political meeting might be intimidated, and designed her guidance and training to empower any woman willing to join the fight against feminism.

Dunaway organized an IWY CRC hospitality suite at the conference hotel, where conservative ladies could rest with cups of coffee in the company of like-minded women. Anyone who came into the suite had to be escorted by "someone we know" or should be able to show proof of CRC membership upon demand. National CRC chair Rosemary Thomson reminded women "to avoid talk about our activities on elevators or at lunch."[21] The suite served as CRC headquarters, where attendees submitted workshop reports and some husbands feverishly compiled the findings into a daily report. Dunaway, Thomson, and national STOP ERA co-chair Elaine Donnelly presented the findings at a press conference at the close of the IWY meeting.[22]

The Georgia IWY hosted workshops on eighteen topics, including Homemakers, Women's Health, Teen Pregnancy, Sports, Foreign Policy, Employment, and Minority Women. Dunaway and her followers put their plan into action, disrupting workshops, forcing votes on their chosen issues, repeatedly calling to adjourn, and sometimes even walking out. They failed to stop the meeting and did not even make a good-faith effort to shape the resolutions.

However, the conservatives managed at least a small victory when, at the end of the meeting, participants elected conservatives Lee Wysong and Beverly Adams among the state's thirty official delegates to the National Women's Conference scheduled to be held in Houston that November. Kathryn Dunaway was an alternate.[23] Despite having given many column inches to understanding Dunaway in the past, *Atlanta Constitution* women's columnist Carole Ashkinaze had no sympathy for the tactics of the IWY CRC crowd, which she described as a "hot-headed minority" displaying "stridency, intolerance, and militancy."[24]

After the state IWY meeting, Dunaway used the women's notes to prepare her own report on perceived ethics and rules violations. Dunaway's report outlined irregularities ranging from materials missing from some participants' registration packets to suspected voting fraud. She protested that keynote speaker Bella Abzug openly endorsed the ERA and even read a telegram of support from President and First Lady Jimmy and Rosalynn Carter. Dunaway offered more detail on individual workshops, asserting that "there was active suppression of views different from IWY." She encouraged other states to "stress [the] importance of enlisting our churches' participation" in recruiting enough conservatives to monitor all panels. Repeating a lesson learned from the NFRW election that Schlafly lost, Dunaway reminded other state leaders to "appoint *poll watchers* inside and outside [the] poll area" and to watch out even in the hallways for harassment of conservative delegates. Her primary advice for other state leaders included "watch for infiltration" and "remain ladies at all times."[25] Dunaway's methods contributed greatly to other states electing even more conservatives to their official Houston delegations.[26]

After her show of leadership at the Georgia IWY meeting, Kathryn Dunaway earned a position with the national STOP ERA organization. As IWY CRC state coordinator, she took the methods she developed in Georgia to train other state leaders in how to disrupt an IWY meeting.[27] As a former officer of the Georgia Federation of Republican Women, Dunaway had more than a decade of experience presenting herself as the conservative underdog staring down a powerful foe. She knew the strategy well enough to teach it to others. Dunaway directed others to follow her example of sending their IWY CRC findings to state and federal legislators as well as to STOP ERA leaders in other states.[28] After years of organizing and volunteering at the local level, she joined the ranks of Georgia conservatives who grew to national leadership roles. Just as Lee Miller rose to prominence in anti-busing work, Dunaway took a major role in anti-feminist organizing. Georgia women were taking their southern brand of conservatism national.

Despite the best efforts of STOP ERA among the states, the Houston IWY meeting went as planned. Two thousand delegates from every state and territory converged on the city, with thousands more joining just to be a part of this historic event that would shape a national women's platform. Three first ladies—Lady Bird Johnson, Betty Ford, and Rosalynn Carter—attended the event, indicating bipartisan and high-level support for the meeting. Rosalynn Carter was introduced as "a southerner who manages to combine the mind of Scarlett and the manner of Melanie," though she was also introduced as "first woman," rather than the more demure "lady." After hearing Carter speak, one attendee declared, "Schlafly can never match this."[29]

The IWY delegates approved twenty-five planks for the National Women's Conference platform, including its support of ratification of the ERA. After debate, the delegates even passed a resolution calling for the end of laws discriminating against homosexuals and lesbians. Even the more liberal members of the Georgia delegation opposed that measure, saying, "We come from a very conservative state.... Our legislators are simply not going to understand this." They worried that this plank, especially, played into the hands of STOP ERA, giving rise, as it would, to fears of gay rights and stereotypes of militant lesbian feminists.[30]

In one of the more powerful moments of the Houston meeting, Atlantan Coretta Scott King, attending in her position as a national commissioner for IWY, presented the "minority issues" resolution, symbolically linking her husband's work for civil rights with the convention's work for women's rights. The plank represented a coalition of Hispanic, Asian American, Indigenous, African American, and other minority groups calling for the end of discrimination in education, housing, and other federal programs. After it passed, the crowd swelled, singing "We Shall Overcome." Despite the enthusiasm of the moment, the vote was not unanimous. An Atlanta reporter noted that "only five men from Mississippi and several Mormon delegates" opposed or abstained.[31]

Protesting against the conference and stealing some of the media attention, Lottie Beth Hobbs of Women Who Want to be Women and Phyllis Schlafly organized a Pro-Life, Pro-Family Rally at another Houston venue. Georgia STOP ERA arranged a bus trip to Houston for women who wanted to attend. Dunaway advertised the trip to ministers throughout the state, asking them to share the opportunity with congregants. STOP ERA had also been successful in asking Democratic governor George Busbee to declare Georgia Family Week to coincide with the Houston IWY meeting. In doing so, Busbee asserted that "the family is the basic unit of society and the foundation of civilization" and a "society of strong families is fortified to combat destructive forces which would otherwise undermine individuals and nations." The gubernatorial declaration did not mention the Equal Rights Amendment, though it appropriated the pro-family language that STOP ERA had used for years. Dunaway also requested that the state's ministers honor Family Week by preaching on a topic related to the Christian family on Sunday, November 20—the final day of the Houston IWY conference.[32]

Thousands of men and women attended the Houston Pro-Family Rally, including a busload of forty-six Georgians. Schlafly opened the meeting, as she often did, with thanks to her husband for allowing her to attend, acknowledging the joy she took in irritating feminists by doing so. In contrast to the IWY meeting, the Pro-Family Rally featured many male speakers. They included several religious figures, emphasizing their idea of America as a Christian nation and of the family, not the individual, as the basic unit of society. Phyllis Schlafly and a number of prominent conservative speakers called for defeat of the ERA, an end to legal abortion, and protection for families from homosexual activists. Florida orange juice spokeswoman, Christian self-help author, and anti-gay rights activist Anita Bryant sent a filmed message to say, "In Houston and all over the nation, the voice of motherhood will be heard." National CRC chairman Rosemary Thomson described the outlook of the group: "We're a pro-family, pro-American, anti-lib, anti-NOW [National Organization for Women] organization." Schlafly contrasted the rally with the IWY meeting, which she predicted "will show them off for the radical, anti-family, pro-lesbian people they are."[33]

Georgia STOP ERA had much to celebrate after Houston. Nationally, they managed to steal some thunder from the IWY conference as the media split its attention to cover both women's meetings. Locally, they attracted a big-name convert to the anti-ERA side when longtime civil rights activist and feminist member of the state IWY committee Eliza Paschall came out against the ERA. The move was so shocking that *Atlanta Constitution* women's columnist Carole Ashkinaze asked, "Eliza Paschall, are your ears burning?" Paschall's shift was hot gossip in the city's feminist circles and Ashkinaze reported some of the theories circulating on Paschall's switch: "Had she been brainwashed? Drugged? Held in a room without windows for days on end by right-wing Bible thumpers and forced to 'recant'?" No matter the mysterious cause, Ashkinaze labeled it "the most startling conversion since Larry Flynt found religion." Speaking for herself, Paschall argued that, while surprising, the decision "hasn't been at all drastic."[34] Drastic or not, it was a triumph for the STOP ERA side to be able to count Atlanta NOW's 1973 Feminist of the Year among their anti-amendment numbers. When Dunaway distributed Paschall's statement opposing the IWY conference, she made sure to note that its author was "a former officer of the National Organization for Women."[35]

Paschall's record of working for civil rights was well known in Atlanta. She first entered the social justice movement while a student at Agnes Scott College in the 1930s. By the 1960s, she was a recognized advocate for improving race relations. In 1960, she published a pro–civil rights and anti-demagogue article in the *Atlantic Monthly*. Paschall served as executive director of the Community Relations Commission of the City of Atlanta, where she supported peaceful yet thorough school desegregation in the early 1960s. Later, she became executive director of the Greater Atlanta Council on Human Relations. She had been on the board of the Atlanta Urban League and Atlanta YWCA—both organizations known for civil rights activity.[36] In 1966, when Paschall had to give a list of personal and professional references, she included National Urban League director Whitney Young, two members of Congress, *Atlanta Journal* editor Jack Spalding, and "Dr. & Mrs. M. L. King, Jr." among others.[37] Her progressive credentials were strong.

In addition to her record on race relations, Paschall had earned a reputation as an Atlanta feminist. After her husband Walter's early death, she was a single mother, working and raising three daughters. While working in the Atlanta office of the U.S. Equal Employment Opportunity Commission (EEOC), she coauthored a guidebook on sex discrimination in the workplace.[38] When she remarried, she kept the name Paschall professionally, using her second husband's surname Morrison socially and always in addition to, never in place of, Paschall. She insisted on the title "Ms." rather than "Mrs." or "Miss."[39] She co-founded the Atlanta Chapter of the National Organization for Women in 1968 and was given the group's Feminist of the Year award five years later.[40] Unlike Dunaway and other STOP ERA members, Paschall identified as "a card-carrying feminist . . . dedicated to the principle of equality between the sexes."[41]

Eliza Paschall must have been one of the least likely converts to ERA opposition. In the early years of the ERA battle, she supported ratification, though she always justified her approval by saying that women needed to understand the rights they already had. She ridiculed claims that the ERA would make women less feminine, saying, "Those men who oppose ERA because they 'like their women to be ladies' must not think much of the women if they believe it takes a law to keep us ladies."[42] In November 1973, she declared herself "all for the ERA," but asserted her belief that many existing legal protections simply needed to be enforced. "There is little gained in getting more legislation, even constitutional amendments," she maintained, "if we are not going to act on the rights which we have all fought so hard to change from privileges to rights."[43] In 1976, Paschall encouraged the acting head of the National Commission on the Status of Women to examine the "objections of those who still work against [the ERA]" in order to pull the amendment from its stalemate.[44]

However, Paschall continually questioned the methods of feminist organizations. Even while she supported the ERA, she loathed the language of second-wave feminism, which she thought promoted the idea of victimization of American women. She criticized reports of the Commission on the Status of Women as being "too anti-men; sounds as if men have it made and all the problems of women stem from the meanness of all men."[45] In a letter opposing the IWY meeting, Paschall explained, "I reject the hypothesis that there are 'women's issues,' because that requires a corollary that there are 'non-women's' issues.' I cannot find any aspect of society which does not affect women." She again asserted that "there is *no* public issue which does not concern women *and* men."[46]

Paschall had built a career struggling against boundaries between Black and white and she feared state Commissions on the Status of Women and IWY commissions threatened to build walls between men and women. She wrote, "I don't want to see us segregated by race, that's what I worked hard & long against. And I don't want to see us segergated [*sic*] by sex."[47] She explained her membership in feminist organizations by saying, "I have granted to certain individuals permission to represent me and to speak for me as a member of that organization." However, she criticized any group that *assumed* the right to speak for her and all women. After the IWY meeting, Paschall summarized her understanding of its goals: "to minimize individual initiative and self reliance [*sic*], to minimize the advantages of the diversity of the nation, to decrease opportunities for solution of communities' problems on state and local levels."[48] In her conversion to conservatism, Paschall voiced concern for diversity but amplified arguments based on individual responsibility and local control.

Paschall also vehemently spoke out against any taxpayer-funded women's organization as a violation of federal laws. She criticized state Commissions on the Status of Women as "self-defeating propositions," asserting that "special 'feminist' activities only move women from one backwater to another."[49] She criticized the commissions for "creating volunteer parallel institutions for women rather than concentrating on integrating women—as policy makers, employers, recipients—into the normal public programs, which happily continue to serve men as they always have." Rather than having specially appointed committees to discuss women's issues, she wanted to ensure women had a place at every table. She thought the Commissions on the Status of Women relegated women to second-class consideration, while "the 'real government' continues to deal with the needs of men."[50] Feminists, she thought, were in effect fighting to deny women access to real power with their demands for separate consideration. Paschall defended her own position on the Georgia Commission for the Status of Women by explaining that she was there to convince others the group was unnecessary.[51]

Paschall railed against all forms of the sex segregation that she believed feminists groups advocated, "While picketing 'men's clubs,' we create new Women's Centers. . . . While calling for the end of Democratic and Republican Women's Clubs, we form a Women's Political Caucus." Paschall highlighted the hypocrisy of the Women's Political Caucus for backing feminist male candidates over more conservative female candidates. Feminists, she chided, mocked housewives who met over coffee to discuss problems, but "we formally schedule sex segregated Rap Sessions for Consciousness Raising, and act as if something new has happened." What feminists wanted, she argued, was not real change, but just a renaming and repackaging of the strategies that women had employed for generations.[52]

Paschall and Dunaway created a fruitful alliance. They met serving as commissioners on the Georgia IWY planning committee. Though they came from vastly different political organizing traditions, they shared a belief that the IWY should not be funded from federal taxes. Paschall also opposed IWY because it sent the message that her concerns "must be filtered through a 'women's issues' screen."[53] Prior to service on the Georgia IWY Commission, Paschall had never communicated with any opponent of the ERA and marveled at the fact that "that's how narrow my friendships had been."[54] After meeting Dunaway, Paschall found more peers among Georgia's conservative women.

Kathryn Dunaway's friendship proved highly influential as Paschall soon spoke out publicly against the amendment and began sending her essays to Dunaway for nationwide STOP ERA distribution. Eliza Paschall began self-publishing a newsletter reporting on the state General Assembly and proposed laws. *Georgia Factfinders* became an indispensable report for the state's conservatives, many of whom first received a copy from Dunaway. In turn, when Dunaway had trouble getting a story in the *Atlanta Journal* or *Atlanta Constitution*, she would call her well-connected friend Eliza, who then called or lunched with a friend at the newspaper.[55] There seemed to be no one in Georgia that the women could not reach.

Paschall wrote enthusiastically and descriptively. Her allegory of IWY, "Alice in Abzugland," spread rapidly among STOP ERA circles. It featured Alice the housewife at a tea party with Comrades Dee and Dum, led by Bella Abzug, the Mad Hatter. Tea Party attendees chanted, "Tax! Tax! Up with her tax!" and told Alice to demand wages and benefits from her husband. They encouraged Alice to think of her own interests, telling her she was "not just an appendage to her husband" and to "forget John." After a series of conflicts, Alice asserted herself to the Mad Hatter, saying, "*You* cannot give me dignity or status. I have to get that for myself." At that, everyone around the table faded away and Alice woke up, apologized to her husband for being grumpy, and vowed to write her congressman.[56] With its Cold War communist references and warnings of higher taxes forcing the destruction of the family unit, the story became a hit among conservatives. Just as housewife Alice woke up, grateful to be with her loving husband, STOP ERA readers hoped the tale would help more women wake up to the dangers of IWY.

In 1978, Paschall accompanied Dunaway to the combined Eagle Forum/

STOP ERA Conference in St. Louis.[57] Her former allies believed Eliza, not Alice, had fallen through the rabbit hole. More than worrying about their friend, though, the ERA supporters had to worry that if an established liberal like Eliza Paschall could be persuaded, what could happen to the undecided legislators?

Even after the momentum of the Houston meeting, the ERA still needed three more states for ratification. As the seven-year deadline approached, pro-amendment groups lobbied Congress for additional time to pass the ERA. Frustrated but not discouraged, Kathryn Dunaway mounted a refocused campaign in 1978, telling STOP ERA women all over Georgia to meet with legislators to convince them to oppose the extension: "We don't care whether he is pro or con on ERA. We only care that he vote against the . . . Time Extension Bill." She mourned, "The plain fact is that, whatever you already did on this subject was NOT enough! . . . Whatever you did before must be multiplied by 100 times."[58]

While most of Georgia's congressional delegation opposed the extension, majorities in the houses of Congress voted for the bill. Pro-ERA groups now had until March 22, 1982, to get the final three states. Undeterred, Phyllis Schlafly still declared victory over the first round of the ERA battle and celebrated with an "End of an E.R.A." gala. Recognizing Dunaway's value to the campaign, Schlafly invited her friend to walk in with her and sit at the head table.[59] In her report for the 1978 Eagle Forum meeting, Dunaway reported that she had fought the ERA and its extension during four television appearances and eight radio spots. Even with the ERA held down in committee, Dunaway never took anything for granted.[60] With the momentum they had built over the first seven years, STOP ERA forces knew they had to keep up their hope and hard work for another three years.

Though the ERA did not come up on the 1979 Georgia legislative agenda, another piece of legislation, one that Dunaway dubbed the "little ERA," did. State Representative Eleanor Richardson introduced a bill to establish a Displaced Homemakers Advisory Council to study the needs of Georgia's "displaced homemakers." This group included housewives in the "middle years," defined as "the years between 40 and 62," who had lost their husbands through divorce, separation, or death. Women with grown children did not qualify for child support or Social Security children's benefits, leaving them with limited means. Divorced women often found themselves with no health insurance, no claim to retirement pensions, and no obvious job skills. In many cases, especially if a woman had been awarded the family home, she was considered too wealthy for welfare. Unpaid work in the home left homemakers unable to collect unemployment. Approximately fifty thousand Georgia women fell into the category of "displaced homemaker." By the end of 1977, fourteen states had passed legislation to fund centers to aid displaced homemakers in making a transition to the workforce. In 1979, Rep. Richardson hoped Georgia would join their ranks.[61]

Conservative women set about opposing legislation to aid displaced homemakers in the name of smaller government, local control, and family protection. Kathryn Dunaway mobilized her state network. In an extended profile in the *Atlanta Journal*, Dunaway explained the women's opposition: "Have you ever seen a little bird protect its nest when there was something frightening? ... Well, we feel our homes are being attacked." She also expressed their fear that the legislation would substitute state funds for a husband's alimony, burdening the state taxpayers.[62]

Dunaway's troops took up their pens once again. Full-time homemaker Patricia Fulton of Jonesboro wrote her state senator, "First, shame on those who do not recognize and value the homemakers' contribution to the welfare and economic stability of society. Second, shame on anyone who thinks that after years of managing a modern household, a person could not readily adapt to a new situation." She listed the services in Clayton County that she would reach out to if she ever found herself in need.[63] Many conservatives similarly argued that displaced homemakers did not need new programs but simply needed to take advantage of public education and welfare programs or private programs offered through churches and charities. It echoed their opposition to the ERA, resting on the belief that new legislation was unnecessary if only women would take advantage of existing policies.

Feminists' declarations that homemaking should be treated as work and its contribution factored into national economic figures fed the fires of opponents. Rather than seeing the bill as recognizing homemakers, conservatives perceived it as a continuation of the anti-family goal of women's economic independence. They worried that the gender-neutral language of the legislation would write married housewives out of the law completely. When asked if the women's movement had affected her life, Kathryn Dunaway replied that it had taken "seven years of my life, time, and finances trying to ... remedy the image and low status created by the W. Lib thrust on the Homemaker. She has been cast in a fictional role as unproductive ... unfulfilled, unimportant, parasitic which in reality she occupies the most exalted position in God's Universe."[64] Of course, her work against the ERA also turned Dunaway into a state and national leader of a political movement, a trailblazer of gendered conservatism, and a respected lobbyist under the gold dome of Georgia's capitol.

Despite her extensive efforts, Dunaway did not speak for all housewives. Georgia Housewives for ERA started with fifty charter members in November 1978.[65] Anne Bowen Follis, founder of the national organization, wanted to reach women "who described themselves as 'Christians' and 'homemakers.'" She blamed sexist translations of the Bible for church teachings against women in ministry.[66] The Georgia Housewives for ERA argued that women needed constitutional protection in order to "enter contracts, engage in their own business without their husband's consent, manage their own property, administer estates, serve on juries," maintain separate lines of credit, and keep their own names if they chose.[67] Pro-ERA homemakers found allies in First Lady Rosalynn Carter and daughter-in-law Judy Carter, both of whom advocated for and with pro-ERA groups to raise support among homemakers. In a late push to garner housewife support, the American Association of University Women launched the campaign "At Ease with ERA" to get out the message that the changes the amendment would bring would help housewives. The literature called women the "Hidden Breadwinners" and suggested the slogan, "Don't confuse protection with repression!"[68]

Richardson's bill for the Displaced Homemakers Advisory Council passed, but without any funding for the program. Rather, Richardson explained, Georgia would start a "clearinghouse" for public and private "programs available around the state."[69] She identified the need, saying, "These women need counseling emotionally before they can be retrained in the job market."[70] Area colleges and community centers offered personal growth courses in topics like "divorce adjustment."[71] The Georgia Department of Labor applied for a grant through the federal Comprehensive Employment Training Act to fund a job training program for displaced homemakers in rural areas of the state.[72] Though conservative women opposed the "little ERA," they relented, since the programs did not require taxpayer support. They would focus on fighting the big ERA.

In 1980, the ERA came to the floor of the Georgia state legislature for the first time since former governor Jimmy Carter had assumed the presidency. However, the Republican Party was also gaining ground in Georgia. West Georgia College professor Newt Gingrich, riding a political movement that conservative Georgia women had built, finally succeeded in his third campaign for a seat in the U.S. House of Representatives, defeating the pro-ERA state senator Virginia Shapard. Gingrich, of course, won with the support of the GFRW. They worked polls and handed out voter material at textile mills. Two members even sent their husbands to go shopping to replace Gingrich's red polyester sport coat and white socks with a navy-blue sport coat and black socks. Then, GFRW member Emma Hinesley recalled, "He looked like a candidate."[73]

As Republican men won more seats, women still volunteered behind the scenes. In late 1979, Schlafly again visited the Atlanta area on a speaking tour, recognizing the value of defeating the amendment in Carter's home state.[74] Privately, Kathryn Dunaway battled stomach cancer, which only seemed to make her push harder to defeat the amendment in her lifetime.

President Jimmy Carter wielded his influence in hopes of securing a much-needed domestic policy victory before a heated campaign season. The Iran hostage crisis dragged on and Carter faced a 1980 primary challenge from Senator Ted Kennedy. Carter received a telegram from a pro-ERA voter in Pennsylvania, charging, "Ted Kennedy is from a ratified state. You aren't. Don't you think that it's about time for Georgia to ratify the ERA?"[75] In an effort to win a major victory and secure women's support, Carter instructed his administration to be aggressive in Georgia. Administration staff went to Georgia to lobby in person while First Lady Rosalynn Carter made several personal phone calls to state legislators. The president phoned Governor George Busbee to ask him to pressure legislators.[76]

Carter's special assistant for women's affairs, Sarah Weddington, readied for a showdown in the Georgia House. She was aware that organizing from the top down would have little effect. Weddington's research on the state's ERA story revealed that "there was strong lobbying by Stop-ERA groups.... Brought in hundreds of people and passed out sandwiches and cake and stayed there until they beat it down. *Good* lobbyists." Dunaway was not mentioned by name, but her strategy was all over the report. An anonymous legislator predicted that "ERA has about as much chance of passing as I do of walking on Lake Lanier." The memo on Georgia offered "a bleak outlook. Sorry."[77] The research turned out to be accurate in its predictions. Despite pressure from the administration in Washington, the Georgia Senate defeated the ERA for a third time on January 21, 1980.

Kathryn Dunaway admitted, "We thought they [the senators] wouldn't resist the pressure. We were looking for the worst, but praise the Lord, we got the best." The most the senators could do was delay the vote for a few minutes. Initially, Carter's supporters in the state senate tried to delay voting by a day so that a defeat would not influence the Iowa caucuses the next day. However, anti-ERA legislators thrice voted down any delays before voting down the amendment itself, 32–23. "It was just wonderful, wonderful, wonderful," gushed Dunaway.[78] Her grassroots efforts had established conservative voting power in local districts and provided a bulwark against pressure from as high up as the White House. ERA advocates in Atlanta and in the Carter administration immediately began to spin their defeat. They explained that the vote was close and that pro-ERA groups had finally begun powerful grassroots organization on the local level to encourage ratification. They failed to mention that Dunaway had been nurturing her grassroots coalition for much longer.

For over twenty years, Dunaway had been building a network of conservative women. By the time ERA left the U.S. Congress for state ratification in 1972, Dunaway already had a strong volunteer base that only grew stronger during the decade. By 1980, the group had developed solid relationships with legislators, pastors, and women all across Georgia. Whatever the pro-ERA forces could accomplish at the grassroots level in a couple of years could not compete with what Dunaway had accomplished over twenty years. Even the efforts of the White House could not prevail against the decades of volunteers' dedication to the conservative women's network. Of course, Dunaway did have the advantage of working in line with what Weddington recognized as "the extremely religious, conservative nature of Georgia."[79] However, even granting the general conservatism of the state, Dunaway managed a skillful campaign against an amendment that had once seemed destined for passage even in Georgia.

Of course, STOP ERA continued to send their personal notes to legislators, but conservative congressional delegates had long ago learned the value of Dunaway's endorsement. Representative from District 40 Paul Coverdell wrote Kathryn Dunaway to "once again express my appreciation to you and your associate for your continued actions on behalf of good government."[80] Conservative women were even starting to run for office themselves. Martha Elrod, running in the 71st District, wrote Dunaway "to solicit your prayers and support in my campaign for State Legislator." Elrod assured her that "I have become very much aware of the direction the humanist[s] are leading our country in."[81] James Tuten in the 153rd District in Brunswick wrote to request STOP ERA information for his concerned constituents.[82] Conservative office-seekers sought out the influential women of local and state STOP ERA for valuable endorsements, volunteers, and information about the amendment.

Kathryn Dunaway's final battle in the Georgia House took place in 1980. She died from stomach cancer on September 16. Earlier that year, Fred Schlafly, Phyllis's husband, praised Dunaway in a personal note, writing, "I love to tell Phyllis and the other wonderful girls in all the states which have defeated ERA that your work is even superior to what everyone else did because you have stopped ERA in Carter's own state for eight hard fought years." He closed with high praise: "What you have accomplished should be described as the greatest political victory of the second half of the twentieth century."[83] Fred Schlafly's flattery summed up the significance of the political work of the Georgia housewife who had turned into a powerful political strategist. Dunaway had organized women throughout the state effectively enough to resist pressure from numerous better-funded groups, national organizations, celebrities, and experienced politicians.

Dunaway did not live to vote for Ronald Reagan in 1980, but she did write to scold him for his decision in "appointing so many women's libbers to [his] women's advisory committee" during his campaign.[84] Even with conservatives, Dunaway remained vigilant.

In the 1981 session of the Georgia General Assembly, legislators recognized the absence of the woman they had come to expect in the halls, greeting them with baked goods and pamphlets. Senate Resolution 177 expressed "deepest sympathy" over Kathryn Dunaway's death. Significantly, the resolution employed vague language to discuss her political work. Instead of spelling out her opposition to civil rights legislation, it celebrated that she had been "actively involved in improving and preserving the educational process and for ten years supported state and national legislation to preserve Georgia's schools from federal control." While it listed her husband's and children's accomplishments and her work for her family, it lumped the unnamed ERA in with "her staunch opposition to legislation which she believed would be detrimental to the State of Georgia." Only in death could Kathryn Dunaway's sharp politics be so vague.[85]

Dunaway's followers honored her legacy by keeping the amendment from passing in Georgia until the extended time period for ratification ended in 1982. Upon Dunaway's death, her friend and longtime co-chair Lee Wysong assumed leadership of Georgia STOP ERA, assuring conservatives and liberals alike that "there won't be any lag in the Stop ERA effort because I think that continuing to oppose ERA and achieve ultimate success would be the greatest tribute we can pay."[86] Phyllis Schlafly again spoke at First Baptist Church of Atlanta in June of 1981.[87] When the state legislature issued the final defeat for the ERA on January 21, 1982, it was once again by a wide margin.[88]

Dunaway's legacy extended further than the defeat of the ERA. She brought a generation of conservative women into politics. Stone Mountain STOP ERA organizer Sue Ella Deadwyler wrote to John Dunaway, "I thank the Lord that Kathryn taught me how to work the Capitol!"[89] Women like Deadwyler all over Georgia now had the skills and confidence to meet with legislators and host political meetings on their own. With the ERA finally laid to rest, the numerous women that Dunaway had trained were now free to carry the conservative movement across Georgia, the nation, and on to future generations.

CONCLUSION

Payment Due

Atlanta Constitution editor Hal Gulliver eulogized the Georgia GOP in 1978, declaring, "The Republican Party of Georgia passed away quietly several years ago, yet no one has really had the decency to bury the poor creature." Gulliver may have penned his premature death notice because he had examined the wrong body. He blamed the party's demise on members who were "not willing to . . . roll up their sleeves and work hard, for long months at a time, to build a real political organization or run an effective campaign." However, the editor had been looking for Republican organizing in "country clubs and other pleasant watering holes."[1]

Had Gulliver looked instead to kitchen tables and living rooms, he might have seen conservatism thriving and the Georgia GOP on the verge of victory. Had he looked to the state capitol building, he might have seen women in red dresses, boasting STOP ERA buttons and placards and offering home-baked goods to staffers and legislators alike, promoting a new conservatism focused on the family.

Perhaps the editor of the *Atlanta Constitution* made the all-too-common error of not recognizing those loaves of bread as political work. He likely was at the office when a GFRW volunteer called his house, looking for the heart of the household rather than the head. He was not alone in this grave error. Democrats, feminists, and scholars have neglected to notice conservative women's contributions for their political significance. Women nurtured the Georgia Republican Party and, over two decades, laid the foundation not only of a strong conservative movement, but also for southern leadership within the New Right.

If Hal Gulliver had paid any attention to women's organizing, then he might have been more prepared for the New Right conservatism that was about to overwhelm his state and the nation. Days after Gulliver wrote the Georgia GOP's obituary in 1978, suburban Atlanta voters sent the freshman congressman Newt Gingrich to Washington, wearing the black socks Emma Hinesley had given him. Gingrich had learned Republican campaigning alongside so many Georgians in 1964 on the Goldwater campaign and the Jack Prince for Congress campaign. Back then, Gingrich had refused women's help with opinion surveys for the Prince campaign, only to realize too late that the Republican women's numbers had been accurate while his were not. By 1978, he sought and received the endorsement of conservative women in STOP ERA. Indeed, Gingrich defeated Virginia Shapard, the State Senate sponsor of the ERA. Sixteen years later, with the 1994 elections, Gingrich would be speaker of the United States House of Representatives. In that position, the Georgia congressman led what would become known as the "Republican Revolution" in Congress and authored a new declaration of conservative orthodoxies he called the Contract with America.[2]

In 1980, voters statewide elected Georgia's first Republican U.S. senator since Reconstruction with their choice of Mack Mattingly. The Savannah Area Republican Women hosted one of Mattingly's first campaign events, even before he had filed his official paperwork to run.[3] The Brunswick, Georgia, Republican did not just score a victory for the GOP, but delivered a crushing defeat for the state's Democratic Party by beating their longtime leader Herman Talmadge, delivering the final blow to the Talmadge machine.

When Mattingly won in 1980, his votes came from the suburban strongholds where women had been organizing the longest. Just outside of Atlanta, he won Cobb County—the first county organized by Lee Ague back in 1963—by nearly forty thousand votes. In neighboring DeKalb, his margin exceeded sixty-five thousand votes. Richmond County around Augusta yielded Mattingly over three thousand more than Talmadge. Columbus and surrounding Muscogee County gave the Republican a majority by over six thousand votes. Additionally, Mattingly won in counties with smaller populations like Towns, Gilmer, and his home county of Glynn on the coast.[4] Each of these counties boasted strong Republican women's organizations with nearly two decades of GOP volunteerism. Many Georgians must have split their tickets for the state to support Democratic native son Jimmy Carter for president and Republican native son Mattingly for Senate. Georgia voters had a record of splitting the ticket, having voted for Republicans Barry Goldwater (1964) and Richard Nixon (1972) at the top of the ticket and Democrats further down.

Another victory for conservatives in 1980—and one that would bring several Schlafly devotees back into the GOP fold—was the national Republican Party's removal of the Equal Rights Amendment from its platform. Conservative women had been waging a nonpartisan right-wing battle against the ERA for nearly a decade. The ERA had been a part of the Republican platform since 1940, but the new social conservatives wielded their influence in 1980. Not only did the new family-values lobby successfully yank the ERA from the

GOP platform, but they replaced it with another of their key issues, support for a constitutional amendment banning abortion.[5]

Aside from a few certificates and trinkets, the volunteer work of Georgia's conservative women remains unpaid and unrecognized, though Georgia's Republican men win elections and headlines. Decades of women's work hosting teas, organizing bake sales, and shuttling male candidates solidified Georgia as a red state on the electoral map, but still left women out of the paid work of politics. In the 1960s, women's volunteer canvassing yielded the data that paid consultants crunched. In the 1970s, women's volunteer surveying gathered the messages from voters that paid consultants smoothed into campaign strategies. Women's grassroots work laid the foundation of a gendered family-values politics around schooling, abortion, gender, and sexuality. After two decades of donating labor, strategy, and skills, Georgia's Republican women had given enough away. By the 1980s, they demanded their due.

Lee Ague Miller returned to Florida, where she established the Miller Consulting Group, with Miller herself as CEO. With three decades of Republican and regional connections, Miller earned business with the 1984 Reagan-Bush reelection. She coordinated the Southern Republican Leadership Conference in Atlanta in January 1984, including an event featuring a "Presidential Ball where the president is expected to attend" along with Vice President Bush, Senator Mack Mattingly, Representative Newt Gingrich, and National Black Republican Council chairwoman LeGree Daniels. Finally, Lee Miller could flaunt her Georgia organizing successes, bringing national leaders to Georgia while also showing off Georgia's own elected Republicans as well.[6]

Though Miller's experience taught her the effectiveness of personal contact, she also knew the limitations of reaching voters one phone call at a time. New technology in the 1980s opened up a new world of voter contact. Campaigns already used robocalls to collect data, but employed humans to analyze the data. After a few sets of incorrect readings, Ague insisted on eliminating the human error, saying, "Until you connect the computers together, you're not going to get the right answers." Once engineers combined data collection with computerized data analysis, at Miller's suggestion, the Reagan campaign began getting more useful data. Leaders at FMG Megadata, the computer contractor, were so impressed with her idea of connecting the systems that they made Miller their new vice president of marketing.[7]

Miller combined her marketing and political experience in her work for Ronald Reagan's reelection campaign. In a 1984 robocall campaign, Ronald Reagan's recorded voice reached 1.7 million voters nationwide. Lee Miller's mother in New York answered one of those calls. After hanging up, she eagerly told her daughter that President Ronald Reagan himself had just called.

Not letting on, Miller asked, "Well, what did he want?" Her mother replied, "He asked me to vote for him." Miller remembered that her Democratic mother was so impressed that the president had taken time to call her that she voted Republican in 1984.[8]

After her success with the Reagan-Bush reelection campaign, Lee Miller won contracts to use the robocall program for thirty-seven other clients, including Jesse Helms in North Carolina and Jeb Bush in Florida. She also worked with corporate clients: General Motors used the technology to announce a recall and *Ms. Magazine* called on her for marketing strategy as well.[9] Strategist Richard Viguerie receives great acclaim (or condemnation by inundated postal customers) for revolutionizing direct mail to advance Republican outreach in the 1970s. Reagan robocalls likewise expanded voter outreach. No longer did women have to sit at their phone, dialing their neighbors and recording tedious statistics. In 1984, Ronald Reagan, thanks to Lee Miller, made his own calls. Miller achieved her dream of closing the gap between Republican politicians and the voters, ushering GOP voices into every home.

Miller continued to seek out new challenges and new applications for her skills. Ever the anti-communist, she accepted a consulting position in Poland to help establish free elections after the end of communism. She left Poland only when her daughter suffered a brain injury and needed full-time care. Again, Miller's motherhood influenced her politics, as she became an advocate for developmentally disabled people like her daughter.[10] Miller passed away in 2015 in Columbus, Georgia.

While Lee Miller robocalled for Reagan, Eliza Paschall went to work in his White House. In 1984, Paschall accepted the position of associate director in the Office of Public Liaison in the Reagan White House. Faith Ryan Whittlesly, director of the office, described Paschall as having "a unique combination of experience" and cited her work in the EEOC and with NOW. Who better than a labor advocate, civil rights activist, and feminist to connect Reagan's conservatism to the public? Paschall, Whittlesley argued, "speaks effectively on the Reagan record on 'Women's Issues.'"[11] In her position, Paschall addressed diverse audiences ranging from the United Daughters of the Confederacy to the annual meeting of Zeta Phi Beta, a historically African American sorority.

At the White House, Paschall focused on the "50 States Project," working with states to remove sexism from state laws. If individual laws caught up, she thought, women would win equality without the Equal Rights Amendment.[12] Paschall retired from the White House in May 1985. After struggling with cancer for several years, she passed away in early 1990.

Evelyn Frazier remained active in the Republican Party, though the Metropolitan Club appears to have dissolved into the Southwest Fulton Federation of

Republican Women. Frazier continued her support for Republican candidates at the top of the ticket. As a guest of the Southern Black Republican Council, Frazier attended the 1985 Inauguration of Ronald Reagan.[13] In 1988, Frazier joined several other prominent Black Republicans to celebrate the opening of the Blacks for Bush campaign headquarters on Martin Luther King Jr. Drive in Atlanta. Portia Scott, niece of original Metropolitan Club member Mrs. W. A. Scott, attended the Blacks for Bush office opening as one of the "'black national surrogates' for the vice president."[14]

When Mrs. W. A. Scott and her friends visited Mamie Eisenhower's White House in 1953, the Black women predicted that women would "resurrect the Republican Party" in Georgia.[15] Perhaps Scott had her niece in mind. Portia Scott grew up to be managing editor of the family's newspaper, the *Atlanta Daily World*, but left in 1986 to run for Congress. Evelyn Frazier and Eliza Paschall served on her campaign steering committee. Scott won her Republican primary with 59.5 percent of the vote, going on to face civil rights leader and former Atlanta city councilman John Lewis in the general election for the Fifth District seat. The 1986 Fifth District race made history as the first Georgia campaign with two African American candidates competing.[16] Portia Scott predicted that if she went to Congress, "it will turn around politics in the South." She hoped that her victory would prove that the Republican Party welcomed both African Americans and women, echoing Evelyn Frazier's hopes a decade earlier.[17] She positioned herself as representing the party of free enterprise and the future, criticizing what she called Lewis's "rhetoric from the past."[18] Unsurprisingly, the *Daily World* endorsed Portia Scott for her congressional run. Evelyn Frazier hosted a fundraising tea for Scott. Even Maureen Reagan, the president's daughter, visited Atlanta to campaign for her.

In November 1986, Portia Scott lost to John Lewis. Scott won about 25 percent of the vote, but announced that her team had won "a moral victory for freedom of the individual voter."[19] Undeterred, Scott remained active in the GOP. In 1991, she acted as co-chair of the NFRW Outreach Program to set an agenda that would attract new Republican voters.[20] Thanks to party-wide minority outreach programs and Scott's leadership, by the end of the century Georgia led the nation in African American Republicans running for office. Even with Scott's record-setting work, though, only twenty-one African American Republicans stood for elections in the local, state, and federal elections across Georgia in 1998.[21] Decades of disguising Massive Resistance behind a mask of motherhood did little to bring Black women into the state party.

In 2020, *Atlanta Journal-Constitution* political columnists blasted, "It's no secret that women have a difficult time surviving Republican primaries in Georgia." Despite a long record of supporting successful male candidates, Republican women have had a harder time breaking into Georgia state politics.

Perhaps conservative women had been too successful in shaping their politics around motherhood and the home, making it difficult for Georgia Republican voters to imagine women balancing the demands of home with legislative commitments.[22]

In 2003, Renee Unterman became the first Republican woman elected to the state senate. She worked her way up through her city council, a stint as Loganville mayor, and state representative office before joining the state senate. Unterman remained the only Republican woman senator until 2017, when Kay Kirkpatrick won a special election in Cobb County. After successfully backing a bill that drastically restricted abortion access in Georgia, Unterman attempted a run for the Seventh District seat in the U.S. Congress in the 2020 elections. She lost in a primary that saw, among other attacks, a flyer that deployed gendered insults, calling her a "bimbo" and criticizing her looks but not her policies.[23]

In 2019, Republicans Unterman and Kirkpatrick joined thirteen Democratic women state senators in a stand of bipartisan feminism rarely seen in twenty-first-century Georgia. The fifteen women stood together against a change in the Georgia Senate rules instituting a two-year limit for filing sexual harassment claims against senators or senate staff. The women also rallied around veteran lawmaker Unterman, who had been stripped of her committee chairmanship despite a successful record of pushing legislation. The women set aside party to complain that the male leadership relegated women to the least powerful committees.[24] When women did succeed in elections, they still had to battle for representation in the male-dominated legislature.

The 2020 elections represented gains for women in Georgia politics, including Republican women. In 2017, Karen Handel made history as the first Republican woman elected to Congress from Georgia, but she has lost twice since then to Democrat Lucy McBath. In 2020, Republican women stood for election in five of Georgia's fourteen congressional districts, though only Marjorie Taylor Greene won her race. Greene stands as another Georgia conservative woman leading a national political shift. She famously embraces the QAnon conspiracy theory, a social media-driven, evidence-free whirlwind of paranoia allegedly guided by an anonymous government informant. *Atlantic* magazine explained, "To believe Q requires rejecting mainstream institutions, ignoring government officials, battling apostates and despising the press." Despite the FBI classifying QAnon as a domestic terror threat in 2019, the theory has taken hold in conservative circles. While as many as twenty QAnon believers ran for office, Marjorie Taylor Greene stands out as one of few winners and a vocal adherent in Congress. In addition to being the only Republican woman from Georgia in Congress, Taylor Greene is one of the most enthusiastic QAnon supporters in the federal government, giving conspiracy-driven conservatism a seat in both the national Republican Party and the United States Congress.[25]

In a historic runoff election in January 2021, Georgians chose between sending a white woman or an African American man to the Senate. Either would have been a first for the state, which has elected only white men to the Senate since 1789. Republican senator Kelly Loeffler lost to her Democratic opponent, Reverend Raphael Warnock, pastor at historic Ebenezer Baptist Church.[26]

Portia Scott's old foe Congressman John Lewis passed away in July 2020, having served the Fifth District for thirty-three years. In 2020, Fifth District voters chose between two African American *women* candidates. A week after joining other African Americans to pray over President Trump, Angela Stanton-King announced her campaign to challenge John Lewis on March 6. She lost to Nikema Williams, a Democratic state senator.[27]

I remember a conversation with Lee Miller in 2011 when we assessed the potential Republican presidential candidates. She was not excited about any of them and did not see a path to beating Barack Obama. She did not live to see the party under Trump or QAnon, and I will not venture to guess what her thought would have been on these shifts. I like to imagine she would be excited to see the Republican women running for office and especially proud of those who hold office. They inherit her legacy—grassroots networks, volunteers, and generations of Republican voters.

Even with GOP women standing for office and a few winning seats, perhaps Miller's, Dunaway's, and the other women's most enduring legacy has been creating a seemingly permanent majority of Republican women voters in Georgia. White women have become the state's most reliably Republican voters. In 2016, 64 percent of Georgia white women voters polled approved of President Donald Trump's work in office. In 2020, 67 percent of Georgia white women cast a vote for Donald Trump's reelection. In the 2018 Georgia gubernatorial race, 70 percent of white women voted for the Republican man, Brian Kemp, over an African American woman on the Democratic side, Stacey Abrams.[28]

Interestingly, the Georgia of 2020 had become nearly a complete flip of Georgia of 1966. Georgia Republican strategist Heath Garrett acknowledged the similarities, saying that in the past, "the Democratic Party had become complacent," and spent too much time on infighting while ignoring demographic shifts—weaknesses Garrett feared in the 2020 Georgia GOP.[29] The Georgia GOP is preparing for its own infighting in 2022 as incumbent GOP governor Brian Kemp faces a primary challenge from former GOP senator David Perdue. More than just the governor's office, the direction of the state GOP is on the ballot. A similarity Garrett missed, though, was that women stood ready to take advantage of the complacency, knocking on doors and finding new voters.

Today, the suburban areas around Atlanta, Savannah, Columbus, Macon, and Augusta pop up in shades of purple and blue, while rural areas glow bright Republican red. Again, women organizing grassroots movements created statewide changes. Notably, former Georgia House minority leader Stacey Abrams inspired a huge push to register new voters when she ran for governor in 2018. Abrams asserted Georgia Democrats lost because they continually sought swing voters rather than new voters.[30] Between 2018 and 2020, over eight hundred thousand new voters registered in Georgia, reflecting Stacey Abrams's belief in investing in new voters.[31] In November 2020, the nation eagerly awaited election results from Georgia, which Joe Biden narrowly won. Many Republicans refuse to admit that their onetime stronghold may be fading to purple.[32] In December 2021, Abrams announced her 2022 candidacy for governor.[33]

While Democrat Joe Biden took the state's sixteen electoral votes in 2020, the state's two seats in the U.S. Senate went to a January 2021 runoff. With such high stakes, both voter registration and voter suppression reached all-time highs. The Cobb County that Lee Ague moved to in 1963 was a county of white-flight migrants from Atlanta and new Sunbelt migrants. Early women of the GFRW turned the county into the heart of the state's Republican shift. The county today is more diverse, white-flight migrants having moved even further out. In the county where Clara Curtis once sat on a ballot box to prevent theft of Republican ballots, now county officials try to close early voting sites in heavily Black and Latinx areas of town.[34] Voter suppression and voter protest in Georgia each have long traditions, with the state showing no sign of stopping either.

The 1960s demographic shift in Georgia involved migrants from Rust Belt states to the southern Sunbelt economy. The twenty-first century's demographic shift in Georgia's population is more global. Yet a demographic shift alone does not explain electoral changes. In the 1950s and 1960s, more diverse neighborhoods led to increased anxiety among white voters, playing into the strengths of the emerging GOP of Barry Goldwater. In the wake of societal change, converting a demographic shift into new voter registrations has contributed to Georgia's new status as a swing state. White voters now make up less than two-thirds of the state's total electorate, with African American voters comprising 29 percent. Asian American, Hispanic American, and other groups make up the rest of Georgia voters, a small percentage but one that can be decisive in close elections.[35]

Converting new American citizens into voters required focused efforts. In Sam Park's 2016 campaign for the state house, campaign manager Bee Nguyen coordinated outreach to register Korean voters in suburban Gwinnett County. Park and Nguyen coordinated an effort to reach voters in their native languages, opening access to voter participation. In 2017, Park became the first Asian American representative in the Georgia House of Representatives. Nguyen joined him later in 2017, when she won a special election to fill Stacey Abrams's old seat. In 2021, six Asian Americans sat in the Georgia legislative chamber.[36] Bee Nguyen has announced her 2022 candidacy to be the first Asian American secretary of state in Georgia, entering a race that will certainly garner nationwide attention over voter registration, access, and equity.

As with the shift from Democratic to Republican strength after 1964, current political upheavals in Georgia come largely because of the unseen, unpaid work of women. After the 2016 Trump victory and the record-setting Women's Marches the day after his 2017 inauguration, progressive women throughout Georgia's suburbs gathered in living rooms and at kitchen tables, strategizing how to turn their disillusionment into change. Historian Ellen Rafshoon calls these pop-up groups "stand-ins for Democratic Party chapters that had dwindled in Georgia since the 1990s."[37] Again, even with record-setting money flooding into Georgia politics, change in Georgia's suburban politics is coming from women meeting in living rooms, writing postcards, and phone banking. Tea parties may serve mandu dumplings or pan dulce now, but the volunteer work of women registering and educating voters to change Georgia remains constant.

In January 2019, GOP state senator Renee Unterman observed, "There's no cultivation in the Republican party to encourage women. They want them to work on campaigns, they want them to lick the envelopes."[38] At the end of that year, Governor Brian Kemp overlooked the elected women serving in local and state offices and appointed Kelly Loeffler to the senate seat vacated by a retiring Johnny Isakson, a longtime supporter of the GFRW. A financial executive, Loeffler vowed to spend "$20 million of her own cash" to hold on to the seat in the 2020 election. Governor Kemp's choice appeared to reach out to the Republican Party base of conservative white women, but he missed the mark. He could have selected any of the Republican women who had won office and established records in state or local office. Further, Kemp ignored the contributions of Republican women organizers, party loyalists who had turned out conservative voters for the past six decades. Expressing her rage over the choice, Atlanta Tea Party founder Debbie Dooley warned, "Hell hath no fury like a base scorned."[39]

In appointing Kelly Loeffler to the Georgia Senate, Kemp attempted to shore up support from suburban white women voters for the Republican Party. In another year, it might have worked. In 2020, however, Kemp, Loeffler, and all Republican candidates ran in the shadow of President Donald Trump. Defying expectations of moderation, Loeffler ran on a "100% Trump voting record" and infamously ran ads declaring herself "more conservative than Attila the Hun."[40] A sports executive, Loeffler clashed with her own WNBA Atlanta Dream players over civil rights and support for the Black Lives Matter movement. Neither the politics nor the issues of 2020 allowed room for moderation. Nearly a day after losing her runoff and hours after insurrectionists stormed the U.S. Capitol, Loeffler finally broke her "100% Trump voting record" and voted to certify the 2020 presidential election for Democrat Joe Biden.

Having lost the state's 2020 presidential electoral votes and both U.S. Senate seats, Georgia Republicans are now scrambling to shore up their party for 2022. On the first day of Black History Month 2021, Kemp and Loeffler joined other GOP leaders to launch a Stop Stacey campaign to oppose Democrat Stacey Abrams before she even announced a 2022 run for governor. Weeks later, Loeffler announced her Greater Georgia program, a conservative response to Abrams's Fair Fight organization, which focuses on voter registration and education campaigns. Loeffler's Greater Georgia seeks to register two million new Republican voters in Georgia.[41]

Despite the historic shift in presidential politics, Georgia remains a strong Republican state, with GOP majorities in both state houses. The GFRW continues to volunteer on campaigns at every level, though other organizations like the Tea Party and QAnon groups have siphoned away some members and attention.

The current generation of Republican legislators owe their dominance to the women in these pages—the Go Bo Girls, the Victory Girls, the women of Operation Lend-An-Ear, and STOP ERA. Through the 1960s and 1970s, white conservative women did the polling and politicking to shift Georgia from the solid Democratic South to being a reliable Republican region, electing GOP men in unprecedented numbers. They did so without ever abandoning the goals of Massive Resistance; they merely softened the path with a language of motherhood and home and the smells of home cooking.

NOTES

Acknowledgments

1. Marjorie Spruill also used Dunaway's papers to tell the story of International Women's Year in her book *Divided We Stand*.

2. My notes in this book refer to the original places in the boxes. The papers have since moved to Georgia State University where they have recently been processed. When I saw them, not all papers were in folders and folders were not labeled. My notes reflect the unprocessed nature of the original collection.

Introduction. "First, Take a Shoebox"

1. Ague Miller interview, May 31, 2014.

2. Ibid. Miller hoped to write books describing her political experience organizing campaigns and another book on her life in Poland, discussed briefly in the conclusion. One of the books she planned to write was to be titled "First, Take a Shoebox." Since Miller passed away in 2015 without writing her books, I title this chapter in gratitude for her generosity with sharing her memories, time, and papers with me. Miller did get to read a copy of my dissertation, which has been the basis for much of this book. When she began campaigning in the 1950s, she was married to Bob Ague. In the late 1960s, she married Gene Miller. In chapters 1–3, she is Lee Ague. In chapter 4, she is Lee Miller.

3. McRae, *Mothers of Massive Resistance*; Brückmann, *Massive Resistance and Southern Womanhood*.

4. Goldwater Girls were usually teenaged girls or young women, dressed in cowgirl outfits consisting of a gold or navy-blue skirt, white shirt, Goldwater kerchief tied on the right side, and a cowboy hat. In Georgia in 1966, the Go Bo Girls and the Victory Girls could be younger but also included the older women of the clubs. Descriptions of these roles are found in chapters 1 and 2. This book grows from the author's dissertation (Morris, "Building the New Right").

5. For more on the NFRW, see Rymph, *Republican Women*.

6. The important history of minority groups and the Republican Party and conservatism has recently been the subject of excellent scholarship. On African Americans and the Republican Party, see Wright Rigueur, *Loneliness of the Black Republican*; Fields, *Black Elephants in the Room*; Dillard, *Guess Who's Coming to Dinner Now?*; and Farrington, *Black Republicans and the Transformation*. On Latinx Americans and the GOP, see Cadava, *Hispanic Republican*. For a more recent history of Native Americans and the New Right, see Smith, *Native Americans and the Christian Right*. In writing the story of Black women in the Georgia GOP, Atlanta's African American newspaper, the *Atlanta*

Daily World, has proven immensely valuable, since the controlling Scott family had a longtime affiliation with the Republican Party as the civil rights party.

7. Founded in 1927, the Women's National Democratic Club (WNDC) was a social club first and political club second, open to women residing in or visiting Washington, D.C. In contrast, the NFRW was founded a decade after the WNDC but began with chapters in eleven states totaling eighty-five member clubs. None were southern. While the WNDC did not admit its first African American member until 1955, the NFRW welcomed four "colored women's clubs" at its inaugural meeting in 1937. Rymph, *Republican Women*, 71–74; Fenzi and Black, *Democratic Women*, 48, 64–65.

8. The political meaning and uses of motherhood have a rich history and deep historiography. Linda K. Kerber examined the uses of motherhood in the early republican—small *r*—period of the United States in "The Republican Mother: Women and the Enlightenment—An American Perspective," in Kerber, *Toward an Intellectual History*. On maternalism and political activism in the twentieth-century United States, see Ladd-Taylor, *Mother-Work*; Linda Gordon, *Pitied but Not Entitled*; Mink, *Wages of Motherhood*; and Koven and Michel, "Womanly Duties." On maternalism in southern women's movements of the Progressive Era, see Spruill Wheeler, *New Women*; Elna C. Green, *Southern Strategies*; Cox, *Dixie's Daughters*; and Gilmore, *Gender and Jim Crow*. On maternalism in more recent international politics, see Jetter, Orleck, and Taylor, *Politics of Motherhood*. On white women's maternalist politics in the era of civil rights and Massive Resistance, see Brückman, *Massive Resistance and Southern Womanhood*.

9. Kevin P. Phillips, *Emerging Republican Majority*, 186.

10. Ibid., 205.

11. Maxwell and Shields, *Long Southern Strategy*, 129.

12. Lee Atwater quoted in Bob Herbert, "The Ugly Side of the GOP," *New York Times*, Sept. 25, 2007 (bracketed text in original).

13. Kruse, *White Flight*, 245. For context on the civil rights movement in Atlanta, which gave rise to the reactionary white flight noted by Kruse, see Brown-Nagin, *Courage to Dissent*. Brown-Nagin explores the "long history" of the movement in Atlanta from 1940 to 1980.

14. See also McRae, *Mothers of Massive Resistance*.

15. On the evolution of color-blindness as a talking point of the Right, see Hall, "Long Civil Rights Movement," 1237–38.

16. Spruill Wheeler, *New Women*; Cox, *Dixie's Daughters*; Gilmore, *Gender and Jim Crow*. Other works on southern women's Progressive activism include Hall, *Revolt against Chivalry*; and Giddings, *Ida*.

17. While I suggest here and in chapter 2 that the 1966 Georgia gubernatorial campaign was a critical step toward the Republican realignment, it is more often analyzed as a victory for the Massive Resistance politics of white supremacy. In *White Flight*, Kevin Kruse dedicates several pages to the election, primarily as a victory for segregationist Lester Maddox. For broader analysis of the 1966 gubernatorial campaign, including the struggle in the Democratic primary as well as the drawn-out general election, see Henderson, "1966 Gubernatorial Election in Georgia."

18. See Gene Miller, "Address of Mrs. Gene Miller to the NFRW Biennial Convention," Washington, D.C., Sept. 27, 1969, folder "Speech Material," box 3, Lee Ague Miller Papers, Unprocessed Record Group, Georgia Archives, Morrow, Ga. (The pre-1974 Miller Papers have since moved to Georgia State University, where the post-1974 papers were and continue to be held; my notes citations to the pre-1974 papers reflect the location in which I found them at the Georgia Archives.)

1. Edward Peeks, "Atlantans Pay Tribute to Lincoln in Friday Program," *Atlanta Daily World*, Feb. 13, 1954, 1. As the city's African American newspaper, the *ADW* gave the women here the title of "Mrs." as a means to assert equality in 1950s Atlanta. Out of respect for the women and the newspaper, I keep that honorific here.

2. Georgia Club List, Folder Georgia 1953, Box 30, National Federation of Republican Women Papers, Eisenhower Presidential Library, Abilene, Kansas.

3. Edward Peeks, "Atlantans Pay Tribute to Lincoln in Friday Program," *Atlanta Daily World*, Feb. 13, 1954, 1.

4. Program of the Annual Awards Banquet of the Metropolitan Atlanta Republican Women, Oct. 27, 1973, folder 8, box 6, series 4, Evelyn J. Frazier Papers, Auburn Avenue Research Library for African American Culture and History, Fulton County Library System, Atlanta, Ga.

5. "GOP Negro on Augusta School Body," *Atlanta Constitution*, Nov. 10, 1952, 9; Bertha Adkins to Mrs. Carroll Kearns, May 29, 1953, folder "Georgia 1953," box 30, NFRW Papers, Eisenhower Presidential Library, Abilene, Kans.

6. African American participation in the Republican Party from Reconstruction through the mid-twentieth century has been studied by several historians. As the Party of Lincoln and the Party of Emancipation, the Republican Party was considered the progressive or civil rights party for several decades. When the Democratic Party would not allow African Americans, the Republican Party admitted them, even if not always on an equal basis. On African American women and voting rights at this time, see Ann D. Gordon et al., *African American Women*; and Nealy, *African American Women Voters*.

7. Mrs. W. A. Scott was the wife of the *Atlanta Daily World* publisher.

8. "Three Atlantans Attending Woman's Meet in D.C.; To Meet Mrs. Eisenhower," *Atlanta Daily World*, Apr. 22, 1953, 4; "U.S. Warned against 'Over Optimism' in Face of Soviet Peace Overtures," *Atlanta Daily World*, Apr. 25, 1953, 1; "President Reveals Awareness of Women's Voting Importance," *Atlanta Daily World*, Apr. 26, 1953, 1.

9. Hattie Greene to Bertha Adkins, June 8, 1953, folder "Georgia 1953," box 30, NFRW Papers, Eisenhower Library. Bertha Adkins was assistant to the chairman of the RNC at that time.

10. Hattie Greene to Mrs. Carroll D. Kearns (NFRW president), Apr. 19, 1954, folder "Georgia 1953," box 30, NFRW Papers, Eisenhower Library.

11. Holly Crenshaw, "Evelyn Jones Frazier, 95, Brought Style, Class to Segregated South," *Atlanta Journal-Constitution*, Sept. 6, 2007, B5.

12. "Republican Women Meet in New Orleans in October," *Atlanta Daily World*, Oct. 5, 1955, 4.

13. NFRW, "About the Federation 1968–69," South Carolina Federation of Republican Women Papers, Louise Pettus Archives, Dacus Library, Winthrop University, Rock Hill, S.C. The other southern states to organize before Georgia were Arkansas (1955), Florida (1953), Kentucky (1947), Louisiana (1953), North Carolina (1953), Tennessee (1955), Texas (1955), Virginia (1953), and West Virginia (1939). Part of Georgia's difficulty in qualifying came from the requirement to have a Republican women's organization in 60 percent of a state's counties, meaning that 95 of Georgia's 159 counties would have needed an organization. Once the requirement changed to require organization in 50–75 percent of a state's congressional districts, Georgia joined. Alaska was the final state to join, in 1962.

14. "Republican Ladies Adopt Plans for November Election," *Atlanta Daily World*, Oct. 20, 1960.

15. On the Republican Party in the post-Reconstruction South, see McMillen, *Dark Journey*; Bullock, "Congressional Voting and the Mobilization"; Watson, "Guess What Came?"; and Leak, *Rac(e)ing to the Right*.

16. Edward Peeks, "Atlantans Pay Tribute to Lincoln in Friday Program," *Atlanta Daily World*, Feb. 13, 1954, 1.

17. Rymph, *Republican Women*, 71–74; Fenzi and Black, *Democratic Women*, 48, 64–65. When the WNDC did admit its first African American member, they allowed only one, and that by a 14–11–1 vote. The National Federation of Democratic Women did not form until 1971.

18. Tennessee's Second District, representing the unionist mountain area, has been held by Republicans since Reconstruction. Florida and "the four mountain states of the peripheral South," which I assume to be Virginia, West Virginia, Tennessee, and Kentucky, ran Republicans who made a strong showing, but lost. Georgia, Mississippi, and South Carolina did not have any Republican gubernatorial or senatorial candidates until at least 1966. Bartley and Graham, *Southern Politics*, 82–110. South Carolina senator Strom Thurmond famously changed parties in 1964 but had run in 1960 as a Democrat. In 1966, he won reelection as a Republican.

19. Key, *Southern Politics in State*, 118–21; Jason W. Gilliland, "The Calculus of Realignment: The Rise of Republicanism in Georgia, 1964-1992," Unpublished Senior Essay, Yale University, 2010; Buchanan, "Effects of the Abolition," 689.

Chapter 1. The Two Party Tea Party

1. Ague Miller interview, Feb. 25, 2010. Robert and Lee Ague divorced in the mid-1960s and she married Gene Miller in the late 1960s.

2. Ibid.

3. Tenth District of Virginia Directory, no folder, box 5, Lee Ague Miller Papers, Unprocessed Record Group, Georgia Archives, Morrow, Ga. (hereafter, Ague Miller Papers). As of summer 2020, these records are processed and in the Activist Women's Collection at Georgia State University. However, as I consulted the papers in their unprocessed state at the Georgia Archives, I have designated location by box and folder as accurately as possible. Where a paper is not in a folder, I have designated that. When a paper is in a folder, I designate by color or other characteristic to aid in finding. Ague was first vice president of the club in 1963 ("first" was part of the position's title, there also being second vice presidents and so on).

4. President's newsletter, CCFRW, April 1964, no folder, box 5, Ague Miller Papers.

5. Ague Miller interview, Feb. 25, 2010. The man who hired Ague told her he would get credit for hiring a woman even though he expected her to leave to have babies soon.

6. Biography of Mrs. Lucas (Marjean) Birt, folder "Fulton County," box 3, Ague Miller Papers.

7. Member profiles, *Distaff*, March 1965, no folder, box 5, Ague Miller Papers.

8. Ague to Bill [no surname], Dec. 13, 1962, no folder, box 5, Ague Miller Papers. Ague wrote this while she and her husband lived in Virginia. There is no record of how she came to be a consultant for the Arkansas GOP.

9. Ague Miller interview, Feb. 25, 2010.

10. Siskind, "Shades of Black and Green." Goldwater and Rockefeller did differ on the

role of the United Nations in Cold War policies, with Rockefeller more supportive of U.S. participation in international organizations.

11. Goldwater, *Conscience of a Conservative*, 24, 34 (emphasis in original). Conservative author L. Brent Bozell is widely credited with ghostwriting this volume (see Perlstein, 61–68). Barry Goldwater also had significant support among right-wing members of the national leadership of the NFRW. Dorothy Elston, elected NFRW president in 1962, was a strong Goldwater supporter. On the NFRW and the Goldwater campaign, see Rymph, *Republican Women*, 160–87.

12. "Goldwater in Georgia on a Tour for GOP," *Atlanta Daily World*, Sept. 17, 1960, 1.

13. "Republicans Charge Alien, Racist Group Seeks to Take Over," *Atlanta Daily World*, Feb. 19, 1964, 1; "Dr. Lee R. Shelton Views Republican Party's Organization," *Atlanta Daily World*, May 20, 1964, 3.

14. "Republicans to Meet Tonight at Frazier's," *Atlanta Daily World*, Feb. 18, 1964, 1; "Republicans Charge Alien, Racist Group Seeks to Take Over," *Atlanta Daily World*, Feb. 19, 1964, 1. The signers of this document are not identified by race.

15. "'Regular' Republicans Maintain Control of Fulton County Group," *Atlanta Daily World*, Feb. 23, 1964, 1.

16. Ague, "Be a GOP Gardener," *Dispatch*, June 1964, no folder, box 6, Ague Miller Papers.

17. Ague to Mrs. Arthur Sandison, November 18, 1964, no folder, box 3; Hope Ayo, "Campaign Activities," *Dispatch*, July 1964, no folder, box 3, Ague Miller Papers.

18. Miller interview, Feb. 25, 2010.

19. In "Tea and Suffrage," Jessica Sewell examines the use of tea in the suffrage movement in California. She analyzes the femininity and elitism of the beverage of tea (as opposed to men's coffee) and shows how the tea and tea parties became important to the suffrage movement.

20. Memo to Two Party Tea Party hostesses from Ague, n.d., folder "Two Party Tea Parties," box 3, Ague Miller Papers. Ague Miller did not hyphenate Two Party in the event name.

21. Ague, "President's Report," *Distaff*, May 1964, no folder, box 5, Ague Miller Papers.

22. Instructions for Victory Girls, newsletter unknown, 7, no folder, box 5, Ague Miller Papers. This page is separated from the front page of the newsletter, so the title and date are missing, though it is from 1966. The source is most likely either a Cobb County Federation newsletter or a Georgia Federation newsletter. When I asked Lee Miller about this, she laughed at the memory that she had ever been skilled enough to sew a Victory Girl uniform.

23. *Distaff*, November 1964, 2, no folder, box 5, Ague Miller Papers.

24. Carolyn Stuedli, "Finance Report," *Distaff*, n.d., unnamed folder, box 5, Ague Miller Papers. Other information in this newsletter suggests that it is the September 1964 issue. It is postmarked to Ague's Spring Drive address, Aug. 27, 1964.

25. Ague, progress report for week ending Sept. 26, 1964, no folder, box 4, Ague Miller Papers.

26. Cumulative report for Georgia state canvass tally, folder "1964 Canvass Data," box 5, Ague Miller Papers; Miller interview, Feb. 25, 2010.

27. Katherine Gunnell to unnamed recipient, Nov. 26, 1964, folder "Correspondence * Ague," box 5, Ague Miller Papers.

28. *The South*, MORE booklet no. 5, Alabama Republican State Executive Committee and RNC, no folder, box 3, Ague Miller Papers.

29. Ague speech, n.d., unnamed folder, box 3, Ague Miller Papers.

30. Miller interview, Feb. 25, 2010.

31. Ibid.

32. Republican Party of Georgia, press release, Apr. 3, 1967, no folder, box 3, Ague Miller Papers.

33. Memo from state canvass chairman [Ague] to county chairmen, "Suggested Instructions to Include with Distribution of Canvass Tally Sheets," no folder, box 5, Ague Miller Papers.

34. Ague Miller interviews, Feb. 25, 2010, and Dec. 11, 2011. She would not go into detail about the woman she employed.

35. *Dispatch*, June 1964, 2, no folder, box 3, Ague Miller Papers.

36. Lee Ague, "Instructions for Couples Canvass"; memo from Lee Ague to county canvass chairmen, "How to Recruit Volunteers"; memo from Lee Ague to county canvass chairmen, "Instructions for a Door-to-Door Canvass"; all in no folder, box 3, Ague Miller Papers. "Brass collar" Democrats were those known by county Republican leaders to be unshakably loyal to the Democratic Party. This identification required familiarity with the people of the area, since most voters had always voted Democratic as a matter of course.

37. Ague handwritten notes, no folder, box 5, Ague Miller Papers. Ague kept informal, handwritten notes from her conversations. The note is dated Oct. 12 and records the conversation was with Jim Tilton.

38. Memo to Joseph Tribble, state chairman, and G. Paul Jones, state Goldwater campaign coordinator, from Lee Ague, Sept. 20, 1964, no folder, box 5, Ague Miller Papers.

39. Ague, weekly report to Joseph Tribble, week of Sept. 13, 1964, no folder, box 5, Ague Miller Papers.

40. "State's Voter Total Estimated at 275,000," *Atlanta Daily World*, May 16, 1964, 1. On civil rights and voter registration in Georgia, see Brown-Nagin, *Courage to Dissent*.

41. Ralph Sutton to Mr. G. Paul Jones, state [GOP] chairman, Oct. 25, 1964, Ague Miller Papers, no folder, box 5. Wilcox County is a rural county in south-central Georgia.

42. Carolyn Wynn Smalley to Paul [Tribble, state Goldwater chairman], Oct. 24, 1964, unnamed folder, box 5, Ague Miller Papers.

43. Mrs. Lee Wash to Ague, Oct. 19, 1964, no folder, box 5, Ague Miller Papers. Clarke County is home to the University of Georgia and the county seat of Athens.

44. M. C. McAlpin, Oct. 14, 1964, unnamed folder, box 3, Ague Miller Papers.

45. Reg Murphy, "Republican Captures State for First Time," *Atlanta Constitution*, Nov. 3, 1963, clipping in Lee Ague scrapbook, box "School Injunction" in box 8, Ague Miller Papers.

46. Goldsmith, *Colleagues*, 113–15. Richard Russell traditionally did not get involved with presidential politics and did not make an exception in 1964.

47. Ayo, "Report on the Cobb County Fair," *Distaff*, November 1964, no folder, box 5, Ague Miller Papers.

48. Julie Anderson, dir., *Mr. Conservative: Goldwater on Goldwater* (New York: Zeitgeist Films, 2006). The documentary includes Hillary Rodham Clinton's memories of being a Goldwater Girl as well as archival footage of the uniforms.

49. *Distaff*, November 1964, no folder, box 5, Ague Miller Papers. The newsletter only says that the Goldwater Girls sang, but unfortunately does not list any women by name nor the songs they sang.

50. Daniel, *Lost Revolutions*, 273.

51. On the construction of white womanhood and its connection to white supremacist movements in the twentieth-century South, see Hale, *Making Whiteness*, 199–297; Dray, *At the Hands*; Hall, *Revolt against Chivalry*; Gilmore, *Gender and Jim Crow*; McRae, *Mothers of Massive Resistance*; and Dailey, "Sex, Segregation, and the Sacred."

52. Joseph Tribble to district chairmen, Sept. 19, 1964, no folder, box 5, Ague Miller Papers.

53. Lee Wash to Lee Ague, Oct. 29, 1964, no folder, box 5, Ague Miller Papers.

54. Cohodas, *Strom Thurmond and the Politics*, 359.

55. The vote was 888 for Blitch and 832 for her opponent. See "More Legislative Leaders to Return," *Atlanta Journal*, n.d., 1, folder 22, "Clippings," box C9, series 6, "Campaign 1954–1958," Iris Blitch Papers, Richard B. Russell Library, University of Georgia Libraries, Athens, Ga. (hereafter, Blitch Papers).

56. Margaret Shannon, "Iris Blitch Turns to GOP and Barry," clipping, unidentified newspaper, n.d., folder 22, "Clippings," box C9, series 6, Blitch Papers.

57. Tenney Griffin, "Blitch Quits Party," clipping, unidentified newspaper, n.d., folder 22, "Clippings," box C9, series 6, Blitch Papers. From references within the article, the newspaper clipping appears to be from the *Valdosta Daily Times*.

58. "Cumulative Report for Georgia State Canvass Tally," 1964 Canvass Data folder, box 5, Ague Miller Papers.

59. Lee Ague, "From Our President," *Distaff*, November 1964, no folder, box 5, Ague Miller Papers.

60. Instructions for Operation Win, no folder, box 5, Ague Miller Papers.

61. Lee Ague, "From Our President," *Distaff*, November 1964, no folder, box 5, Ague Miller Papers (emphasis in original).

62. *Distaff*, November 1964, 1–2, no folder, box 5, Ague Miller Papers.

63. Lee Ague to county canvass chairmen, "Telephone Instructions for Election Day—November 3," and "Turning Out Our Vote—The Victory Squad," no folder, box 3, Ague Miller Papers; Clara Curtis to County Election Day Chairmen, n.d., no folder, box 5, Ague Miller Papers.

64. Lee Wash to Lee Ague, Oct. 29, 1964, no folder, box 5, Ague Miller Papers.

65. Final Goldwater Report, Second Congressional District Republican Committee, Oct. 30, 1964, no folder, box 5, Ague Miller Papers. This report includes information on a training by Lee Ague as well as directions from Second District chairman R. E. Kaliher.

66. Memo from Ague to county canvass chairmen, "Why Not Victory? Ballot Security," no folder, box 3, Ague Miller Papers.

67. Telegram from Ralph Ivey to Lee Ague, Nov. 2, 1964, no folder, box 6, Ague Miller Papers.

68. Memo from Ague to county canvass chairmen, "Why Not Victory? Ballot Security," no folder, box 3, Ague Miller Papers (emphasis in original).

69. Ague Miller interview, Feb. 25, 2010.

70. Reg Murphy, "Republican Captures State for First Time," *Atlanta Constitution*, Nov. 3, 1963, clipping in Lee Ague scrapbook, box "School Injunction" in box 8, Ague Miller Papers. On Atlanta residential segregation and its effect on voting trends, see Kruse, *White Flight*.

71. Handwritten notes, no title, folder "Correspondence * Ague," box 5, Ague Miller Papers.

72. Ague, "President's Message," *Dispatch*, January 1965, no folder, box 4, Ague Miller Papers.

73. Barry Goldwater to Lee Ague, November 18, 1964, folder "Correspondence * Ague," box 5, Ague Miller Papers.

74. Holmes Alexander, "The Bo Callaway Story," folder 3, box II-A-1, series 2, Howard H. (Bo) Callaway Papers, Richard B. Russell Library for Political Research and Studies, University of Georgia, Athens, Ga. (hereafter, Callaway Papers).

75. "Callaway Campaigns in Lee County," Callaway for Congress news release, n.d., folder 58, "Callaway for Congress—News Releases—Sept. 26, 1964–Nov. 4, 1964," box IA2, series 1: Congressional, Callaway Papers.

76. See Callaway kickoff rally speech, September 26, 1964, Columbus, Ga., folder 58, "Callaway for Congress—News Releases—Sept. 26, 1964–Nov. 4, 1964," box IA2, series 1: Congressional, Callaway Papers; Cook, *Carl Sanders*, 210–13; and Henderson, *Politics of Change in Georgia*, 225–27.

77. Callaway kickoff rally speech, September 26, 1964, Columbus, Ga., folder 58, "Callaway for Congress—News Releases—Sept. 26, 1964–Nov. 4, 1964," box IA2, series 1: Congressional, Callaway Papers.

78. Lee Ague, "Complaints against GFRW," n.d., no folder, box 5, Ague Miller Papers.

79. Ague to NFRW, n.d., folder "Correspondence * Ague," box 5, Ague Miller Papers.

80. "Choice Asked in GOP Split," article clipping, n.d., folder "Correspondence * Ague," box 5, Ague Miller Papers. This clipping looks to be from the *Atlanta Times*, a short-lived newspaper begun by Roscoe Pickett Jr. as a conservative alternative to the *Journal-Constitution*. See also Charles Pou, "Goldwaterites and Moderates Set First Skirmish for Macon," clipping, unidentified newspaper, n.d., no folder, box 5; Reg Murphy, n.d., box "School Injunction," in box 8, Ague Miller Papers.

81. President of the Muscogee Republican Women's Club to Dorothy Elston, Nov. 25, 1964, no folder, box 3, Ague Miller Papers. This is a carbon copy of the letter which is unsigned by the author.

82. Hallie McCormick Kendall to Dorothy Elston, Dec. 5, 1964, no folder, box 3, Ague Miller Papers.

83. Ague to Mrs. John A. Cauble of Cherokee Federation; Ague to Mrs. John C. Swann of Jefferson County Federation; Ague to Mrs. Janis Rosser of Fourth District FRW, Atlanta; Ague to Mrs. J. W. (Clara) Martin of Hall County FRW; Ague to Mrs. A. G. Baxter of Gwinnett County Federation; Ague to Mrs. George (Katherine) Gunnell of Douglass County FRW; Ague to Mrs. Hallie McCormick Kendall of College Park, all letters dated Dec. 17, 1964, no folder, box 3, Ague Miller Papers.

84. Ague to Mrs. Skeeters, May 13, 1964, no folder, box 6, Ague Miller Papers.

85. Dorothy Elston, "Official Call for First Reorganization Meeting of Georgia Federation of Republican Women, February 20, 1965," no folder, box 4, Ague Miller Papers; Elston to Ague, Jan. 5, 1964, no folder, box 4, Ague Miller Papers; Ague, "From Our President," *Distaff*, February 1965, no folder, box 4, Ague Miller Papers.

86. Ague to Republican women leaders, Mar. 1, 1965, no folder, box 4, Ague Miller Papers.

87. Ague to Republican women leaders, Feb. 28, 1965, folder "Correspondence * Ague," box 5, Ague Miller Papers.

88. Reg Murphy, "Goldwater Women Tighten Grip on State," *Atlanta Constitution*, Feb. 22, 1965, 5–A.

89. Unsigned article, "History Committee," and Nancy Geiger, "A Message from Your President," *GOPeople* 1, no. 1, February 1965, 4, 1, no folder, box 4, Ague Miller Papers.

90. Mrs. W. C. (Ruby) LeShanna, letter to the editor, *GOPeople* 1, no. 1, February 1965, 3, no folder, box 4, Ague Miller Papers.

91. *Distaff*, March 1965, 5, no folder, box 4; Clara Curtis to delegates, n.d., folder "Correspondence * Ague," box 5, Ague Miller Papers.

92. Lee Ague for President flyer, no folder, box 5; Ague to Republican women leaders, Mar. 1, 1965, no folder, box 4, Ague Miller Papers.

93. Clara Curtis to GFRW presidents, n.d., box "School Injunction" in box 8, Ague Miller Papers.

94. *Distaff*, March 1965, 5, no folder, box 4, Ague Miller Papers.

95. Lisa Battle, "Mrs. Robert Ague Elected President of State Federation of GOP Women," *Columbus, Ga., Sunday Ledger-Enquirer*, Mar. 7, 1965, D9, box "School Injunction" in box 8, Ague Miller Papers.

96. "Mrs. Ague to Lead GOP Women," *Atlanta Journal*, Mar. 8, 1965, clipping in unnamed folder, box 5, Ague Miller Papers. Halcyon Bell of Atlanta had been GFRW president from 1959 to 1961.

97. Ague, "From Our President" column, *Distaff*, March 1965, 1, no folder, box 4, Ague Miller Papers.

98. Minutes of Regional Meeting, Mar. 27, 1965, folder "Bd. Meeting, March 27, 1965," no folder, box 3, Ague Miller Papers.

99. Ibid. These birdhouses came from the Lookout Mountain chapter, which not only included Georgia residents but pulled members across the state border from Tennessee. Rock City, just south of the border, was a tourist attraction operated by Georgia Seventh District Republican congressional candidate Ed Chapin.

Chapter 2. The Go Bo Girls

1. Memo from Estelle Lee Ague to All GOP district chairmen and co-chairmen, county chairmen and co-chairmen, n.d., folder "Canvass Misc. 1964," box 9, Ague Miller Papers. The fact that Ague was GFRW president at the time and the content of her text shows that this memo was most likely distributed in 1965, despite the marking on the folder.

2. On Massive Resistance and school desegregation in Georgia, see Kruse, *White Flight*. On white women in Massive Resistance, see McRae, *Mothers of Massive Resistance*. On Massive Resistance regionwide, see Lassiter and Lewis, *Moderates' Dilemma*; and Bartley, *Rise of Massive Resistance*.

3. Newsletter, Toco Hills FRW, April 1965, no folder, box 2, Ague Miller Papers.

4. Hope Ayo, *Distaff*, 2, March 1965, no folder, box 4, Ague Miller Papers. Though the federal right of eighteen-year-olds to register to vote did not pass until 1971, Georgia law allowed eighteen-year-olds to vote.

5. *GOPeople*, 2, no folder, box 4, Ague Miller Papers.

6. Dunaway testimony before Senate Foreign Relations Committee, Feb. 22, 1965, folder 2, box 3, Kathryn Fink Dunaway Papers, Manuscripts and Rare Books Library, Robert W. Woodruff Library, Emory University, Atlanta, Ga. (hereafter, Dunaway Papers).

7. Ibid.

8. Ibid.

9. Critchlow, *Phyllis Schlafly and Grassroots Conservatism*, 119–25.

10. Ibid., 133–35; Dunaway testimony before Senate Foreign Relations Committee, Feb. 22, 1965, folder 2, box 3, Dunaway Papers; Newsletter, Toco Hills FRW, April 1965, no folder, box 2, Ague Miller Papers. This newsletter shows Kathryn Dunaway as a guest at the May 11 meeting of the Toco Hills (DeKalb County) club. See also Dunaway testi-

mony before Senate Foreign Relations Committee, Feb. 22, 1965, folder 2, box 3, Dunaway Papers.

11. *Troup County Trumpet*, May 1965, no folder, box 3, Ague Miller Papers.

12. Ibid.

13. Newsletter, Toco Hills FRW, April 1965, no folder, box 2, Ague Miller Papers.

14. Newsletter, Cherokee Federation of Republican Women, May 1965, no folder, box 3, Ague Miller Papers.

15. NFRW Southeastern Regional Conference flyer, Oct. 22, 1965, no folder, box 3, Ague Miller Papers. On Strom Thurmond's conversion from Democrat to Republican, see Crespino, *Strom Thurmond's America*, 165–84.

16. Ague to Elston, Feb. 3, 1966, folder "Correspondence to 11/8/66," box 3, Ague Miller Papers.

17. Lee Ague, "President's Report to the Board," no folder, box 9, Ague Miller Papers. When I asked her about balancing her political activity with motherhood, Miller curtly replied, "I had help," but she did not elaborate on who cared for her children while she traveled. Ague Miller interview, Feb. 25, 2010.

18. John H. Friend Co., "Instructions for Surveys," no folder, box 9, Ague Miller Papers.

19. Mrs. Hill Blackett, n.d., folder "Memos to Jim Files," box 5, Ague Miller Papers.

20. Mrs. George Brewton to Ague, n.d., no folder, box 9, Ague Miller Papers. Martinez was in the Tenth District, a suburb of Augusta in Richmond County.

21. John H. Friend Co., "Instruction Kit for Volunteer Interviewers," Georgia Opinion Survey, July 1965, no folder, box 2, Ague Miller Papers.

22. Ibid. (emphasis in original).

23. Ibid. See also "Current Population Reports: Consumer Income," Aug. 10, 1966, series P-60, no. 49, Bureau of the Census, U.S. Department of Commerce, www2.census .gov/prod2/popscan/p60–049.pdf.

24. John H. Friend Co., "Instruction Kit for Volunteer Interviewers," Georgia Opinion Survey, July 1965, no folder, box 2, Ague Miller Papers.

25. Ibid.

26. Ibid. The results of this round of surveys are not in the files of either Lee Ague Miller or Bo Callaway. I have not located archival holdings, nor have I been able to determine if such records even exist, for the John H. Friend Company, which, in 1966, changed its name to the Jim Files Company to avoid any conflict of interest with Friend's campaign for a position in the Alabama state legislature. The results for other rounds of the 1966 campaign surveys are analyzed in other parts of this chapter.

27. Maddox, *Speaking Out*, 56–58; Galphin, *Riddle of Lester Maddox*, 47–54, 55–85.

28. "Negroes in South Test Rights Act; Resistance Light," *New York Times*, July 4, 1964, 1; "Race Barriers Fall in Much of Dixie," *Hartford Courant*, July 4, 1964, 1; "Rights Reaction Varied," *Chicago Tribune*, July 4, 1964, 1; "First Rights Bill Tests in South Quiet; Many Facilities Desegregate," *Washington Post*, July 4, 1964, A1; "Violence Greets Ga. Rights Test," *Philadelphia Tribune*, July 7, 1964, 1. The *New York Times* and *Hartford Courant* ran the same photo of Maddox with his pistol on page 1; the *Chicago Tribune* ran the story on page 1 and the photo on page 4. Brown-Nagin, *Courage to Dissent*, 222–23.

29. "Restaurateur Defiant," *New York Times*, Aug. 11, 1964, 24.

30. Henderson, "1966 Gubernatorial Election in Georgia," 59.

31. "GOP Women Predict Gubernatorial Effort," *Augusta Chronicle*, Oct. 22, 1965, 1, no folder, box 9, Ague Miller Papers.

32. Lee Ague, "President's Report to the Board," Feb. 19, 1966, no folder, box 9, Ague Miller Papers.

33. G. Paul Jones to Dr. John A. Cauble, June 3, 1966, no folder, box 5, Ague Miller Papers. The first Republican woman to run for Congress in Georgia was Karen Handel, who ran in the special election for Congressman Tom Price's seat after Donald Trump appointed Price to head the Department of Health and Human Services. Handel won the special election in 2017 but lost in the next election in 2018.

34. John H. Friend, "Proposal: Political Opinion Poll with Professional Supervision of Volunteer Interviewers in Georgia," John H. Friend Co., Mobile, Ala., no folder, box 9, Ague Miller Papers. "County by County Analysis," www.georgiastats.uga.edu, Georgia Statistics Center of the Center for Agribusiness and Economics Development, Department of Agricultural and Applied Economics and Cooperative Extension Service, University of Georgia.

35. Frances Durham to Ague, n.d., folder "Survey: Tenth District," box 9, Ague Miller Papers.

36. Gladys Green to Lee Ague, Aug. 2, 1966, folder "Survey 4," box 7, Ague Miller Papers.

37. Note from Kathleen [no surname] to Lee Ague, July 12, 1965, unnamed folder, box 2, Ague Miller Papers. This note is on the back of survey results from Mrs. V. C. Wade of Valdosta, but the survey was done in Echols County in District 8. Because surveyors turned in results to district chairwomen, I do not assume that Kathleen is Mrs. V. C. Wade.

38. Lee Ague to Bill [Amos], Mar. 25, 1966, no folder, box 9, Ague Miller Papers. Ague does not mention the Metropolitan Club in her recruitment or survey files.

39. Naomi Roughton to Lee Ague, n.d., folder "Survey 4," box 7, Ague Miller Papers.

40. Jane Pruett, Survey 9 feedback form, n.d., folder "Opinion survey to be Filed #9," box 5, Ague Miller Papers (emphasis in original).

41. John H. Friend Co., "Political Opinion Surveys," no folder, box 1, Ague Miller Papers. The long-form statistical data for Districts 1, 3, 4, 6, 8, 9, and 10 are in Ague Miller's files. While other files indicate that the women did conduct the surveys in Districts 2, 5, and 7, there is not a binder of this data preserved in the archives.

42. Ibid.

43. Ibid.

44. Ibid.

45. Talmadge with Winchell, *Talmadge*, 306–7; Robert Sherrill, "Nixon's Man in Dixie," *New York Times*, Sept. 15, 1968, SM32.

46. John H. Friend Jr., "Callaway has 2-to-1 Lead over Arnall at this Time," July 1966, no folder, box 9, Ague Miller Papers, 1.

47. Ibid.

48. Vera E. Martin to Ague, Aug. 2, 1966, folder "Survey #4," box 7, Ague Miller Papers.

49. William G. Amos, "Notice to Editors—Confidential—Notification that Congressman Howard H. (Bo) Callaway will announce his candidacy for Governor on Monday, July 4th at 5pm in Columbus at the Fairgrounds," n.d., folder 54, box II-A-7, series 2, Howard H. (Bo) Callaway Papers, Richard B. Russell Library for Political Research and Studies, University of Georgia, Athens, Ga. (hereafter, Callaway Papers).

50. "Women's Activities Chairman Named by Callaway," press release, July 19, 1966, folder 50, box II-A-7: News Releases July 4, 1966–October 31, 1966, series 2, Callaway Papers.

51. Ague, Handwritten notes for women in campaign work, 1966, unnamed folder, box 5, Ague Miller Papers.

52. *Republican Candidate's Wives Manual*, folder: Publications, box 3, Ague Miller Papers. A note of acknowledgment in the back thanks Congressman and Mrs. Bob Dole for their help in getting the information from incumbent congressmen and their wives.

53. Ague, *The Women in Your Political Life: A Candidate's Primer*, April 1965, no folder, box 5, Ague Miller Papers.

54. Margaret Dickerson to Ague, Sept. 23, 1966; Mimi Austin to Ralph Watson, Oct. 7, 1966; Ague, "Beth's Schedule," folder: Beth's Schedule, box 3, Ague Miller Papers. Signs around rural Georgia announced "This is Maddox Country!" in support of the segregationist Atlanta Democrat. The strategy of using women's spaces for political organizing has a long history. For example, Vera Pigee in Clarksdale, Mississippi, used beauty appointments as a time for African American voter education. See Hamlin, *Crossroads at Clarksdale*. Glenda Elizabeth Gilmore also traces how white and black women in North Carolina used these women's spaces to challenge Jim Crow in her book *Gender and Jim Crow*.

55. Ague, *The Women in Your Political Life: A Candidate's Primer*, April 1965, no folder, box 5, Ague Miller Papers.

56. Hope Ayo to Callaway, Feb. 24, 1966, and Callaway to Ayo, March 2, 1966, folder 33, box 24, series 2-b, Callaway Papers.

57. "Demo's Wife Endorses Callaway," Callaway Press Release, Oct. 5, 1966, folder 33, box II-A-7, series 2, Callaway Papers.

58. Letter from Mrs. John A. Cauble, Sept. 20, 1966, folder: Publications, box 3, Ague Miller Papers. This letter is on Bo Callaway gubernatorial campaign letterhead.

59. Ralph Wilson and Lee Ague to Terrell Jones, Sept. 26, 1966, folder "Beth's Schedule," box 3, Ague Miller Papers.

60. Albany FRW, *Trunk Line*, November 1966, no folder, box 5 Ague Miller Papers.

61. Anne Tutt to Bill Woodall, July 8, 1966, folder "Correspondence to 11/8/66," box 3, Ague Miller Papers.

62. Decatur County Republican Party to teachers, n.d., folder: Publications, box 3, Ague Miller Papers. Decatur County is separate from the city of Decatur which is in suburban DeKalb County.

63. Barbara King to Lee Ague, Sept. 30, 1966, folder "Survey 8," box 7, Ague Miller Papers.

64. Charlotte Milford to Lee Ague, Aug. 24, 1966, folder "Surveys # Assigned," box 9, Ague Miller Papers.

65. "Reports from 1966 GFRW State Meeting," July 19, 1966, unnamed folder, box 3, Ague Miller Papers.

66. Dorothy Elston to Lee Ague, Oct. 13, 1966, no folder, box 3, Ague Miller Papers.

67. NFRW, *Women on the Warpath* newsletter, no folder, box 3, Ague Miller Papers. There is no date on this material, but it does refer to the November 8 election, which indicates that the material was mailed during preparations for the 1966 elections.

68. "Reports of Local Federations, Board of Directors Meeting," July 9, 1966, unnamed folder, box 3, Ague Miller Papers.

69. Maria Downs to Lee Ague, Sept. 15, 1966; Marjean Birt, "Report of State Membership Chairmen," no folder, box 3 Ague Miller Papers. Birt's report includes mentions LBJ supermarkets in the counties.

70. "Bacon Ad Stirs Sizzle," *Atlanta Constitution*, June 24, 1966, Ague scrapbook, box "School Injunction" in box 8, Ague Miller Papers.

71. No name, feedback forms to Lee Ague, no folder, box 9, Ague Miller Papers. There is no date or county on this form, but the reference to farmers and a mention of Maddox shows that it is September or October 1966 in a rural county.

72. "Mother Plans to Protest," *Atlanta Journal and Constitution*, Oct. 2, 1966, 9E. Before the 2001 completion of their step-by-step merger of staff and publications, the *Journal* and *the Constitution* ran a joint issue on Sundays.

73. Lee Ague, "Women's Activities—June," no folder, box 9, Ague Miller Papers. Ague marked her notes for each county for June and then added other summer months at the end, so the document reflects the full summer.

74. Henderson, "1966 Gubernatorial Campaign in Georgia," 169, 173.

75. Grady-Willis, *Challenging U.S. Apartheid*, 117–20.

76. Henderson, "1966 Gubernatorial Election in Georgia," 173–78; Bartley and Graham, *Southern Elections*, 104–6.

77. Henderson. "1966 Gubernatorial Election in Georgia," 178.

78. Ibid., 181.

79. Mrs. Allen M. Pool, Ft. Valley, Ga., to Callaway, Oct. 10, 1966, no folder, box 9, Ague Miller Papers.

80. Kruse, *White Flight*, 231.

81. Bartley, *From Thurmond to Wallace*, 67–83; Henderson and Roberts, *Georgia Governors in an Age*, 198–201; Kruse, *White Flight*, 231–33; Boyd, "1966 Election in Georgia."

82. W. Frank Branch to an unidentified women's group, n.d., folder 26, box II-A-7, series 2, Callaway Papers.

83. Henderson, "1966 Gubernatorial Election in Georgia," 227–29.

84. "Stop Maddox!! Stop Callaway!!" flyer, n.d., folder 5, box II-A-4, series 2, Callaway Papers.

85. Margaret M. Thrower to Evelyn Frazier, Oct. 18, 1966, folder 7, box 5, series 4, Evelyn J. Frazier Papers, Auburn Avenue Research Library on African American Culture and History, Fulton County Library System, Atlanta, Ga.

86. Duane Riner, "Suit Will Ask Right to Use Stickers in Arnall Write-In," *Atlanta Constitution*, Oct. 17, 1966, 1; Henderson, "1966 Gubernatorial Election in Georgia," 232–34.

87. John H. Friend Company, Political Opinion Surveys, Oct. 10 and 11, 1966, no folder, box 9, Ague Miller Papers.

88. Mrs. Tom Weathers to Lee Ague, Aug. 10, 1966; Mrs. Carl Ponder to Ague, n.d.; Bootsie Calhoun to Ague, n.d.; Vera E. Martin to Ague, Aug. 23, 1966; Gladys W. Blackett to Ague, n.d.; Charlotte Milford to Ague, Aug. 24, 1966; Maryliza [no surname] to Ague, n.d.; all in folder "Surveys # Assigned," box 9, Ague Miller Papers.

89. Gladys Green to Lee Ague, Aug. 2, 1966, folder "Survey 4," box 7, Ague Miller Papers.

90. Allen Jones to Callaway staff, June 29, 1966, folder "Office Memo", box 3, Ague Miller Papers.

91. "Re: Calloway [*sic*] Parade and Kick-Off Rally on September 30th," memo, Sept. 6, 1966, and "Callaway Parade Order," folder 8, box 8, series 2-a, Callaway Papers.

92. Ibid.

93. Lee Ague to Mrs. Mary Brooks, assistant chairman RNC, Oct. 3, 1966, no folder, box 3, Ague Miller Papers.

94. Mrs. John T. Salmon, NFRW membership director, to Ague, Oct. 3, 1966; Ague to Elston, Oct. 3, 1966, folder "Correspondence to 11/8/66," box 3, Ague Miller Papers.

95. Ague to volunteers, n.d., folder "Memos from Surveys," box 7, Ague Miller Papers.

96. Ague Miller interview, May 31, 2014.

97. Barbara King to Ague, Sept. 30, 1966, folder "Survey 8," box 7, Ague Miller Papers.

98. Ague to volunteers, n.d., folder "Memos from Surveys," box 7, Ague Miller Papers.

99. Henderson, "1966 Gubernatorial Election in Georgia," 235–41, 244.

100. Robert P. Hey, "Dirksen Whips Up Republican Zeal in Georgia," *Christian Science Monitor*, Oct. 28, 1967, 5.

101. Miller interview, May 31, 2014.

102. Henderson, "1966 Gubernatorial Election in Georgia," 261–63.

103. Bo Callaway to Lee Ague, Feb. 18, 1967, no folder, box 5, Ague Miller Papers.

104. Gunnell to Ague, Feb. 1, 1967, unlabeled brown envelope, box 5, Ague Miller Papers.

105. Ague, "President's Report to NFRW Board of Directors Meeting," Jan. 24–25, 1967, no folder, box 4, Ague Miller Papers.

106. *Distaff*, newsletter of the Cobb County FRW, March 1967, no folder, box 7, Ague Miller Papers.

Chapter 3. Fighting Factions

1. Brennan, *Turning Right in the Sixties*, 109–12. Brennan examines the position of RNC chairman Ray Bliss as the architect of the purge of extremists as well as the target of the extremists who sought to retain power. In one of his first acts as RNC chair, Bliss issued a statement "denouncing right-wing radicals" and naming the John Birch Society specifically (110). Donald T. Critchlow and Catherine Rymph also cite the central role of Bliss in the NFRW campaigns of 1967. Sociologist Sara Diamond examines the role of conservative groups that supported Republican candidates while officially unaffiliated with the GOP itself. Young Americans for Freedom, the American Conservative Union, and similar groups, she argues, pulled the party further right. Diamond, *Roads to Dominion*, 111–13. One such group, the Eagle Forum, developed out of the intraparty fighting in 1967 and will be discussed in greater depth in chapter 5.

2. Critchlow, *Phyllis Schlafly and Grassroots Conservatism*, 138.

3. Rymph, *Republican Women*, 180. Though Elston's term should have expired in 1966, the board of directors instituted a rule change to shift NFRW national conventions to odd-numbered years in order to enable women to stay focused on campaigns at home.

4. William Rusher, "The Plot to Steal the GOP," *National Review* 18, Nov. 12, 1968, 668–71; Charles Pou, "Georgia Politics," *Atlanta Journal and Constitution*, May 14, 1967, 14, no folder, box 5, Ague Miller Papers.

5. Georgia Federation of Republican Women, program of the Biennial Convention, Apr. 20, 1967, Atlanta, Ga., no folder, Ague Miller Papers.

6. Schlafly, *Choice, Not an Echo*, 23–29, 96–116.

7. Ibid., 117.

8. Critchlow, *Phyllis Schlafly and Grassroots Conservatism*, 144.

9. Rymph, *Republican Women*, 180–81; Critchlow, *Phyllis Schlafly and Grassroots Conservatism*, 148.

10. Barry Goldwater to Dorothy Elston, Mar. 27, 1967, no folder, box 5, Ague Miller Papers.

11. Copies of *A Choice, Not an Echo* are in box 13, Kathryn Fink Dunaway Papers, Manuscripts and Rare Books Library, Robert W. Woodruff Library, Emory University, Atlanta, Ga. (hereafter, Dunaway Papers).

12. Critchlow, *Phyllis Schlafly and Grassroots Conservatism*, 138–39. Critchlow writes that Schlafly passed out suggested reading lists.

13. *Troup County Trumpet*, May 1965, no folder, box 3, Ague Miller Papers.

14. Mrs. V. C. Wade and Mrs. L. T. McVey of Valdosta, Georgia, to Lee Ague, Apr. 14, 1967, no folder, box 5, Ague Miller Papers. Wade and McVey wrote in Ague's name in the salutation and added handwritten notes at the bottom which read, "We thought you might like to see the letter we wrote. — K" (Kathleen Wade) and "See you in Atlanta Wednesday. — C" (Clara McVey).

15. Rosalind K. Frame to "Fellow Republican," Mar. 27, 1967, no folder, box 5, Ague Miller Papers.

16. Georgia Federation of Republican Women, program of the Biennial Convention, Apr. 20, 1967, Atlanta, Ga., no folder, Ague Miller Papers. The convention proceedings included reports from all committees, the election of officers, and a keynote address from Schlafly. The program does not mention any workshops, which generally happened at the level of local clubs.

17. Republican Party of Georgia, "Mrs. Estelle Lee Ague of Smyrna is State Finance Chairman," press release, Apr. 3, 1967, no folder, box 8, Ague Miller Papers.

18. Georgia Federation of Republican Women, program of the Biennial Convention, Apr. 20, 1967, Atlanta, Ga., no folder, Ague Miller Papers.

19. Program, NFRW Convention, May 5–6, 1967, Washington, D.C., no folder, box 5, Ague Miller Papers. The states with the most delegate votes were Ohio with 462, New York with 100, and Pennsylvania with 393. These large states were considered friendlier toward O'Donnell's moderation than Schlafly's conservatism. However, delegates cast individual ballots, meaning that state delegations could split. Texas had 67 votes; Alabama, 54; South Carolina, 24.

20. Ibid.

21. Rymph, *Republican Women*, 178–80; Critchlow, *Phyllis Schlafly and Grassroots Conservatism*, 142–47.

22. Pennsylvania Council of Republican Women to Mrs. Charles L. Brooks, n.d., and Bobbie Ames (Alabama FRW) to Mrs. John Glaze, Apr. 17, 1967, folder 6, box 1, Dunaway Papers; *Singalong for Phyllis Schlafly*, brochure, n.d., folder 8, box 7, Dunaway Papers (emphasis in original).

23. This GFRW battle is covered in greater detail at the end of chapter 1.

24. Gladys O'Donnell to Lee Ague, Apr. 22, 1967, no folder, box 6, Ague Miller Papers. The letter is on "GOP Unity" letterhead, again stressing the message that support for the national nominee O'Donnell was also a vote for NFRW unity.

25. Digna Yurick, clipping from *Success* 11, no. 6, Apr. 10, 1967, 9, folder 5, box 7, Dunaway papers; Marie Smith, "Two GOP Rivals Unbutton Gloves," *Washington Post and Times Herald*, May 3, 1967, D1.

26. Muriel Dobbin, "2 Hostile but Polite Women Battle for GOP Leadership," *Baltimore Sun*, May 3, 1967, A1.

27. Ibid.; Marie Smith, "Two GOP Rivals Unbutton Gloves," *Washington Post and Times Herald*, May 3, 1967, D1.

28. Rymph, *Republican Women*, 181.

29. Evelyn Frazier, "Report of the Metropolitan Club," February 18, 1968, folder "February 17, 1968 Fed. Board Meeting," box 3, Ague Miller Papers.

30. Charles Pou, "Georgia Politics," *Atlanta Journal and Constitution*, May 14, 1967, 14, no folder, box 5, Ague Miller Papers. The *Atlanta Journal* and *Atlanta Constitution* ran a joint issue on Sundays.

31. Critchlow, *Phyllis Schlafly and Grassroots Conservatism*, 155–57. Quotation of Isaiah 40:31 is from the King James Version. Various artists recorded different songs ti-

tled "P.S. I Love You," so those wearing the ribbon may have been referring to either the Beatles or the Frank Sinatra song, probably depending on the generation of the wearer. Others may have thought of Billie Holiday's version of the same song Sinatra covered. The Schlafly campaign literature does not make a distinction among the artists or composers, though. *Singalong for Phyllis Schlafly* includes rewritten lyrics for "P.S. I Love You," but does not specify which of these songs they are based on. *Singalong for Phyllis Schlafly*, brochure, n.d., folder 8, box 7, Dunaway Papers.

32. Critchlow, *Phyllis Schlafly and Grassroots Conservatism*, 157.

33. Rymph, *Republican Women*, 181–82; Critchlow, *Phyllis Schlafly and Grassroots Conservatism*, 157–58.

34. Isabelle Shelton, "Phyllis Schlafly's Strategy," *Baltimore Sun*, June 4, 1967, FC4; Schlafly quoted in Critchlow, *Phyllis Schlafly and Grassroots Conservatism*, 158.

35. Shelton, "Phyllis Schlafly's Strategy," *Baltimore Sun*, June 4, 1967, FC4.

36. Ibid.

37. Kathryn F. Dunaway, report to the GFRW board of directors, September 9, 1967, envelope addressed to Mrs. Al McEachin, box 5, Ague Miller Papers. This envelope held several materials and appeared to be more for storage than for organization. However, as this document was in the envelope, I have made note of it here.

38. Phyllis Schlafly to "Friend," August 1, 1967; *Phyllis Schlafly Report*, August 1967, October 1967, folder 8, box 1, Dunaway Papers.

39. Mrs. William T. Smith, Tift County FRW report to the board, February 17, 1968, and Eloise M. Cumbaa, Columbus Area Republican Woman's Club report to the board, February 17, 1968, folder "FEBRUARY 17, 1968 Fed. Board Meeting," box 3, Ague Miller Papers. At this meeting, board presidents presented their activity reports for the full previous year. Phyllis Schlafly to Kathryn Dunaway, October 30, 1967, folder 8, box 1, Dunaway Papers.

40. Gladys O'Donnell to Lee Ague, May 17, 1967, no folder, box 8, Ague Miller Papers.

41. Frank Troutman to Lee Ague, July 31, 1967; Bo Callaway to Lee Ague, July 24, 1967; G. Paul Jones to Lee Ague, July 19, 1967; all in no folder, box 8, Ague Miller Papers.

42. Kathryn Dunaway, "Report to GFRW Board," Feb. 17, 1968, folder "February 17, 1968 Fed. Board Meeting," box 3, Ague Miller Papers.

43. Mrs. Lucas E. (Marjean) Birt, "Report of State Membership Chairman," Feb. 17, 1968, folder "February 17, 1968, Fed. Board Meeting," box 3, Ague Miller Papers.

44. Few Mixon, "Report of the Third District Chairman"; Blanche Wynne, "Report of the Fourth District Chairman"; Oleeta Aspinwall, "Report of Troup County FRW"; Barbara L. Monous, "Report of Cherokee County FRW"; Louise Wofford, "Hall County FRW"; all in folder "February 17, 1968 Fed. Board Meeting," box 3, Ague Miller Papers.

45. Mrs. W. F. Norton, "Report of Richmond County FRW," folder "February 17, 1968 Fed. Board Meeting," box 3, Ague Miller Papers.

46. Republican Party of Georgia, press release, Nov. 8, 1967, folder "Press Releases," box 5, Ague Miller Papers.

47. Republican Party of Georgia, press release, Feb. 9, 1968, folder "Press Releases," box 5, Ague Miller Papers.

48. Eleanor Alexander, "Report of Bibb County FRW," folder "February 17, 1968 Fed. Board Meeting," box 3, Ague Miller Papers.

49. The Pickett family had a long tradition in the state Republican Party, which included much experience with party division. In 1916, Roscoe Pickett Sr. ran on the Republican ticket on the issues of a protective tariff for the state's cotton manufacturers and opposition to Prohibition. The Georgia GOP that year also endorsed an anti-

lynching platform, proposing legislation that would require a county to pay a lynching victim's family ten thousand dollars and make the sheriff ineligible for reelection. Pickett lost the race but remained active in the state GOP. The senior Pickett also had experience with division within the Georgia Republican Party. In 1916, 1920, 1928, and 1930, the *Atlanta Constitution* reported on the state's Republican factionalism. Pickett Sr. led a factional group in all but 1916, when he was the party candidate. The disruptions involved pledged votes. In 1928, Pickett led a faction that supported "Joe Watson, negro" over "Ben J. Davis, negro." The younger Pickett followed in his father's footsteps when he assumed leadership of a faction that in 1952 submitted a list of electors committed to Robert Taft rather than Dwight Eisenhower for Republican presidential nominee. Pickett withdrew the slate after much national attention. Thus, the showdown for Pickett Jr. in 1967 fit in the same way with the family tradition of GOP factionalism. "Two Conventions Held Wednesday by Georgia GOP," *Atlanta Constitution*, Apr. 13, 1916; "Roscoe Pickett Now in Governor's Race," *Atlanta Constitution*, Oct. 15, 1916; "Showdown Seen in GOP Fight," *Atlanta Constitution*, Aug. 11, 1928; "Georgia Revolt Ends: Anti-Eisenhower Group Withdraws Elector Slate," *New York Times*, Aug. 12, 1952.

50. "A Split Develops in Georgia G.O.P." *New York Times*, Dec. 3, 1967.

51. Cecilia Smith, Tifton, Ga., to Hon. H. P. Callaway [sic], Pine Mountain, Ga., n.d., folder 1, "Republican Party of Georgia," box II-B-24, series 2, Howard H. (Bo) Callaway Papers, Richard B. Russell Library for Political Research and Studies, University of Georgia, Athens, Ga.

52. Galphin, *Riddle of Lester Maddox*, 158, 202–4. In 1966, George Wallace's wife Lurleen won the gubernatorial election, effectively allowing for another George Wallace governorship. Legal restrictions prevented George Wallace from holding the office for consecutive terms. Goldwater's insult dismissed not only Maddox's politics, but also his food. Maddox's restaurant had featured fried chicken, not hot dogs.

53. Robert Sherrill, "Nixon's Man in Dixie," *New York Times*, Sept. 15, 1968, SM32.

54. Jack Nelson, "Romney Confers with Georgia GOP Leaders," *Los Angeles Times*, Sept. 27, 1967, 16; Robert P. Hey, "Dirksen Whips Up Republican Zeal in Georgia," *Christian Science Monitor*, Oct. 28, 1967, 5.

55. Kevin P. Phillips, *Emerging Republican Majority*, 211–32, 287n, 287.

56. Carter, *Politics of Rage*, 326.

57. Lassiter, *Silent Majority*, 227.

58. Robert Sherrill, "Nixon's Man in Dixie," *New York Times*, Sept. 15, 1968, SM32.

59. Ibid.

60. Virginia Estes to Dee Hardin, Nov. 11, 1968, folder "Lamar County," box 5, Ague Miller Papers.

61. "GOP Women Can Attend Convention," *Atlanta Daily World*, Jan. 24, 1968.

62. Perlstein, *Nixonland*, 297.

63. "The Metropolitan Atlanta Republican Women Salutes America" 1971, folder 8, box 6, series 4, Evelyn J. Frazier Papers, Auburn Avenue Research Library for African American Culture and History, Fulton County Library System, Atlanta, Ga. Upon honoring Frazier in 1971, the club retold the story of her participation at the 1968 GOP convention.

64. Roena Sawyer, "Report of Houston County FRW" box 4, Ague Miller Papers.

65. Report of the Cobb County FRW, Sept. 21, 1968, folder "Minutes, Federation Board Meeting, September 21, 1968," box 4, Ague Miller Papers. The Cobb County FRW president is not named in the minutes.

66. Lyn W. Thornton, "Clarke County Report," Sept. 21, 1968, folder "Minutes, Federa-

tion Board Meeting, September 21, 1968," box 4, Ague Miller Papers. The Tenth District coordinator is not named in the minutes.

67. Roena Sawyer, "Report of Houston County FRW"; Mrs. Grace Haddock, "Peach County FRW"; Eleanor Alexander, "Bibb County Report," Federation Board Meeting, Sept. 21, 1968, box 4, Ague Miller Papers.

68. Bessie M. Militades, "Report of the First and Tenth Districts," Federation Board Meeting, Sept. 20, 1968, folder "Minutes, Federation Board Meeting, 09/21/1968," box 4, Ague Miller Papers.

69. "Tenth District Report," Federation Board Meeting, Sept. 20, 1968, folder "Minutes, Federation Board Meeting, 09/21/1968," box 4, Ague Miller Papers. The Tenth District coordinator is not named in the minutes.

70. JoAnne Williams, "The Wallace Phenomenon," *Distaff*, March 1968, folder 9, box 12; Mike McKenzie to CCFRW and Williams to McKenzie, reprinted in *Distaff*, June 1968, folder 9, box 12, Dunaway Papers.

71. Bartley and Graham, *Southern Elections*, 95, 363; "1968 Presidential Election Results—Georgia," Dave Leip's Atlas of U.S. Elections, http://www.uselectionatlas.org /RESULTS/state.php?f=0&fips=13&year=1968.

72. Virginia Estes to Dee Hardin, Nov. 11, 1968, folder "Lamar County," box 5, Ague Miller Papers. This correspondence is in this file, despite its lack of relevance to Lamar County.

73. "GFRW . . . Today," May 3, 1969, folder "Biennial Convention," box 3, Ague Miller Papers.

74. Critchlow, *Phyllis Schlafly and Grassroots Conservatism*, 159; "Minutes of the Board of Directors Meeting of the GFRW," Sept. 21, 1968, at Callaway Gardens, Ga., folder "GFRW Board meeting 2/15/69," box 3, Ague Miller Papers. While the folder is designated as the 1969 spring meeting date, the document itself has the 1968 autumn date.

75. Dunaway's post-GFRW work is analyzed in greater depth in chapters 5 and 6, which focus on her work against the Equal Rights Amendment in Georgia.

Chapter 4. Thousands of Mothers Make a Movement

1. Richard M. Nixon, "First Inaugural Address," Jan. 20, 1969, reprinted in *U.S. Presidential Inaugural Addresses* (Bibliobazaar, 2006, Kindle); Elly Peterson, "Participation by Women," *Focus*, newsletter published by the NFRW, Washington, D.C., vol. 2, no. 6, Jun.–Jul. 1969, 1.

2. "Very Confidential Memo" from Harry Dent to Bob Haldeman and John Ehrlichman, Feb. 3, 1969, folder 6, box 10, location 2/B/2/1, Harry Dent Files, White House Special Files, Staff Member Office Files, Richard Nixon Presidential Library and Museum, National Archives and Records Administration, Yorba Linda, Calif.

3. Ague Miller interview, May 31, 2014; Raymonde Alexander, "Green Acres: A Former City Slicker from New York Discovers What Rural Life is All About," *Atlanta Constitution*, May 27, 1976, 3B. In our interview, Lee Miller told me that Gene adopted her children. She did not want to talk about her divorce from Bob Ague.

4. Ague Miller interview, May 31, 2014; Lassiter, *Silent Majority*, 244–45, 131–47; Kruse, *White Flight*, 239–47; Douglas, *Reading, Writing, and Race*. Lee Miller's local work focused on Columbus, Georgia. For more on the busing plans and legal battles in Atlanta, see Brown-Nagin, *Courage to Dissent*, 360–408, 418–29.

5. Perlstein, *Nixonland*, 300. *Swann v. Charlotte-Mecklenburg Board of Education* be-

came the Supreme Court case that ruled busing constitutional in 1971. In 1968, the case was still awaiting decision in the federal courts.

6. Ibid.

7. "Gladys O'Donnell Establishes Education Committee," NFRW press release, May 22, 1969, folder "Press Release—Ga. Governor & General Press clipping," box 4, Lee Ague Miller Papers, Unprocessed Record Group, Georgia Archives, Morrow, Ga. (hereafter, Ague Miller Papers).

8. "Hotline Kickoff Set Today," *Columbus Ledger*, May 26, 1969, clipping in folder "Focus," box 4, Ague Miller Papers. Dee Hardin moved to Columbus and lived in the Millers' house during the OLAE campaign, Ague Miller interview, May 31, 2014. While Miller designed the work of OLAE to support Republican political movements against busing, she had inherited a legacy of white southern women before her who had been the voices of segregationist demonstrations since the 1954 *Brown v. Board* decision. In *Massive Resistance and Southern Womanhood*, historian Rebecca Brückmann analyzes the roles of white women in school segregation movements in Arkansas, Louisiana, and South Carolina in the 1950s–60s. She argues that "[white] women's activism in Little Rock and New Orleans emerged out of an impending crisis, one they helped create" (11). Lee Miller was working in the context those women created and continued to foster a perceived crisis of busing and integration for the social purpose of white supremacy and the political purpose of increasing GOP influence in the South.

9. "Operation Lend-An-Ear" survey, *Athens Banner-Herald*, June 6, 1969, clipping in folder "Press—EAC," box 4, Ague Miller Papers.

10. Operation Lend-An-Ear survey form, no folder, box 3, Ague Miller Papers.

11. Lee Miller to Mrs. Jill Dover of Ft. Lauderdale, Fla., Oct. 8, 1969, unlabeled folder, box 3, Ague Miller Papers.

12. Letter from Bette Bannister, Georgia EAC coordinator, to Educational Advisory Committee members, n.d., unlabeled folder, box 3, Ague Miller Papers.

13. Harry S. Dent to Lee Miller, June 19, 1969, no folder, box 3, Ague Miller Papers.

14. Mattie Fiske, Quitman, Ga., returned survey, and P. H. Thompson, Newton, Ga., returned survey, both in no folder, box 4, Ague Miller Papers.

15. Mrs. Gene Miller, "Address of Mrs. Gene Miller to the NFRW Biennial Convention," Washington, D.C., Sept. 27, 1969, folder "Speech Material," box 3, Ague Miller Papers. The women collected the surveys, but did not record the official count of surveys. In order to reach a million Georgians, however, they would have had to reach just over 20 percent of Georgia's 4,589,575 people. More likely, they reached tens of thousands. Georgia population figure from 1970 United States Census, census.gov/population /cencounts/ga190090.txt.

16. Mrs. W. B. Mitchell to Lee Miller, Sept. 29, 1969, unlabeled folder, box 3, Ague Miller Papers.

17. Handwritten note from Joel Fisher to "Lee, Gene, Dee, and Kids," July 22, 1969, no folder, box 8, Ague Miller Papers. The note is handwritten on White House stationery. Fisher was assistant deputy counsel to the president. "A Community Involvement Plan: National 'I Care About People' Program," n.d., no folder, box 8, Ague Miller Papers. "I Care about People" is crossed out, with "Be a Doer" handwritten beneath it (emphasis in original).

18. Confidential memo from Joel M. Fisher to Harry S. Dent, "Re: Voluntary Action Programs (Preliminary Report #3)," July 23, 1969, no folder, box 4, Ague Miller Papers.

19. On the effect of desegregation cases, and particularly busing cases, in southern

cities, see Brown-Nagin, *Courage to Dissent*, 357–408; and Lassiter, *Silent Majority*, 160–97. Brown-Nagin focuses on the Black community's response in Atlanta while Lassiter analyzes the suburban politics of Charlotte, N.C., at the time of the court case bearing that city's name.

20. Kevin P. Phillips, *Emerging Republican Majority*, 463, 467–68; Lassiter, *Silent Majority*, 250–74. Lassiter called the 1970 midterm elections the "Failure of the Southern Strategy." The women of the GFRW, though, considered themselves to be in the middle of a revolution. OLAE was a means of building their conservative arsenal.

21. Nickerson, *Mothers of Conservatism*, xiii.

22. "Local Toastmistress Wins for Third Time," *Sunday Ledger-Enquirer*, Columbus, Ga., May 4, 1969, E-10, no folder, box "School Injunction" in box 8, Ague Miller Papers.

23. Ibid.

24. Mrs. Gene Miller, "Address of Mrs. Gene Miller to the NFRW Biennial Convention," Washington, D.C., Sept. 27, 1969, folder "Speech Material," box 3, Ague Miller Papers.

25. Ibid.

26. Mrs. Gene Miller to Mrs. Betty Shattles of Americus, Ga., Oct. 8, 1969, unlabeled folder, box 3, Ague Miller Papers. On Strom Thurmond and busing, see Crespino, *Strom Thurmond's America*, 256–58. Crespino notes that, like Miller, Thurmond began to view and discuss busing as a national rather than a regional issue.

27. Lee Miller to Sen. Jacob Javits, Oct. 8, 1969, unlabeled folder, box 3, Ague Miller Papers.

28. Constance Armitage to Lee Miller, Oct. 7, 1969, no folder, box 3, Ague Miller Papers. In this letter, Armitage also welcomes Miller back to NFRW events and mentions that she is looking well after her illness. OLAE was Lee Ague Miller's triumphant return to NFRW activism.

29. Lee Miller to Mrs. Jill Dover of Ft. Lauderdale, Fla., Oct. 8, 1969, unlabeled folder, box 3, Ague Miller Papers.

30. Ibid.

31. Miller to Barbara Walters, Nov. 13, 1969, and Miller to Mrs. David Delbridge, Jan. 12, 1970, no folder, box 2, Ague Miller Papers.

32. OLAE responses from Stevens Point, Wisc., unlabeled brown envelope, box 5, Ague Miller Papers.

33. OLAE surveys mailed from Mrs. R. W. Wackley, Calabasas, Calif., to Mrs. Gene Miller, Columbus, Ga., in original envelope, no folder, box 4, Ague Miller Papers. On conservative women's work and influence in southern California, see McGirr, *Suburban Warriors*; and Nickerson, *Mothers of Conservatism*.

34. Draft of article from Lee Miller to Edie [no surname], n.d., unlabeled folder within folder "National Republican Committee," box 5, Ague Miller Papers.

35. Ibid.

36. Ibid. The separate Department of Education was established in 1979. Ronald Reagan proposed to eliminate the department, and elimination of the Department of Education has been a conservative campaign talking point in many recent primaries and elections.

37. Frank Miller was a state senator representing DeKalb County, a suburb of Atlanta and a stronghold of Republican votes in the past three elections. Lester Maddox had briefly considered following his friend George Wallace's example and running his wife for the governorship, but Maddox apparently decided against that.

38. Ed Rogers, "G.O.P.'s Suit Confers with President Nixon," *Atlanta Daily World*, Sept.

27, 1970, 1; "Suit Proposes $6,500 Pay as Minimum for Teachers," *Atlanta Daily World*, Oct. 29, 1970, 1.

39. "Hal Suit Opens Westside Headquarters," *Atlanta Daily World*, Oct. 1, 1970, 1; "We Again Commend Mr. Suit," *Atlanta Daily World*, Oct. 29, 1970, 6.

40. "Republican Women Hold Banquet Friday Night," *Atlanta Daily World*, Oct. 29, 1970, 1; Evelyn Frazier, notes for speech, folder 7, box 5, series 4, Evelyn J. Frazier Papers, Auburn Avenue Research Library for African American Culture and History, Fulton County Library System, Atlanta, Georgia (hereafter, Evelyn J. Frazier Papers).

41. "Eleven Negroes Elected to Legislature; Carter Over Suit; Thompson Over Young," *Atlanta Daily World*, Nov. 5, 1970, 1. On the Democratic primary in which Andrew Young beat Lonnie King, see Brown-Nagin, *Courage to Dissent*, 357–58.

42. Kevin P. Phillips, *Emerging Republican Majority*, 464.

43. "What Is the Black Silent Majority?" folder 4, box 5, series 4, Evelyn J. Frazier Papers.

44. Ibid. In *Loneliness of the Black Republican*, Leah Wright Rigueur addresses the origins and work of the National Black Silent Majority Committee (207–12). The group was founded on July 4, 1970, and within two years had grown to 8,500 members in thirty states.

45. Mrs. Jesse Hargro Kelly to Evelyn Frazier, Feb. 19, 1970, folder 8, box 6, series 4, Evelyn J. Frazier Papers.

46. "The Metropolitan Atlanta Republican Women Salutes America," folder 8, box 6, series 4, Evelyn J. Frazier Papers.

47. "Parade Program—WSB Television's Salute to America Parade," July 5, 1971, folder 9, box 6, series 4, Evelyn J. Frazier Papers. The parade was held on July 5 because the 4th fell on a Sunday.

48. "Virgin Islands Gov. Cites Danger for Negroes Staying in One Party," *Atlanta Daily World*, Nov. 23, 1971, 1.

49. Ibid.; Awards list, folder 8, box 6, series 4, Evelyn J. Frazier Papers. C. A. Scott assumed the leadership of the *Atlanta Daily World* upon his brother W. A. Scott's death.

50. Frazier to Andrew Young, Nov. 29, 1972, folder 7, box 5, series 4, Evelyn J. Frazier Papers.

51. Frazier to Richard Nixon, Dec. 26, 1972, folder 8, box 5, series 4, Evelyn J. Frazier Papers.

52. "Large, Festive Crowd Observes President Nixon's Inauguration," *Atlanta Daily World*, Jan. 21, 1973, 1. Other Atlanta attendees included chairman of the Georgia Black Committee for Re-Election of the President Dr. C. Clayton Powell and his wife, *Atlanta Daily World* publisher C. A. Scott, Metropolitan Club member Ruth Simmons, Lowell Dicker, Herman Russell, Richard Rowe, Mr. and Mrs. T. M. Alexander, and Mr. and Mrs. T. M. Alexander Jr. The chair of the Political Science Department at Morris Brown College, Charles E. Price, also attended with his wife. Price had been one of the twelve Republican electors from Georgia in the last presidential election. "To Cast Electoral Vote for President Nixon," *Atlanta Daily World*, Dec. 14, 1972, 1.

Chapter 5. The Cause of American Womanhood

1. Telephone message from Lee Miller to Jill Ruckelshaus, folder 6 "Jill Ruckelshaus, Patricia Lindh, Jean Spence File," box 20, Anne Armstrong Papers, Nixon Presidential Library. The date on the memo is March 13, though there is no year. From mate-

rial around it, this phone call would have been made in 1973. This is the only record I have found of Lee Miller mentioning the Equal Rights Amendment. In our oral history, she said that she did not support it, but she was never active either way. This memo suggests she supported it, at least as a Nixon White House and NFRW goal. During the years of the ERA battles, Lee Miller led anti-busing movements in Georgia and nation-wide, covered in Chapter 4.

2. The House passed the ERA bill in a 354–23 vote on Oct. 12, 1971. The Senate followed with a vote of 84–8 on Mar. 22, 1972. Eileen Shanahan, "Equal Rights Amendment Passed by House, 354–23," Oct. 12, 1971, *New York Times*, 1; "Equal Rights Amendment is Approved by Congress," Mar. 23, 1972, *New York Times*, 1. See Felsenthal, *Sweetheart of the Silent Majority*, 234.

3. "Georgia Senate Votes Suffrage for Women," *New York Times*, Feb. 17, 1970, 10.

4. O'Donnell to all state presidents and board members, June 15, 1970, folder 8, box 2, South Carolina Federation of Republican Women Papers, Louise Pettus Archives, Dacus Library, Winthrop University, Rock Hill, S.C. Hereafter, SCFRW papers.

5. Mrs. J. Lloyd O'Donnell, "Women in Government" (1970), folder 8, box 2, SCFRW papers; Gladys O'Donnell to Beverly [no surname], Feb. 4, 1971, folder 8, box 2, SC-FRW papers. O'Donnell was a longtime feminist trailblazer and was one of the original ninety-nine members of the Ninety-Nines: International Organization of Women Pilots, founded in 1929.

6. Warren Weaver Jr., "Defeated Leader Sets Up a Rival Group for Republican Women," *New York Times*, Aug. 9, 1967, 21.

7. Felsenthal, *Sweetheart of the Silent Majority*, 193–94.

8. Schlafly interview, June 8, 2009.

9. Phyllis Schlafly, "What's Wrong with 'Equal Rights' for Women?," *Phyllis Schlafly Report* (hereafter, PSR), February 1972, box 11, Kathryn Fink Dunaway Papers, Manuscripts and Rare Books Library, Robert W. Woodruff Library, Emory University, Atlanta, Ga. (hereafter, Dunaway Papers). Cognitive scientist and linguist George Lakoff has studied this rhetorical difference in American political discourse. He suggests that conservatives view the family as the basic unit of society while liberals believe it is the individual. See Lakoff, *Moral Politics*.

10. Schlafly, "What's Wrong with 'Equal Rights' for Women?," PSR, February 1972, box 11, Dunaway Papers.

11. Ibid.

12. Ibid. For analyses of household technology and its effects on both American capitalism and women's household labor, see Cowan, *More Work for Mother*; Coontz, *Way We Never Were*; and May, *Homeward Bound*.

13. Ibid. (emphasis in original).

14. Critchlow, *Phyllis Schlafly and Grassroots Conservatism*, 23; Marshall Dunaway (Kathryn's youngest son) interview, August 2006.

15. Felsenthal, *Sweetheart of the Silent Majority*, 269. Marjorie Spruill (*Divided We Stand*, 81) addresses the power of Schlafly's sharp sarcasm in these early newsletters, as they set the tone for the later fight against the ERA.

16. Judy Klemesrud, "Opponent of E.R.A. Confident of Its Defeat," *New York Times*, Dec. 15, 1975, 53.

17. Schlafly interview, June 8, 2009.

18. Kathryn Dunaway and Lee Wysong first became friends in the DAR, but carried the friendship over when they both became active in Georgia Republican politics in the 1960s. Wysong interview, August 15, 2006.

19. Ibid.

20. Ibid.

21. Ibid.

22. Ibid.

23. "Stop ERA's Katherine [*sic*] Dunaway Spends Her Time Rallying Her 'Girls,'" *Atlanta Constitution*, May 2, 1979, B1. Clipping in folder 5, box 5, Dunaway Papers.

24. Wysong interview, August 15, 2006.

25. Historians have examined the ERA battles in key states like Sam Ervin's North Carolina and Schlafly's Illinois. Mathews and De Hart's *Sex, Gender, and the Politics of ERA* examines the two sides of the ERA debate in North Carolina over the course of the decade. Critchlow's *Phyllis Schlafly and Grassroots Conservatism* analyzes not only Schlafly's national work, but also her political activism in her home state of Illinois.

26. Letter from Jeanne Cahill to Georgia Commission on the Status of Women, Feb. 6, 1974, folder 3; Minutes of the Commission on the Status of Women meeting, Nov. 28, 1972, folder 2; both in Georgia Commission on the Status of Women Papers, Department of Human Relations, Georgia Archives, Morrow, Ga. (hereafter, CSW Papers).

27. Minutes of the Georgia Commission on the Status of Women, Sept. 19, 1972, folder 1, "1972," CSW Papers.

28. Dunaway marked a list of all speakers at a Georgia Women's Forum "SOW" to indicate their appointments to the commission (folder 3, box 5, Dunaway Papers); Schlafly regularly used "SOW" to refer to the commissions, as in her story on "The Arkansas SOWs" in "Are You Financing Women's Lib and ERA?," PSR, Feb. 7, 1974, box 11, Dunaway Papers.

29. Minutes of the Georgia Commission on the Status of Women, Sept. 19, 1972, folder 1, "1972," CSW Papers.

30. Ibid.

31. On the wage gap, see O'Neill, "Trend in the Male-Female Wage Gap." The figure of 64 cents to the dollar represents wages adjusted for hours as presented in O'Neill's article on page S94.

32. "How E.R.A. Will Hurt Men," PSR, May 1975, box 11, Dunaway Papers.

33. "The Fraud Called the Equal Rights Amendment," PSR, May 1972, box 11, Dunaway Papers. The underlying charge that girls would be preyed upon in schools hearkens back to the fearmongering surrounding white girls' sexuality in school-integration debates of the previous two decades. On the portrayal of white girls as both pawns and provocateurs in segregation movements, see Daniel, *Lost Revolutions*, 272–83; and Dailey, "Sex, Segregation, and the Sacred."

34. Mrs. John A Dunaway, "Con: ERA Is a Power Grab By Washington Lawmakers," *Atlanta Constitution*, Jan. 15, 1977, 1B.

35. Schlafly interview, June 8, 2009.

36. Quoted in Critchlow, *Phyllis Schlafly and Grassroots Conservatism*, 212–13.

37. Atlanta Women Who Want to be Women, "Ladies! Have You Heard?," n.d., folder 4, box 4, Dunaway Papers.

38. "ERA and Homosexual 'Marriages,'" PSR, September 1974, box 11, Dunaway Papers. The kidnapping of Patty Hearst by the Symbionese Liberation Army happened in February 1974. Singer Anita Bryant launched her campaign against gay teachers in Miami-Dade County in 1976, embracing many of the same arguments about traditional American families that Schlafly had been promoting. Bryant wrote about the anti-gay campaign in *The Anita Bryant Story*. For historical analysis and placement of Bryant among her contemporaries, see Johnson, *This Is Our Message*.

39. "How Will ERA Change State Laws?," PSR, April 1973, box 11, Dunaway Papers.

40. "S.O.S. memorandum" from Dorothy Gibson to members of the Commission on the Status of Women, Jan. 18, 1973, folder 2– 1973, CSW papers (emphasis in original).

41. Bill Montgomery, "Women's Rights Backers Say Men's Room is Safe," *Atlanta Journal*, Feb. 7, 1973, 2–A.

42. "Protest Equal Rights Bill," *Tri-State Defender* (Memphis, Tenn.), Feb. 17, 1973, 5, in Georgia files, Eagle Forum Library and Archives, St. Louis, Mo. Deb Pentecost, archivist at the Eagle Forum Archives, generously photocopied all files related to Georgia. The files did not indicate folder numbers.

43. Ibid.

44. J. B. Stoner, "Dangers Posed by Women's Lib Amendment," n.d., photocopy in the STOP ERA Georgia files, Eagle Forum Library and Archives, St. Louis, Mo.

45. Bill Montgomery, "Women's Rights Backers Say Men's Room is Safe," *Atlanta Journal*, Feb. 7, 1973, 2A.

46. Maxwell and Shields, *Long Southern Strategy*, 9.

47. STOP ERA of Georgia, "Check List for Witnesses to Speak against ERA," n.d., folder 8, box 4, Dunaway Papers.

48. Spruill discusses how southern progressives made the link between racism and anti-feminism in *Divided We Stand*, 304–8.

49. Quoted in "Can a State Rescind Ratification of ERA?," PSR, June 1973.

50. The question of rescission may become relevant again in months or years after this book's publication. Virginia ratified the ERA in January 2019, becoming the thirty-eighth state to do so, though after the 1982 deadline covered in the next chapter. Debates over the deadline's legality will almost surely come alongside debates over the rights of states to rescind their votes for ERA ratification. Five states—Nebraska (1973), Tennessee (1974), Idaho (1977), Kentucky (1978), and South Dakota (1979)—voted to rescind their previous approval of ERA. In Georgia, the amendment remains unratified. On possible futures of the ERA since the Virginia vote, see Garrett Epps, "The Equal Rights Amendment Strikes Again," *Atlantic*, January 20, 2019, https://www.theatlantic.com /ideas/archive/2019/01/will-congress-ever-ratify-equal-rights-amendment/580849.

51. "Section 2 of the Equal Rights Amendment," PSR, May 1973, in box 11, Dunaway Papers.

52. Mrs. Allen Jones to Kathryn Dunaway, Dec. 27, 1973, folder 26, box 1, Dunaway Papers.

53. Margaret Scharmitzky to Kathryn Dunaway, Jan. 12, 1974, folder 27, box 1, Dunaway Papers.

54. Erin Sherman to Kathryn Dunaway, folder 29, box 1, Dunaway Papers.

55. Schlafly to state STOP ERA chairmen, Feb. 14, 1974, folder 19, box 1, Dunaway Papers. Recall that STOP ERA used the "chairman" title regardless of the sex of the office-holder. On evangelical women's political awakening in the 1970s, see Johnson, *This is Our Message*.

56. Williams, *God's Own Party*, 105–10, 157–58. Johnson's *This is Our Message* profiles the work of individual women in the New Right.

57. "E.R.A.'s Assist to Abortion," PSR, December 1974, box 11, Dunaway Papers. Interestingly, this is the newsletter from December, a month during which she easily could have linked to religious holidays and religious ideas about birth.

58. "E.R.A.'s Purpose: To Shrink Population," PSR, December 1974, box 11, Dunaway Papers. Schlafly also addressed abortion and zero population growth in several other issues, including those of June 1975, July 1975, October 1975, December 1979, and August

1980. Maxwell and Shields (*Long Southern Strategy*, 191–92) discuss how anti-feminism and "southern Christian moralism" joined around issues like abortion, birth control, and, especially, the federal court decisions that enabled more American women to access them.

59. *The Abortion Connection*, published by Eagle Forum, n.d., folder 1, box 3, Dunaway Papers. The quotes from this pamphlet are listed as from 1975, so the piece likely came out in 1975 or 1976.

60. Mary Kelly to Kathryn Dunaway, Nov. 8, 1973, folder 27, box 1, Dunaway Papers.

Chapter 6. Breadmaker Politics

1. "Stop ERA's Katherine [*sic*] Dunaway Spends Her Time Rallying Her 'Girls,'" *Atlanta Constitution*, May 2, 1979, B1.

2. Kathryn Dunaway to Chester Gray, Feb. 6, 1974, folder 20, box 1, Kathryn Fink Dunaway Papers, Manuscripts and Rare Books Library, Robert W. Woodruff Library, Emory University, Atlanta, Ga. (hereafter, Dunaway Papers).

3. Schlafly to state STOP ERA chairmen, Feb. 14, 1974, folder 19, box 1, Dunaway papers.

4. Cake tag, folder 7, box 2, Dunaway Papers.

5. Wysong interview, August 15, 2006.

6. Marshall Dunaway interview. He remembered that his mother was known for her devil's food cake.

7. "Stop ERA's Katherine [*sic*] Dunaway Spends Her Time Rallying Her 'Girls,'" *Atlanta Constitution*, May 2, 1979, B1.

8. Rosalynn Carter, *First Lady from Plains*, 102–3.

9. Sam Miller, "Equal Rights Amendment Defeated by Ga House," *Atlanta Daily World*, Jan. 31, 1974, 2.

10. Letter from Jeanne Cahill to commission members, Feb. 6, 1974, Georgia Commission on the Status of Women Papers, Department of Human Resources, Georgia Archives, Morrow, Ga.

11. Kathryn Dunaway to Canter Brown, Feb. 6, 1974, folder 20, box 1, Dunaway Papers.

12. Form letter from Kathryn Dunaway and Lee Wysong to "Mr. Legislator," Feb. 6, 1974, folder 2, box 7, Dunaway Papers.

13. Examples of these thank-you notes are in folder 20, box 1, Dunaway Papers.

14. Mrs. William R. Bass to Kathryn Dunaway, Jan. 31, 1974, folder 27, box 1, Dunaway Papers.

15. Mrs. R. W. Patterson, College Park, Ga., to Kathryn Dunaway, Jan. 30, 1974, folder 24, box 1, Dunaway papers.

16. Mrs. John Preston Younger to Kathryn Dunaway, Jan. 30, 1974, folder 29, box 1, Dunaway Papers.

17. Loretta Vitale to Kathryn Dunaway, Apr. 3, 1973, folder 29, box 1, Dunaway Papers.

18. Lena Fay Parish to Kathryn Dunaway, Jan. 17, 1974, folder 26, box 1, Dunaway Papers.

19. Angelynn McGuff to Kathryn Dunaway, n.d., folder 26, box 1, Dunaway Papers.

20. Mrs. R. K. (Jean) Stovall to Kathryn Dunaway (via *Atlanta Journal*), Mar. 22, 1974, folder 27, box 1, Dunaway Papers.

21. Kathryn Dunaway and Lee Wysong to "Friend," June 1, 1974, folder 23, box 1, Dunaway Papers.

22. Lee Wysong to candidates, September 1974, folder 2, box 7, Dunaway Papers.

23. Leonard B. Brown to STOP ERA, n.d., folder 2, box 7, Dunaway Papers.

24. Wysong to candidates, September 1974, folder 2, box 7, Dunaway Papers.

25. Kathryn Dunaway and Lee Wysong to STOP ERA members, Nov. 1974, folder 2, box 7, Dunaway Papers.

26. Sarah Cash, "How the ERA Battle was Lost," *Atlanta Journal and Constitution*, Mar. 2, 1975, 4G.

27. Georgia STOP ERA Committee, editorial for Channel 5, Jan. 9, 1975, folder 2, box 7, Dunaway Papers. Earlier versions of this research appeared in Robin Morris, "Kathryn Dunaway (1906–1980): Grassroots Conservatism and the STOP ERA Campaign," in *Georgia Women: Their Lives and Times*, vol. 2, eds. Ann Short Chirhart and Kathleen Ann Clark (Athens: University of Georgia Press, 2014).

28. William Cotterell, "ERA Rejected by Georgia Senate," *Washington Post*, Feb. 18, 1975, A2. Though "lady" and "woman" may frequently be used as synonyms, they carry different power, with connotations of class and race. In her history of politically active southern women, Anne Firor Scott asserts, "Slavery had a good deal to do with the idea of the southern lady." The ability to own an enslaved person elevated a woman's status as it enshrined her whiteness. However, she remained beneath white men because, as Scott writes, "Obedient, faithful, submissive women strengthened the image of men who thought themselves vigorous, intelligent, commanding leaders." Scott, *Southern Lady*, 16–21. This image of a "lady" as submissive, higher-status, and white lingers in the twentieth century usage by these Georgia politicians.

29. Fred Schlafly to Catherine [*sic*] Dunaway, Feb. 18, 1975, folder 4, box 2, Dunaway papers.

30. "North Dakota is 34th State to Back Equal Rights Bid," *New York Times*, Feb. 4, 1975, 31.

31. Evaluations of Kathryn Dunaway, folder 5, box 4, Dunaway Papers. Lee Wysong told me that they usually wore red to communicate the message of "stop." In photos at the Capitol, Dunaway is always in red.

32. "Be a Voice, Not an Echo," folder 8, box 4, Dunaway Papers.

33. Georgia STOP ERA, "Tips When You Go on Television," n.d., folder 5, box 3, Dunaway Papers.

34. Letter from Atlanta Women's Chamber of Commerce to STOP ERA, Oct. 15, 1975, folder 17, box 6, Dunaway Papers.

35. "Outline for Speech," n.d., folder 24, box 5, Dunaway Papers.

36. American Mothers Committee, Inc., "Rules," folder 8, box 2, Dunaway Papers. I discuss Dunaway as a Cold War mother in chapter 2.

37. Tom Murphy to Georgia Mother's Committee, Nov. 7, 1975, folder 10, box 2, Dunaway Papers. Murphy went on to be the longest-serving speaker of any state's legislative body, serving as Georgia's speaker of the house from 1974 to 2002. He remained a staunch opponent of ERA and one of Dunaway's best assets in the Georgia legislature. Waskey, "Tom Murphy."

38. "Georgia Mother's Committee, Mother of the Year 1976," folder 8, box 2, Dunaway Papers.

39. Chairman's report on Constitution Week, 1975, folder 15, box 7, Dunaway Papers.

40. Wysong interview, August 15, 2006.

41. Chuck Edwards to STOP ERA, n.d., folder 2, box 7, Dunaway Papers. Wysong's note is handwritten on this letter.

42. Wade C. Hoyt III to Dunaway and Wysong, Aug. 6, 1976, folder 2, box 7, Dunaway Papers (emphasis in original).

43. Diane L. Fowlkes, assistant professor, Political Science Department, Georgia State University, to Kathryn Dunaway, Oct. 18, 1976, folder 6, box 2, Dunaway Papers.

44. Letters from Dunaway to Charles Stanley, Herschel Turner, and Curtis Hutson, Jan. 17, 1977, folder 7, box 2, Dunaway Papers.

45. Form letter from Kathryn Dunaway to unnamed persons, Jan. 31, 1977, folder 4, box 2, Dunaway Papers. On the history of women's activism in evangelical politics, see Williams, *God's Own Party*, 104–32; and Johnson, *This Is Our Message.*

46. STOP ERA organizational chart, folder 8, box 5, Dunaway papers. Kathryn Dunaway was a Methodist. Lee Wysong was Catholic.

47. Kathryn Dunaway and Lee Wysong, "May We Share with You Some of Our STOP ERA Activities," Jan. 26, 1977, folder 6, box 6, Dunaway Papers.

Chapter 7. The End of an ERA

1. Douglas E. Kneeland, "Boycott by Equal Rights Backers Puts Squeeze on Convention Cities," *New York Times*, Nov. 13, 1977, 1.

2. Carole Ashkinaze, "Impact of the ERA," *Atlanta Constitution*, Oct. 29, 1977, 4B. Among the national organizations boycotting unratified states were the League of Women Voters, the National Association of Social Workers, the American Library Association, and the Modern Language Association. These boycotts affected major convention cities like Atlanta, Chicago, Las Vegas, and New Orleans.

3. Kathryn Dunaway speech to Georgia Association of Broadcasters, Inc., Apr. 20, 1978, folder 3, box 1, Kathryn Fink Dunaway Papers, Manuscripts and Rare Books Library, Robert W. Woodruff Library, Emory University, Atlanta, Ga. (hereafter, Dunaway Papers).

4. "Corporate Responsibility Planning Service Report #580–49," June 11, 1979, folder 18, box 16, Papers of the Office of the First Lady, Jimmy Carter Presidential Library and Museum, Atlanta, Ga.

5. Spruill, *Divided We Stand*, 54. For the transition from the United Nations International Women's Year in 1975 to the U.S. IWY in 1977, see Spruill, 50–59. For background on the 1975 global events of a truly International Women's Year, see Jocelyn Olcott, *International Women's Year: The Greatest Consciousness-Raising Event in History* (New York: Oxford University Press, 2017).

6. Spruill, *Divided We Stand*, 58.

7. Phyllis Schlafly, "Federal Financing of a Foolish Feminist Festival," *Daughters of the American Revolution Magazine* 112, no. 3 (March 1978): 192; Spruill, *Divided We Stand*, 54–57.

8. "International Women's Year Commission—Report on ERAmerica Formation," Jan. 15, 1976, subject file "1976–1982," box 132, Records of ERAmerica, Manuscript Division, Library of Congress, Washington, D.C.; Spruill, *Divided We Stand*, 50–58.

9. Sam Nunn to Kathryn Dunaway, May 20, 1976, folder 1, box 1, Dunaway Papers. See Spruill, *Divided We Stand*, 69–70.

10. Resolution introduced at Republican Party of Georgia Convention, n.d., folder 18, box 4, Dunaway Papers.

11. "STOP ERA Fundraising Project," n.d., folder 2, box 3, Dunaway Papers.

12. Carole Ashkinaze, "Something for Every Georgia Woman," *Atlanta Constitution*, Mar. 5, 1977, 3B.

13. Georgia Coordinating Committee on the Observance of International Women's

Year letterhead, example found in folder 22, box 4, Dunaway Papers. In 1978, Committee member Eliza Paschall voiced her opposition to the ERA. Dunaway's papers do not give any insight into how or why she was selected for the committee.

14. Spruill, *Divided We Stand*, 135–46; and Thomson, *Price of LIBerty*, 94.

15. STOP ERA of Georgia and Eagle Forum Georgia, "Dear Friends," Apr. 7, 1977, folder 10, box 1, Dunaway Papers.

16. Ibid. First Baptist Church of Atlanta was pastored by Charles Stanley, one of the pastors Dunaway had reached out to earlier.

17. "Instructions for Workshop Leaders," folder 1, box 4, Dunaway Papers. For more on the Eagle Forum training for public speaking and media appearances, see chapter 6.

18. "Agenda Told for IWY Meeting Fri," *Atlanta Daily World*, Apr. 28, 1977, 2; and Lyn Martin, "Push for Rights, Women Urged," *Atlanta Constitution*, May 7, 1977, 3A. On Bella Abzug, her role in the IWY, and her antagonistic relationship with anti-ERA groups, see Zarnow, *Battling Bella*, 275–95.

19. "IWY Workshop Report Form," folder 1 box 4, Dunaway Papers.

20. International Women's Year Citizen's Review Committee, handout to Georgia delegates, folder 1, box 4, Dunaway Papers; and Carole Ashkinaze, "ERA Opponents Rail against Women's Meeting," *Atlanta Constitution*, May 14, 1977, 9B.

21. Rosemary Thomson to Citizens' Review Committee chairman, June 5, 1977, folder 2, box 1, Dunaway Papers.

22. "Instructions for IWY Conference" n.d., folder 1 box 4, Dunaway Papers.

23. Portia S. Brookins, "Women Seek Consensus on Majority of Issues at State Meeting Here," *Atlanta Daily World*, May 12, 1977, 2; Beverly Adams, "Forget 'Rights': Attack Specifics," *Atlanta Constitution*, Dec. 3, 1977, 1B; and Carole Ashkinaze, "National Women's Conference to Begin Friday in Houston," *Atlanta Constitution*, Nov. 17, 1977, 7B. Eleven of Georgia's thirty delegates were African American women.

24. Carole Ashkinaze, "ERA Opponents Rail against Women's Meeting," *Atlanta Constitution*, May 14, 1977, 9B. Ashkinaze covered Dunaway in numerous articles and columns, even allowing Dunaway to write a guest column ("Con: ERA Is a Power Grab by Washington Lawmakers," *Atlanta Constitution*, Jan. 15, 1977, 1B).

25. Georgia Eagles to Eagle Forum members in other states, "Be Prepared for the IWY Meetings," n.d., folder 9, box 4, Dunaway Papers. For more on the 1967 NFRW election, see chapter 3.

26. On individual state meetings and the rising power of conservatives in later meetings, see Spruill, *Divided We Stand*, 166–88.

27. Georgia Eagles to Eagle Forum members in other states, "Be Prepared for the IWY Meetings."

28. See Spruill, *Divided We Stand*, 184–85; and Thomson, *Price of LIBerty*. Thomson's book, published in 1978, describes the IWY CRC work in detail.

29. Carole Ashkinaze, "Carter Women Get Cheers in Houston," *Atlanta Constitution*, Nov.19, 1977, 1A.

30. Carole Ashkinaze, "In Houston, ERA OK Seemed Just a Matter of Time," *Atlanta Constitution*, Nov. 26, 1977, 3B.

31. Martha Fleming, "Coretta King Hails Women's Conference Minority Resolution," *Atlanta Daily World*, Nov. 24, 1977, 2; and Carole Ashkinaze, "Women Choose 25 Targets for 'Action,'" *Atlanta Daily World*, Nov. 22, 1977, 8A. On the male Mississippi delegation and the Mormon representatives to the National Women's Conference, see Spruill, *Divided We Stand*, 170–72, 251–54.

32. George Busbee, "Proclamation, Family Day Family Week," Nov. 8, 1977, folder 8,

box 4; and letter from Kathryn Dunaway to pastors, Nov. 9, 1977, folder 4, box 2, Dunaway papers.

33. Susan Fraker, "Women vs. Women," *Newsweek*, July 25, 1977, 34; Carole Ashkinaze, "God Stronger than Carter, Stop-ERA Leader Declares," *Atlanta Constitution*, Nov. 20, 1977, 12C. Ashkinaze also reported on disputes over crowd size. While rally organizers claimed ten thousand in attendance with two thousand unable to get into the arena, she found only twenty people outside the arena, getting fresh air. Anita Bryant described her anti-gay political work in her memoir *The Anita Bryant Story: The Survival of Our Nation's Families and the Threat of Militant Homosexuality* (Old Tappan, N.J.: Revell, 1977). Historian Emily Suzanne Johnson examined Bryant's position in the New Christian Right in *This Is Our Message: Women's Leadership in the New Christian Right* (New York: Oxford University Press, 2019), 38–67.

34. Carole Ashkinaze, "Can You Be for the ERA and Favor Women's Rights?," *Atlanta Journal and Constitution*, Mar. 4, 1978, 3B. Larry Flynt was the publisher of the pornographic magazine *Hustler*. In early 1978, he claimed to have converted to Christianity under the guidance of Ruth Carter Stapleton, Jimmy Carter's sister. "Self-Styled Pornographer Says He's Changed, But Not into a Traditional Christian: 'Turned off by Pornography,'" *New York Times*, Feb. 2, 1978, A16.

35. Eliza Paschall, "Summary of the Intent of the Sixteen Recommendations to be Voted on by All State IWY Conferences," folder 20, box 4, Dunaway Papers.

36. Biographical information of Eliza K. Paschall, folder 5, box 36, Eliza King Paschall Morrison Papers, Stuart A. Rose Manuscript, Archives, and Rare Book Library, Emory University (hereafter, Paschall Papers, Emory). Paschall also left a small collection of papers at the Ronald Reagan Presidential Library in Simi Valley, California. I cite these papers in the conclusion, where they are defined as Eliza Paschall Papers, Reagan Library. While at Agnes Scott College, Paschall attended interracial meetings with Atlanta University students—an action that led white supremacist watchdogs to notify her parents and the college president.

37. Eliza King Paschall résumé, December 1966, folder 5, box 29, Paschall Papers, Emory.

38. Eliza Paschall to Linda Hartsock, Jan. 23, 1976, folder "IWY-AAUW," box 35, Paschall Papers, Emory.

39. Eliza Lydia King Paschall Morrison (Mrs. William Morrison) to editor of the newsletter of the Atlanta-Fulton County League of Women Voters, Jan. 27, 1975, folder 3, box 29, Paschall Papers, Emory. Paschall pointed out that Georgia law did not leave women much choice about the title. "Mrs." indicated a married woman. "Miss," according to Georgia law—at least in Paschall's reading—had to mean a virgin or a criminal, since fornication outside marriage was illegal. She argued that "Ms." gave her the freedom to keep her sex life private and allowed her to keep her first husband's name, upon which she had built her professional reputation.

40. Biographical information of Eliza K. Paschall, folder 5, box 36, Paschall Papers, Emory.

41. "A Feminist Protest against Backwater Feminism," n.d., folder "IWY-General #1," box 35, Paschall Papers, Emory.

42. Eliza Paschall Morrison to editor of *Christian Science Monitor*, Jan. 19, 1973, folder 4, box 29, Paschall Papers, Emory.

43. Eliza K. Paschall to Ms. Lucy Wilson Benson, president of the League of Women Voters, Nov. 13, 1973, folder 4, box 29, Paschall Papers, Emory.

44. Eliza Paschall to Fran Henry, May 1, 1976, folder 4, box 29, Paschall Papers, Emory.

45. Letter to Kay [no surname], July 3, 1977, yellow folder, box 35, Paschall Papers, Emory.

46. Letter from Eliza Paschall to Jimmy Carter, Herman Talmadge, Sam Nunn, Elliott Levitas, George Busbee, Zell Miller, Pierre Howard, and John Hawkins, June 27, 1977, folder "IWY-General #1," box 35, Paschall Papers, Emory.

47. Eliza Paschall to Raymond [surname illegible], Feb. 10 [no year], folder 3, box 29, Paschall papers; and Eliza Paschall, "To Whom It May Concern," n.d., folder 9, box 3, Dunaway Papers. Paschall typed her own materials and often made errors, seemingly due more to the great passion with which she put her ideas on paper rather than ignorance of spelling or punctuation.

48. Eliza Paschall, "Summary of the Intent of the Sixteen Recommendations to Be Voted On by All State IWY Conferences," folder 20, box 4, Dunaway Papers.

49. "A Feminist Protest against Backwater Feminism," n.d., folder "IWY-General #1," box 35, Paschall Papers, Emory.

50. Ibid.

51. Eliza Paschall Morrison to Mr. Harris [no first name], Feb. 3, 1974, folder 3, box 29, Paschall Papers, Emory.

52. Ibid.

53. Letter from Eliza Paschall to Jimmy Carter, Herman Talmadge, Sam Nunn, Elliott Levitas, George Busbee, Zell Miller, Pierre Howard, and John Hawkins, June 27, 1977, folder "IWY-General #1," box 35, Paschall Papers, Emory.

54. Carole Ashkinaze, "Can You Be for the ERA and Favor Women's Rights?," *Atlanta Journal and Constitution*, Mar. 4, 1978, 3B.

55. Wysong interview, August 15, 2006.

56. "Alice in Abzugland," folder "IWY-General #1," box 35, Paschall Papers, Emory (emphasis in original).

57. Dunaway registration, 1978 Eagle Council/Eagle Forum/STOP ERA Conference, folder 8, box 8, Dunaway Papers. On a list of conference events, Dunaway wrote "Eliza" next to entries for panels on "How to Get Your Message across in the Media" and "How to Lobby Effectively." She did not indicate whether Paschall was attending the forums or leading them.

58. Kathryn Dunaway to STOP ERA "friend," May 23, 1978, folder 3, box 1, Dunaway Papers.

59. Phyllis Schlafly to Kathryn Dunaway, Mar. 17, 1979, folder 3, box 1, Dunaway Papers.

60. Dunaway registration, 1978 Eagle Council/Eagle Forum/STOP ERA Conference, folder 8, box 8, Dunaway Papers.

61. Memo from Eleanor Richardson Re: HR 438–1274, Feb. 16, 1978, folder 2, box 2, Janet Cukor Papers, Donna Novak Coles Georgia Women's Movement Archives, Georgia State University Library, Atlanta, Ga. (hereafter, Cukor Papers); "Displaced Homemakers Need Key to Open Doors to Employment," *Atlanta Daily World*, Aug. 11, 1978, 3; Harriet Stix, "Experimental Job Project for Former Homemakers," *Los Angeles Times*, Jan. 27, 1977, photocopy in folder 2, box 2, Cukor Papers; and "League of Women Voters Examines Problems of 'Displaced Homemakers,'" *Atlanta Daily World*, Dec. 18, 1979, 3. For more on the national campaign for displaced homemakers legislation, see Lisa Levenstein, "'Don't Agonize, Organize!': The Displaced Homemakers Campaign and the Contested Goals of Postwar Feminism," *Journal of American History* 100, no. 4 (2014): 1114–38; on Schlafly's coordination of the opposition, see pages 1134–36.

62. "Stop ERA's Katherine [*sic*] Dunaway Spends Her Time Rallying Her 'Girls,'" *Atlanta Constitution*, May 2, 1979, B1.

63. Patricia M. Fulton to Hon. Haskew H. Brantley Jr., Feb. 17, 1978, folder 4, box 2, Dunaway Papers. In the letter, Fulton says she is thirty years old.

64. Kathryn Dunaway, responses to unidentified questionnaire regarding the women's movement, n.d., folder 20, box 2, Dunaway Papers.

65. Membership list, Georgia Housewives for ERA, Nov. 1978, folder 2, box 5, Donna Novak Coles Papers, Donna Novak Coles Georgia Women's Movement Archives, Georgia State University Library, Atlanta, Ga. (hereafter, Coles Papers).

66. Carole Ashkinaze, "President of Housewives for ERA Finds Biblical Support," *Atlanta Constitution*, May 30, 1981, photocopy in folder 9, box 4, Carole Ashkinaze Papers, Donna Novak Coles Georgia Women's Movement Archives, Georgia State University Library, Atlanta, Ga.

67. Georgia Housewives for ERA pamphlet, dated 1979–80, folder 2, box 5, Coles Papers.

68. "AAUW Week: Action for Equity," brochure, March 1980, folder 4, box 33, Sarah Weddington Files, Presidential Papers of Jimmy Carter, Jimmy Carter Presidential Library and Museum, Atlanta, Ga.

69. Memo from Eleanor Richardson Re: HR 438–1274, Feb. 16, 1978, folder 2, box 2, Cukor Papers; and "Displaced Homemakers Need Key to Open Doors to Employment," *Atlanta Daily World*, Aug. 11, 1978, 3.

70. "Displaced Homemakers Need Key to Open Doors to Employment," *Atlanta Daily World*, Aug. 11, 1978, 3.

71. "'Evening at Emory' Offers Many Courses," *Atlanta Daily World*, Dec. 18, 1975, 2; "Ga. State Offers Special Courses Winter Quarter," *Atlanta Daily World*, Jan. 4, 1976, 2; and "New Courses Offered at Phyllis Wheatley YWCA," *Atlanta Daily World*, Jan. 4, 1976, 3.

72. "Ga. Develops Displace [*sic*] Homemaker Program," *Atlanta Daily World*, Sept. 25, 1979, 3.

73. Hinesley interview, July 2016.

74. Memo from Linda Tarr-Whelan to Judy Carter, July 28, 1979, folder 1 "ERA-Georgia [2]," box 31, Sarah Weddington Files, Office of the Special Assistant for Women's Affairs, White House Central Files, Jimmy Carter Presidential Library and Museum, National Archives and Records Administration, Atlanta, Ga. (hereafter, Weddington Papers).

75. Patricia Mollo, Catasqua, Pa., to Jimmy Carter, June 15, 1979, folder 10, box 33, Weddington Papers.

76. "First Lady's Telephone Calls," January 19, 1980, and "President's Calls," January 19, 1980, folder 1, box 31, Weddington Papers.

77. "Background on Georgia," unsigned memorandum, Jan. 1, 1980, folder 1, box 31, Weddington Papers,

78. Jerry Schwartz, "Georgia Senators Say No to ERA," *Atlanta Constitution*, Jan. 22, 1980, 7–A. Carter won the Iowa Caucus in 1980.

79. Ibid.

80. Paul Coverdell to Kathryn Dunaway, Apr. 21, 1980, folder 7, box 2, Dunaway Papers. Coverdell later won election to become U.S. senator from Georgia in 1992 and 1998.

81. Mrs. Martha Elrod to Kathryn Dunaway, Aug. 19, 1980, folder 7, box 2, Dunaway Papers.

82. James R. Tuten to Kathryn Dunaway, May 13, 1980, folder 7, box 2, Dunaway Papers.

83. Fred Schlafly to Kathryn Dunaway, Jan. 3, 1980, folder 11, box 1, Dunaway Papers.

84. "Georgia STOP ERA Chairman Dies," newspaper clipping, unknown source, n.d., ERA Georgia files, Eagle Forum Library and Archives, St. Louis, Mo. Because the Eagle Forum files were unavailable at the time of the request, archivist Deb Pentecost graciously photocopied and mailed all files related to Georgia. However, only the collection name indicates the location of the files.

85. Georgia Senate Resolution 117, "A Resolution Expressing Regrets at the Untimely Passing of Mrs. Kathryn Dunaway," ERA Georgia files, Eagle Forum Library and Archives, St. Louis, Mo.

86. Tony Cooper, "Leading ERA Opponent Kathryn Dunaway Dies," *Atlanta Constitution*, Sept. 17, 1980, 1C–2C.

87. Phyllis Schlafly to "Georgia Friend," June 29, 1981, folder 7, box 2, Dunaway Papers. Schlafly did not mention Dunaway's passing in the mailing, but did write, "I feel it is so important that all of us get together that I am making a special effort to come to your state." RSVPs went to Wysong.

88. "ERA Defeated in Georgia House; Third Major Setback in 2 Weeks," *Miami Herald*, Jan. 22, 1982, 8A, photocopy in ERA-Georgia Collection, Eagle Forum Library and Archives, St. Louis, Mo.

89. Sue Ella Deadwyler to John Dunaway, no date, folder 7, box 2, Dunaway Papers. Deadwyler later rose to be president of the Georgia Eagle Forum and editor of the conservative newsletter *Georgia Insight*.

Conclusion. Payment Due

1. Hal Gulliver, "Late Lamented Republican Party," *Atlanta Constitution*, Nov. 1, 1978, clipping in folder 8, box 2, series VI, Mack Mattingly Papers, Richard B. Russell Collection, University of Georgia Libraries, Athens, Ga. (hereafter, Mattingly Papers).

2. Hinesley interview, July 2016; Kruse and Zelizer, *Fault Lines*, 216; Strahan and Palazzolo, "Gingrich Effect," 95–97.

3. Savannah Area Republican Women, invitation, Aug. 17, 1979, folder 1, box 3, series VI, Mattingly Papers.

4. "Voting Results, 1980 Election," folder 1, box 8, series VI, Mattingly Papers.

5. Donald T. Critchlow, "Mobilizing Women: The 'Social' Issues," in Brownlee and Graham, *Reagan Presidency*, 301.

6. "Republican Leadership Conference Jan. 26–29," *Atlanta Daily World*, Jan. 8, 1984, 1.

7. Miller interview, May 31, 2014.

8. Ibid.

9. Ibid.

10. Lee Miller's daughter was injured in a motor scooter accident and I feel certain Lee would want me to remind readers always to wear a helmet. She advocated job training for Georgians with developmental disabilities and worked on education campaigns. One of her allies in her work for disabled Georgians was Bobbie Goldberg, a staff member of ERA sponsor Cathey Steinberg. Miller had supported ERA, though not enthusiastically. Support for developmentally disabled children proved to be a common ground for mothers who were active in different political parties. In 2012, GSU women's movement archivist Morna Gerrard and I visited Lee Miller at her home in Columbus and collected more boxes covering her work in Poland and then in disabled

activism. These boxes are rich in material, but would have moved this book into biography rather than a story of grassroots activism and the GOP. I hope future scholars will look at these papers to document the important disability histories of our state.

11. Faith Ryan Whittlesly to Lisa DeGrandi (RNC), Sept. 25, 1985, folder 1: "Action," box 1, series I: "Subject Files," Eliza K. Paschall Papers, Ronald Reagan Presidential Library, Simi Valley, Calif (hereafter, Paschall Papers, Reagan Library). Eliza Paschall's files from her time of White House employment are housed at the Ronald Reagan Presidential Library. Her personal papers remain at the Stuart A. Rose Manuscript, Archives, and Rare Book Library at Emory University in Atlanta (cited elsewhere as Paschall Papers, Emory).

12. Memo from Eliza Paschall to Faith Ryan Whittlesly Re: 50 States Project, Apr. 5, 1985, folder 1, box 8, series II: "Correspondence," Eliza K. Paschall Papers, Reagan Presidential Library.

13. Portia A. Scott, "Reagan-Bush Inaugurated," *Atlanta Daily World*, Jan. 22, 1985, 1.

14. "'Blacks for Bush' Open Headquarters," *Atlanta Daily World*, Oct. 27, 1988, 1.

15. Edward Peeks, "Atlantans Pay Tribute to Lincoln in Friday Program," *Atlanta Daily World*, Feb. 13, 1954, 1.

16. "Portia Brings Two-Party System to 5th: Lewis Wins District Post in Long Battle," *Atlanta Daily World*, Nov. 6, 1986, 1.

17. See chapter 4 for more about Evelyn Frazier's work with the Metropolitan Club and especially her balancing an interest in civil rights with her membership in the Republican party.

18. "Portia Renews Cause for Strong Two-Party System," *Atlanta Daily World*, Sept. 5, 1986, 1.

19. "Portia Tells Supporters to Continue Two-Party System," *Atlanta Daily World*, Nov. 13, 1986, 1.

20. "Women Gather at Summit Today in Nation's Capital," *Atlanta Daily World*, Feb. 7, 1991, 1. On the gap between Black men and Black women Republicans, see Wright Rigueur, "Major Difference."

21. Hattie Powell, "Georgia Tops in Black GOP Candidates," *Atlanta Daily World*, July 16–17, 1998, 12. Georgia had twenty-one candidates running, four of whom were women. Sunny Warren ran for U.S. Congress in District 4; Portia Scott ran again for State Senate in District 38; Catherine Gilliard ran for State House Seat 70, and Jewel Johnson ran for Fulton County commissioner. California had the second most African Americans running.

22. Nationally, the numbers of Republican women lag behind the numbers of Democratic women in Congress. The 2020 elections set a record of 26 Republican women elected to the U.S. Congress, though that is far behind the 105 Democratic women serving at the same time. Party recruitment, support, and funding may explain a part of this difference. The PAC Emily's List was founded in 1985 to support Democratic women. The Republican counter, E-PAC, did not form until 2018. "Number of Women in the U.S. Congress," website of the Center for American Women and Politics, Eagleton Institute of Politics, Rutgers University, New Brunswick, N.J., updated Dec. 7, 2020, https://cawp.rutgers.edu/election2020-results-tracker; and Danielle Kurtzleben, "How a Record Number of Republican Women Got Elected to Congress," Georgia Public Broadcasting, Nov. 13, 2020, https://www.gpb.org/news/2020/11/13/how-record -number-of-republican-women-got-elected-congress.

23. Jim Galloway, Greg Bluestein, and Tia Mitchell, "The Jolt: A 'Bimbo' Eruption in a GOP Congressional Race," *The Jolt* (blog), *Atlanta Journal-Constitution*, May 22, 2020,

https://www.ajc.com/blog/politics/the-jolt-bimbo-eruption-gop-congressional-race
/JvEhNinODI28OcLfiEFUUL/.

24. Jim Galloway, "The Women at the Well: #MeToo Comes to the State Senate," *Atlanta Journal-Constitution*, Jan. 18, 2019, https://www.ajc.com/blog/politics/the
-women-the-well-metoo-comes-the-state-senate/nnucQMTLvapCIjx7rXdaiL/.

25. Matthew Rosenberg, "QAnon Supporter Is Headed to Congress," *New York Times*, updated Nov. 6, 2020, https://www.nytimes.com/2020/11/03/us/politics/qanon
-candidates-marjorie-taylor-greene.html; and LaFrance, "Prophecies of Q."

26. Georgia elections go to a runoff when a candidate fails to achieve a majority of votes. This law can be traced back to 1968, when the Georgia legislature unanimously passed legislation requiring a runoff rather than sending the choice to the state legislature. The gubernatorial election of 1966 between Lester Maddox and Bo Callaway, recounted in chapter 2, led the legislators to make the change. Sam Hopkins, "House Votes to Get Assembly Off Hook in Governor's Race," *Atlanta Constitution*, Jan. 18, 1968, 1.

27. Office of the White House Press Secretary, "Statement from the Press Secretary Regarding Executive Grants of Clemency," Feb. 18, 2020, https://www.whitehouse
.gov/briefings-statements/statement-press-secretary-regarding-executive-grants
-clemency-2; and Ernie Suggs, "After Getting Trump Pardon, Angela Stanton-King Sets Eyes on Lewis," *Atlanta Journal-Constitution*, Mar. 6, 2020, https://www.ajc.com/news
/after-getting-trump-pardon-angela-staton-king-sets-sights-lewis
/FEhk2wJ9KBIBr6Vj48cnWJ/.

28. Jim Galloway, "White Women Voters Are Sticking—Not Just with Kemp, but Trump, Too," Oct. 12, 2018, *Political Insider* (blog), *Atlanta Journal-Constitution*, https://
www.ajc.com/blog/politics/white-women-voters-are-sticking-not-just-with-kemp-but
-trump-too/tG6ypbHIcNNUJW2tL4MGYL/; "2018 Voter Poll Results: Georgia," *Washington Post*, last updated Nov. 30, 2018, https://www.washingtonpost.com/graphics
/2018/politics/voter-polls/georgia.html; and "Exit Poll Results and Analysis from Georgia," *Washington Post*, Nov. 3, 2020, https://www.washingtonpost.com/elections
/interactive/2020/exit-polls/georgia-exit-polls/.

29. Emma Hurt, "Georgia GOP Fears Changing Demographics Could End Party's Long Dominance," National Public Radio, June 7, 2020, https://www.npr.org/2020
/06/07/870947158/georgia-gop-fears-changing-demographics-could-end-partys-long
-dominance.

30. Abrams interview.

31. After losing her gubernatorial bid in 2018, Stacey Abrams founded Fair Fight, which has focused on registering and turning out new voters. Abrams's work in reaching communities of color as Georgia becomes a more diverse state will prove to be critical in understanding the next phase of Georgia politics. "Former Georgia Gubernatorial Candidate on a Push for Voter Turnout," *All Things Considered*, National Public Radio, Nov. 2, 2020, https://www.npr.org/2020/11/02/930504055/former-georgia
-gubernatorial-candidate-on-a-push-for-voter-turnout.

32. As of this writing in December 2020, Georgia's ballots have been counted three times—twice by machine and once by hand—with the final tally showing Democratic candidate Biden's margin of victory at 14,122 votes. Despite the three counts and the Republican secretary of state certifying the results, many Georgia Republicans refuse to accept the results and continue to pursue heretofore unsuccessful lawsuits and to apply political pressure on elected officials to annul the ballots.

33. Greg Bluestein, "Stacey Abrams Is Running for Georgia Governor in 2022," *At-*

lanta Journal-Constitution, Dec. 1, 2021, https://www.ajc.com/politics/politics-blog
/breaking-stacey-abrams-is-running-for-georgia-governor-in-2022/.

34. The stories of Lee Ague moving to Cobb County and Clara Curtis sitting on the
ballot box are in chapter 1. Vanessa Williams, "Voting Rights Groups Alarmed after
Cobb County Cuts Half of Its Early-Voting Sites for Ga. Senate Runoffs," *Washington
Post*, Dec. 7, 2020, https://www.washingtonpost.com/politics/2020/12/07/voting
-rights-groups-alarmed-after-cobb-county-reduced-early-voting-sites-ga-senate
-runoffs/; Vanessa Williams, "After Criticism, Georgia's Cobb County Restores Some
Early-Voting Sites for Senate Runoffs," *Washington Post*, Dec. 9, 2020, https://www
.washingtonpost.com/politics/2020/12/09/after-criticism-cobb-county-restores-some
-early-voting-sites-ga-senate-runoffs/.

35. Greg Bluestein, "Analysis Shows Surge in Asian, Hispanic Voters Helped Biden
Capture Georgia," *Political Insider* (blog), *Atlanta Journal-Constitution*, Nov. 17, 2020,
https://www.ajc.com/politics/politics-blog/analysis-shows-surge-in-asian-hispanic
-voters-helped-capture-georgia/.

36. Nguyen interview, July 27, 2018; Sabrina Tavernise, "A New Political Force Emerges
in Georgia: Asian-American Voters," *New York Times*, Nov. 24, 2020, https://www
.nytimes.com/2020/11/25/us/georgia-asian-american-voters.html.

37. Rafshoon, "Pave It Blue," 378.

38. Jim Galloway, "The Women at the Well: #MeToo Comes to the State Senate," *Atlanta Journal-Constitution*, Jan. 18, 2019, https://www.ajc.com/blog/politics/the
-women-the-well-metoo-comes-the-state-senate/nnucQMTLvapCIjx7rXdaiL/.

39. Jim Galloway, Greg Bluestein, and Tia Mitchell, "The Jolt: A 'Bimbo' Eruption in
a GOP Congressional Race," *The Jolt* (blog), *Atlanta Journal-Constitution*, May 22, 2020,
https://www.ajc.com/blog/politics/the-jolt-bimbo-eruption-gop-congressional-race
/JvEhNinODI28OcLfiEFUUL/; and Doug Richards, "Tea Party Founder: Gov. Kemp's
U.S. Senate Choice Is a 'Fiasco,'" WXIA-TV, Nov. 29, 2019, https://www.11alive.com/article
/news/kemp-pick-senate/85−9fdbd290−5b0d-45f5-afb8−231b5a07abe9.

40. Sudhin Thanawala, "Loeffler's Wealth, Trump Loyalty Face Scrutiny in Georgia,"
Associated Press, Dec. 21, 2020 https://apnews.com/article/kelly-loeffler-georgia
-senate-elections-7297622933c169ae093327e8b0e1ee75.

41. Greg Bluestein, "Kemp Allies Start 'Stop Stacey' Group as Possible 2022 Rematch
Looms," *Political Insider* (blog), *Atlanta Journal-Constitution*, Feb. 1, 2021, https://www
.ajc.com/politics/politics-blog/kemp-allies-start-stop-stacey-group-as-possible-2022
-rematch-looms/TSIUNQEB3VFLBFSY35SEUVEUGQ/; and Greg Bluestein, "Loeffler
Launches Group to Boost GOP Turnout, Promote, 'Big Tent' Policies," *Political Insider*
(blog), *Atlanta Journal-Constitution*, Feb. 22, 2021, https://www.ajc.com/politics
/politics-blog/loeffler-launches-group-to-boost-gop-turnout-promote-big-tent
-policies/LDK7XT55FJFGDGDUQ3B3737R2U/.

BIBLIOGRAPHY

Primary Sources
MANUSCRIPT COLLECTIONS

ABILENE, KANSAS

Dwight D. Eisenhower Presidential Library

National Federation of Republican Women Papers

ANN ARBOR, MICHIGAN

Gerald Ford Presidential Library

Anne Armstrong Files
Patricia Lindh and Jeannie Holm Files
Elizabeth M. O'Neill Files
President Ford Committee Files

ATHENS, GEORGIA

*Richard B. Russell Library for Political Research and
Studies, University of Georgia Libraries*

Iris Faircloth Blitch Papers
Howard H. (Bo) Callaway Papers
Mack Mattingly Papers

ATLANTA, GEORGIA

*Archives Division, Auburn Avenue Research Library on African
American Culture and History, Fulton County Library System*

Evelyn J. Frazier Papers

Jimmy Carter Presidential Library

Midge Costanza Files, Office of the Assistant for Public Liaison, White House Central
    Files
Office of the First Lady, White House Central Files
Sarah Weddington Files, Office of the Special Assistant for Women's Affairs, White
    House Central Files

Kenan Research Center, Atlanta History Center

Living Atlanta Oral History Recordings

Special Collections and Archives, Georgia State University Libraries

Lee Ague Miller Papers
Donna Novak Coles Georgia Women's Movement Archives
    Carole Ashkinaze Papers, W043
    Jeanne Taylor Cahill Papers, W003
    Donna Novak Coles Papers
    Janet Cukor Papers
    Dorothy Gibson-Ferrey Papers, W007
    Nancy Nowak Papers, W076
    Beth S. Schapiro Papers, W002
    Cathey W. Steinberg Papers, W042

Manuscripts and Rare Books Library,
Robert W. Woodruff Library, Emory University

Kathryn Fink Dunaway Papers
Eliza King Paschall Morrison Papers

State Department of Archives and History

Lee Ague Miller Papers (moved 2011 to Special Collections and Archives, Georgia State University)
Commission on the Status of Women Annual Report and Other Files, 1970–1976, Department of Human Relations Papers, 80/17/47

LAWRENCEVILLE, GEORGIA

Louise Dunaway Grovensteen Papers (personal collection of Laura Dunaway Green)

MORROW, GEORGIA

Georgia Archives

Lee Ague Miller Papers (pre-1974; since moved to Georgia State University in Atlanta)

ROCK HILL, SOUTH CAROLINA

Special Collections and Archives, Dacus Library, Winthrop University

South Carolina Federation of Republican Women Papers

SIMI VALLEY, CALIFORNIA

Ronald Reagan Presidential Library

Lee Atwater Files, Office of Political Affairs
Eliza King Paschall Papers, Office of Public Liaison, White House Central Files

ST. LOUIS, MISSOURI

Eagle Forum Archives, Eagle Forum

STOP ERA Archives, Eagle Forum

WASHINGTON, D.C.

ERAmerica records, 1974–1982, Manuscripts Division, Library of Congress

YORBA LINDA, CALIFORNIA
Richard Nixon Presidential Library

Anne L. Armstrong Papers, White House Central Files
Harry S. Dent Papers, White House Special Files, Staff Member Office Files
Barbara Franklin Papers, White House Central Files

ORAL HISTORIES

Stacey Abrams, April 5, 2017. Interviewed by the author, Atlanta, Ga.
Lee Ague Miller, February 25, 2010. Interviewed by the author, Marietta, Ga.
———, December 11, 2011. Interviewed by the author, Atlanta, Ga. Digital recording and transcript available at Activist Women Oral History Project, Special Collections Department and Archives, Georgia State University, Atlanta, Ga.
———, May 31, 2014. Interviewed by the author, Columbus, Ga. Transcript available at Activist Women Oral History Project, Special Collections Department and Archives, Georgia State University, Atlanta, Ga.
Marshall Dunaway, August 2006. Interviewed by the author, Thomasville, Ga.
Emma Hinesley, July 2016. Interviewed by the author, Newnan, Ga.
Kay Kirkpatrick, June 7, 2017. Interviewed by the author, Marietta, Ga.
Bee Nguyen, July 27, 2018. Interviewed by the author, Atlanta, Ga.
Millie Rogers, June 2016. Interviewed by the author, Marietta, Ga.
Phyllis Schlafly, June 8, 2009. Interviewed by the author, St. Louis, Mo.
Shirley Spellerberg, September 8, 2009. Interviewed by the author via email.
Takosha Swann, July 11, 2018. Interviewed by the author, Decatur, Ga.
Lee Wysong, August 15, 2006. Interviewed by the author, Atlanta, Ga.

NEWSPAPERS AND PERIODICALS

Atlanta Constitution
Atlanta Daily World
Atlanta Journal
Atlanta Journal-Constitution
Atlanta Magazine
Chicago Tribune
Los Angeles Times
National Review
New York Times
Newsweek
Time
Washington Post

BOOKS AND MANUSCRIPTS, PUBLISHED PRIMARY

Arnall, Ellis Gibbs. *The Shore Dimly Seen*. Philadelphia: J. B. Lippincott, 1946.
———. *What the People Want*. Philadelphia: J. B. Lippincott, 1947.
Brown, Barbara A., Thomas I. Emerson, Gail Falk, and Ann E. Freedman. "The Equal Rights Amendment: A Constitutional Basis for Equal Rights for Women." *Yale Law Journal* 80, no. 5 (April 1971): 871–985.
Bryant, Anita. *The Anita Bryant Story: The Survival of Our Nation's Families and the Threat of Militant Homosexuality*. Old Tappan, N.J.: Fleming H. Revell, 1977.
Carter, Jimmy. *Why Not the Best?* Nashville: Broadman, 1975.
Carter, Rosalynn. *First Lady from Plains*. Boston: Houghton Mifflin, 1984.
Daniel, Frank, ed. *Addresses of Lester Garfield Maddox, Governor of Georgia, 1967–1971*. Atlanta: Georgia Department of Archives and History, 1971.
Dent, Harry S. *The Prodigal South Returns to Power*. New York: John Wiley and Sons, 1978.
Felsenthal, Carol. *The Sweetheart of the Silent Majority: The Biography of Phyllis Schlafly*. Garden City, N.Y.: Doubleday, 1981.

Fenzi, Jewell, and Allida Black. *Democratic Women: An Oral History of the Woman's National Democratic Club*. Washington, D.C.: WNDC Educational Foundation, 2000.

Follis, Anne Bowen. *"I'm Not a Women's Libber, But..."* Nashville: Abingdon, 1981.

Goldwater, Barry. *The Conscience of a Conservative*. Shepherdsville, Ky.: Victor, 1960.

Maddox, Lester Garfield. *Speaking Out: The Autobiography of Lester Garfield Maddox*. Garden City, N.Y.: Doubleday, 1975.

Morgan, Marabel. *The Total Woman*. Old Tappan, N.J.: Fleming H. Revelle, 1973.

Murphy, Reg, and Hal Gulliver. *The Southern Strategy*. New York: Scribner, 1971.

Phillips, Kevin P. *The Emerging Republican Majority*. New Rochelle, N.Y.: Arlington House, 1969.

Schlafly, Phyllis. *A Choice, Not an Echo*. Alton, Ill.: Pere Marquette Press, 1964.

——, ed. *Pornography's Victims*. Westchester, Ill.: Crossway Books, 1987.

——. *The Power of the Christian Woman*. Cincinnati: Standard, 1981.

——. *The Power of the Positive Woman*. New Rochelle, N.Y.: Arlington House, 1977.

——. *Safe—Not Sorry*. Alton, Ill.: Pere Marquette Press, 1967.

——, ed. *Who Will Rock the Cradle? Two Conferences on Child Care*. Washington, D.C.: Eagle Forum Education and Legal Defense Fund, 1989.

Schlafly, Phyllis, and Chester Ward. *The Gravediggers*. Alton, Ill: Pere Marquette Press, 1964.

Talmadge, Herman E., with Mark Royden Winchell. *Talmadge: A Political Legacy, A Politician's Life; A Memoir*. Atlanta, Ga.: Peachtree, 1987.

Thomson, Rosemary, *The Price of LIBerty*. Carol Stream, Ill.: Creation House, 1978.

White, F. Clifton, with William J. Gill. *Suite 3505: The Story of the Draft Goldwater Movement*. New Rochelle, N.Y.: Arlington House, 1967.

Secondary Sources

Andrew, John A., III. *The Other Side of the Sixties: Young Americans for Freedom and the Rise of Conservative Politics*. New Brunswick, N.J.: Rutgers University Press, 1997.

Baker, Paula. "The Domestication of Politics: Women and American Political Society, 1780–1920." *American Historical Review* 89, no. 3 (June 1984): 620–647.

Bartley, Numan V. *From Thurmond to Wallace: Political Tendencies in Georgia, 1948–1968*. Baltimore: Johns Hopkins University Press, 1970.

——. *The Rise of Massive Resistance: Race and Politics in the South during the 1950s*. 1969; rpt., Baton Rouge: Louisiana State University Press, 1999.

Bartley, Numan V., and Hugh D. Graham. *Southern Elections: County and Precinct Data, 1950–1972*. Baton Rouge: Louisiana State University Press, 1978.

——. *Southern Politics and the Second Reconstruction*. Baltimore: Johns Hopkins University Press, 1975.

Bass, Jack, and Walter De Vries. *The Transformation of Southern Politics: Social Change and Political Consequence since 1945*. New York: Basic Books, 1976.

Belvin, William. L., Jr. "The Georgia Gubernatorial Primary of 1946." *Georgia Historical Quarterly* 50, no. 1 (March 1966): 37–53.

Berry, Mary Frances. *Why ERA Failed: Politics, Women's Rights, and the Amending Process of the Constitution*. Bloomington: Indiana University Press, 1988.

Black, Earl. *Southern Governors and Civil Rights: Racial Segregation as a Campaign Issue in the Second Reconstruction*. Cambridge, Mass.: Harvard University Press, 1976.

Black, Earl, and Merle Black. *The Rise of Southern Republicans*. Cambridge, Mass.: Belknap Press of Harvard University Press, 2003.

———. *The Vital South: How Presidents Are Elected.* Cambridge, Mass.: Harvard University Press, 1992.

Boyd, Tim. "The 1966 Election in Georgia and the Ambiguity of the White Backlash." *Journal of Southern History* 75, no. 2 (May 2009): 305–40.

Brennan, Mary C. *Turning Right in the Sixties: The Conservative Capture of the* GOP. Chapel Hill: University of North Carolina Press, 1995.

Brown, Ruth Murray. *For a "Christian America": A History of the Religious Right.* Amherst, N.Y.: Prometheus Books, 2002.

Brownlee, W. Elliot, and Hugh Davis Graham, eds. *The Reagan Presidency: Pragmatic Conservatism and Its Legacies.* Lawrence: University Press of Kansas, 2003.

Brown-Nagin, Tomiko. *Courage to Dissent: Atlanta and the Long History of the Civil Rights Movement.* New York: Oxford University Press, 2011.

Brückmann, Rebecca. *Massive Resistance and Southern Womanhood: White Women, Class, and Segregation.* Athens: University of Georgia Press, 2021.

Brundage, W. Fitzhugh. "White Women and the Politics of Historical Memory in the New South, 1880–1920." In *Jumpin' Jim Crow: Southern Politics from Civil War to Civil Rights*, edited by Jane Dailey, Glenda Elizabeth Gilmore, and Bryant Simon, 115–39. Princeton, N.J.: Princeton University Press, 2000.

Buchanan, Scott E. "The Effects of the Abolition of the Georgia County-Unit System on the 1962 Gubernatorial Election." *Southeastern Political Review* 25, no. 4 (December 1997): 687–704.

Bullock, Charles S., III. "Congressional Voting and the Mobilization of a Black Electorate in the South." *Journal of Politics* 43, no. 3 (August 1981): 662–82.

Cadava, Geraldo. *The Hispanic Republican: The Shaping of an American Political Identity, from Nixon to Trump.* New York: Ecco, 2020.

Carter, Dan T. *From George Wallace to Newt Gingrich: Race in the Conservative Counterrevolution, 1963–1994.* Baton Rouge: Louisiana State University Press, 1996.

———. "More Than Race: Conservatism in the White South since V. O. Key Jr." In *Unlocking V. O. Key Jr.: "Southern Politics" for the Twenty-First Century*, edited by Angie Maxwell and Todd Shields, 129–60. Little Rock: University of Arkansas Press, 2011.

———. *The Politics of Rage: George Wallace, the Origins of the New Conservatism, and the Transformation of American Politics.* New York: Simon & Schuster, 1995.

Chirhart, Ann Short, and Kathleen Ann Clark. *Georgia Women: Their Lives and Times.* Vol 2. Athens: University of Georgia Press, 2014.

Cohodas, Nadine. *Strom Thurmond and the Politics of Southern Change.* Macon, Ga.: Mercer University Press, 1993.

Cook, James F. *Carl Sanders: Spokesman of the New South.* Macon, Ga.: Mercer University Press, 1993.

Coontz, Stephanie. *The Way We Never Were: American Families and the Nostalgia Trap.* New York: Basic Books, 1992.

Cosman, Bernard. *Five States for Goldwater: Continuity and Change in Southern Presidential Voting Patterns.* University, Ala.: University of Alabama Press, 1966.

Cott, Nancy F. "What's in a Name? The Limits of 'Social Feminism'; or, Expanding the Vocabulary of Women's History." *Journal of American History* 76, no. 3 (December 1989): 809–29.

Cowan, Ruth Schwartz. *More Work for Mother: The Ironies of Household Technology from the Open Hearth to the Microwave.* New York: Basic Books, 1983.

Cox, Karen L. *Dixie's Daughters: The United Daughters of the Confederacy and the Preservation of Confederate Culture.* Gainesville: University Press of Florida, 2003.

Crespino, Joseph. *In Search of Another Country: Mississippi and the Conservative Counterrevolution*. Princeton, N.J.: Princeton University Press, 2007.

——. *Strom Thurmond's America*. New York: Hill and Wang, 2012.

Critchlow, Donald T. *The Conservative Ascendancy: How the GOP Right Made Political History*. Cambridge, Mass.: Harvard University Press, 2007.

——. *Phyllis Schlafly and Grassroots Conservatism: A Woman's Crusade*. Princeton, N.J.: Princeton University Press, 2005.

Cuordileone, K. A. "'Politics in an Age of Anxiety': Cold War Political Culture and the Crisis in American Masculinity, 1949–1960." *Journal of American History* 87, no. 2 (September 2000): 515–45.

Dailey, Jane. "Sex, Segregation, and the Sacred after *Brown*." *Journal of American History* 91, no. 1 (June 2004): 119–44.

Daniel, Pete. *Lost Revolutions: The South in the 1950s*. Chapel Hill: University of North Carolina Press, 2000.

De Hart, Jane Sherron. "Gender on the Right: Meanings behind the Existential Scream." *Gender and History* 3, no. 3 (Autumn 1991): 246–67.

——. "Second Wave Feminism(s) and the South: The Differences that Differences Make." In *Women of the American South: A Multicultural Reader*, edited by Christie Anne Farnham, 273–301. New York: New York University Press, 1997.

Diamond, Sara. *Not by Politics Alone: The Enduring Influence of the Christian Right*. New York: Guilford, 1998.

——. *Roads to Dominion: Right-Wing Movements and Political Power in the United States*, New York: Guilford, 1995.

Dillard, Angela D. *Guess Who's Coming to Dinner Now? Multicultural Conservatism in America*. New York: New York University Press, 2001.

Donaldson, Gary. *Liberalism's Last Hurrah: The Presidential Campaign of 1964*. Armonk, N.Y.: M. E. Sharpe, 2003.

Douglas, Davison M. *Reading, Writing, and Race: The Desegregation of the Charlotte Schools*. Chapel Hill: University of North Carolina Press, 1995.

Dray, Philip. *At the Hands of Persons Unknown: The Lynching of Black America*. New York: Modern Library, 2003.

Ducat, Stephen. *The Wimp Factor: Gender Gaps, Holy Wars, and the Politics of Anxious Masculinity*. Boston: Beacon, 2004.

Evans, Sara. *Personal Politics: The Roots of Women's Liberation in the Civil Rights Movement and the New Left*. New York: Vintage Books, 1980.

——. *Tidal Wave: How Women Changed America at Century's End*. New York: Free Press, 2003.

Farber, David, and Jeff Roche, eds. *The Conservative Sixties*. New York: Peter Lang, 2003.

Farrington, Joshua D. *Black Republicans and the Transformation of the GOP*. Philadelphia: University of Pennsylvania Press, 2016.

Fields, Corey D. *Black Elephants in the Room: The Unexpected Politics of African American Republicans*. Oakland: University of California Press, 2016.

Fite, Gilbert C. *Richard B. Russell, Jr., Senator from Georgia*. Chapel Hill: University of North Carolina Press, 1991.

Flippen, J. Brooks. *Jimmy Carter, the Politics of Family, and the Rise of the Religious Right*. Athens: University of Georgia Press, 2011.

Foxworth, Laura. "'No More Silence!': Feminist Activism and Religion in the Second Wave." In *The Legacy of Second-Wave Feminism in American Politics*, edited by Angie Maxwell and Todd Shields, 71–96. New York: Palgrave Macmillan, 2018.

Frederickson, Kari. *The Dixiecrat Revolt and the End of the Solid South, 1932–1968.* Chapel Hill: University of North Carolina Press, 2001.

Freeman, Jo. *A Room at a Time: How Women Entered Party Politics.* Lanham, Md.: Rowman & Littlefield, 2000.

Galphin, Bruce. *The Riddle of Lester Maddox.* Atlanta, Ga.: Camelot, 1968.

Giddings, Paula. *Ida: A Sword among Lions; Ida B. Wells and the Campaign against Lynching.* New York: HarperCollins, 2008.

Gilmore, Glenda Elizabeth. *Gender and Jim Crow: Women and the Politics of White Supremacy in North Carolina, 1896–1920.* Chapel Hill: University of North Carolina Press, 1996.

Glotzer, Paige. *How the Suburbs Were Segregated: Developers and the Business of Exclusionary Housing, 1890–1960.* New York: Columbia University Press, 2020.

Goldsmith, John A. *Colleagues: Richard B. Russell and His Apprentice, Lyndon B. Johnson.* Washington, D.C.: Seven Locks, 1993.

Gordon, Ann D., with Bettye Collier-Thomas, John H. Bracey, Arlene Voski Avakian, and Joyce Avrech Berkman, eds. *African American Women and the Vote, 1837–1965.* Amherst: University of Massachusetts Press, 1997.

Gordon, Linda. *Pitied but Not Entitled: Single Mothers and the History of Welfare, 1890–1935.* New York: Free Press, 1994.

Gould, Lewis L. *Grand Old Party: A History of the Republicans.* New York: Random House, 2003.

Grady-Willis, Winston A. *Challenging U.S. Apartheid: Atlanta and Black Struggles for Human Rights, 1960–1977.* Durham, N.C.: Duke University Press, 2006.

Green, Elna C. *Southern Strategies: Southern Women and the Woman Suffrage Question.* Chapel Hill: University of North Carolina Press, 1997.

Green, John C., Mark J. Rozell, and Clyde Wilcox, eds. *The Christian Right in American Politics: Marching to the Millennium.* Washington, D.C.: Georgetown University Press, 2003.

Hale, Grace Elizabeth. *Making Whiteness: The Culture of Segregation in the South, 1890–1940.* New York: Vintage Books, 1999.

Hall, Jacquelyn Dowd. "The Long Civil Rights Movement and the Political Uses of the Past." *Journal of American History* 91, no. 4 (March 2005): 1233–63.

———. *Revolt against Chivalry: Jesse Daniel Ames and the Women's Campaign against Lynching.* New York: Columbia University Press, 1979.

Hamlin, Françoise N. *Crossroads at Clarksdale: The Black Freedom Struggle in the Mississippi Delta after World War II.* Chapel Hill: University of North Carolina Press, 2012.

Harrison, Cynthia Ellen. *On Account of Sex: The Politics of Women's Issues, 1945–1968.* Berkeley: University of California Press, 1988.

Henderson, Harold Paulk. "The 1966 Gubernatorial Election in Georgia." PhD diss., University of Southern Mississippi, 1982.

———. *The Politics of Change in Georgia: A Political Biography of Ellis Arnall.* Athens: University of Georgia Press, 1991.

Henderson, Harold Paulk, and Gary L. Roberts, eds. *Georgia Governors in an Age of Change: From Ellis Arnall to George Busbee.* Athens: University of Georgia Press, 1988.

Hewlett, Sylvia Ann. *A Lesser Life: The Myth of Women's Liberation in America.* New York: William Morrow, 1986.

Horowitz, Daniel. *Betty Friedan and the Making of the Feminine Mystique: The American Left, the Cold War, and Modern Feminism.* Amherst: University of Massachusetts Press, 1998.

Jeansonne, Glen. *Women of the Far Right: The Mothers' Movement and World War II*. Chicago: University of Chicago Press, 1996.

Jetter, Alexis, Annelise Orleck, and Diana Taylor, eds. *The Politics of Motherhood: Activist Voices from Left to Right*. Hanover, N.H.: Dartmouth College Press, an imprint of University Press of New England, 1997.

Johnson, Emily Suzanne. *This Is Our Message: Women's Leadership in the New Christian Right*. New York: Oxford University Press, 2019.

Kabaservice, Geoffrey M. *Rule and Ruin: The Downfall of Moderation and the Destruction of the Republican Party, from Eisenhower to the Tea Party*. New York: Oxford University Press, 2012.

Kerber, Linda K. *Toward an Intellectual History of Women: Essays*. Chapel Hill: University of North Carolina Press, 1997.

Key, V. O. *Southern Politics in State and Nation*. New York: Knopf, 1949.

Klatch, Rebecca. *Women of the New Right*. Philadelphia: Temple University Press, 1987.

Koven, Seth, and Sonya Michel. "Womanly Duties: Maternalist Politics and the Origins of Welfare States in France, Germany, Great Britain, and the United States, 1880–1920." *American Historical Review* 95, no. 4 (October 1990): 1076–108.

Kruse, Kevin M. *One Nation under God: How Corporate America Invented Christian America*. New York: Basic Books, 2015.

———. *White Flight: Atlanta and the Making of Modern Conservatism*. Princeton, N.J.: Princeton University Press, 2005.

Kruse, Kevin M., and Julian E. Zelizer. *Fault Lines: A History of the United States since 1974*. New York: W. W. Norton, 2019.

Kuhn, Clifford M., Harlon E. Joye, and E. Bernard West. *Living Atlanta: An Oral History of the City, 1914–1948*. 1990; repr., Athens: University of Georgia Press, 2005.

Ladd-Taylor, Molly. *Mother-Work: Women, Child Welfare, and the State, 1890–1930*. Urbana: University of Illinois Press, 1995.

LaFrance, Adrienne. "The Prophecies of Q." *Atlantic*, June 2020. https://www.theatlantic.com/magazine/archive/2020/06/qanon-nothing-can-stop-what-is-coming/610567.

Lakoff, George. *Moral Politics: How Liberals and Conservatives Think*. 2nd ed. Chicago: University of Chicago Press, 2002.

Lamis, Alexander P. *The Two-Party South*. New York: Oxford University Press, 1984.

Lassiter, Matthew D. "Big Government and Family Values: Political Culture in the Metropolitan Sunbelt." In *Sunbelt Rising: The Politics of Space, Place, and Region*, edited by Michelle Nickerson and Darren Dochuk, 82–109. Philadelphia: University of Pennsylvania Press, 2011.

———. *The Silent Majority: Suburban Politics in the Sunbelt South*. Princeton, N.J.: Princeton University Press, 2006.

Lassiter, Matthew D., and Joseph Crespino, eds. *The Myth of Southern Exceptionalism*. New York: Oxford University Press, 2010.

Lassiter, Matthew D., and Andrew B. Lewis. *The Moderates' Dilemma: Massive Resistance to School Desegregation in Virginia*. Charlottesville: University Press of Virginia, 1998.

Leak, Jeffrey B., ed. *Rac(e)ing to the Right: Selected Essays of George S. Schuyler*. Knoxville: University of Tennessee Press, 2001.

Lowndes, Joseph E. *From the New Deal to the New Right: Race and the Southern Origins of Modern Conservatism*. New Haven, Conn.: Yale University Press, 2008.

Mansbridge, Jane J. *Why We Lost the ERA*. Chicago: University of Chicago Press, 1986.

Mathews, Donald G., and Jane Sherron De Hart. *Sex, Gender, and the Politics of* ERA: *A State and the Nation*. New York: Oxford University Press, 1992.

Matthews, Glenna. *The Rise of Public Woman: Woman's Power and Woman's Place in the United States, 1630–1970*. New York: Oxford University Press, 1992.

Maxwell, Angie. *The Indicted South: Public Criticism, Southern Inferiority, and the Politics of Whiteness*. Chapel Hill: University of North Carolina Press, 2014.

Maxwell, Angie, and Todd Shields, eds. *The Legacy of Second-Wave Feminism in American Politics*. New York: Palgrave Macmillan, 2017.

———. *The Long Southern Strategy: How Chasing White Voters in the South Changed American Politics*. New York: Oxford University Press, 2019.

———, eds. *Unlocking V.O. Key Jr.: "Southern Politics" for the Twenty-First Century*. Little Rock: University of Arkansas Press, 2011.

Maxwell, Angie, Todd Shields, and Jeannie Whayne, eds. *The Ongoing Burden of Southern History: Politics and Identity in the Twenty-First-Century South*. Baton Rouge: Louisiana State University Press, 2012.

May, Elaine Tyler. *Homeward Bound: American Families in the Cold War Era*. New York: Basic Books, 1988.

McEnaney, Laura. "He-Men and Christian Mothers: The America First Movement and the Gendered Meanings of Patriotism and Isolationism." *Diplomatic History* 18, no. 1 (Winter 1994): 47–57.

McGirr, Lisa. *Suburban Warriors: The Origins of the New American Right*. Princeton, N.J.: Princeton University Press, 2001.

McMillen, Neil R. *Dark Journey: Black Mississippians in the Age of Jim Crow*. Urbana: University of Illinois Press, 1990.

McRae, Elizabeth Gillespie. *Mothers of Massive Resistance: White Women and the Politics of White Supremacy*. New York: Oxford University Press, 2018.

Meyerowitz, Joanne. "Beyond the Feminine Mystique: A Reassessment of Postwar Mass Culture, 1946–1958." *Journal of American History* 79, no. 4 (March 1993): 1455–82.

———, ed. *Not June Cleaver: Women and Gender in Postwar America, 1945–1960*. Philadelphia: Temple University Press, 1994.

Mink, Gwendolyn. *The Wages of Motherhood: Inequality in the Welfare State, 1917–1942*. Ithaca: Cornell University Press, 1995.

Morris, Robin M. "Building the New Right: Georgia Women, Grassroots Organizing, and Party Realignment, 1950–1980." PhD diss., Yale University, 2012.

———. "Organizing Breadmakers: Kathryn Dunaway's ERA Battle and the Roots of Georgia's Republican Revolution." In *Entering the Fray: Gender, Politics, and Culture in the New South*, edited by Jonathan Daniel Wells and Sheila R. Phipps, 161–83. Columbia: University of Missouri Press, 2010.

Nealy, Lisa Nikol. *African American Women Voters: Racializing Religiosity, Political Consciousness and Progressive Political Action in U.S. Presidential Elections from 1964 through 2008*. Lanham, Md.: University Press of America, 2009.

Nickerson, Michelle. *Mothers of Conservatism: Women and the Postwar Right*. Princeton, N.J.: Princeton University Press, 2012.

Nickerson, Michelle, and Darren Dochuk, eds. *Sunbelt Rising: The Politics of Space, Place, and Region*. Philadelphia: University of Pennsylvania Press, 2011.

Olcott, Jocelyn. *International Women's Year: The Greatest Consciousness-Raising Event in History*. New York: Oxford University Press, 2017.

O'Neill, June. "The Trend in the Male-Female Wage Gap in the United States." *Journal of Labor Economics* 3, no. 1, part 2 (January 1985): S91–S116.

Perlstein, Rick. *Before the Storm: Barry Goldwater and the Unmaking of the American Consensus*. 2001; repr., New York: Nation Books, 2009.

——. *The Invisible Bridge: The Fall of Nixon and the Rise of Reagan*. New York: Simon & Schuster, 2014.

——. *Nixonland: The Rise of a President and the Fracturing of America*. New York: Scribner, 2008.

——. *Reaganland: America's Right Turn, 1976–1980*. New York: Simon & Schuster, 2020.

Phillips, Patrick. *Blood at the Root: A Racial Cleansing in America*. New York: W. W. Norton, 2016.

Rafshoon, Ellen G. "Pave it Blue: Georgia Women and Politics in the Trump Era." In *Suffrage at 100: Women in American Politics since 1920*, edited by Stacie Taranto and Leandra Ruth Zarnow, 377–93. Baltimore: Johns Hopkins University Press, 2020.

Rymph, Catherine E. *Republican Women: Feminism and Conservatism from Suffrage through the Rise of the New Right*. Chapel Hill: University of North Carolina Press, 2006.

Schulman, Bruce J. *From Cotton Belt to Sunbelt: Federal Policy, Economic Development, and the Transformation of the South, 1938–1980*. Durham, N.C.: Duke University Press, 1994.

——. *The Seventies: The Great Shift in American Culture, Society, and Politics*. Cambridge, Mass.: Da Capo Press, 2002.

Schulman, Bruce J., and Julian E. Zelizer, eds. *Rightward Bound: Making America Conservative in the 1970s*. Cambridge, Mass.: Harvard University Press, 2008.

Scott, Ann Firor. *Making the Invisible Woman Visible*. Urbana: University of Illinois Press, 1984.

——. *The Southern Lady: From Pedestal to Politics, 1830–1930*. Chicago: University of Chicago Press, 1970.

Seagull, Louis M. *Southern Republicanism*. New York: John Wiley and Sons, 1975.

Self, Robert O. *All in the Family: The Realignment of American Democracy since the 1960s*. New York: Hill and Wang, 2012.

Sewell, Jessica. "Tea and Suffrage." *Food, Culture, and Society* 11, no. 4 (December 2008): 487–507.

Siskind, Peter. "Shades of Black and Green: The Making of Racial and Environmental Liberalism in Nelson Rockefeller's New York." *Journal of Urban History* 34, no. 2 (2008): 243–65.

Smith, Andrea. *Native Americans and the Christian Right: The Gendered Politics of Unlikely Alliances*. Durham, N.C.: Duke University Press, 2008.

Spruill, Marjorie. *Divided We Stand: The Battle over Women's Rights and Family Values that Polarized American Politics*. New York: Bloomsbury, 2017.

——. "Feminism, Anti-feminism, and the Rise of a New Southern Strategy in the 1970s." In *The Legacy of Second-Wave Feminism in American Politics*, edited by Angie Maxwell and Todd Shields, 39–70. New York: Palgrave Macmillan, 2018.

Spruill Wheeler, Marjorie. *New Women of the New South: The Leaders of the Woman Suffrage Movement in the Southern States*. New York: Oxford University Press, 1993.

Stout, Lee. *A Matter of Simple Justice: The Untold Story of Barbara Hackman Franklin and a Few Good Women*. University Park, Pa.: Pennsylvania State University Libraries, 2012.

Strahan, Randall, and Daniel J. Palazzolo. "The Gingrich Effect." *Political Science Quarterly* 119, no. 1 (Spring 2004): 89–114.

Sugrue, Tomas. "Crabgrass Politics: Race, Rights, and Reaction against Liberalism in the Urban North, 1940–1964," *Journal of American History* 82, no. 2 (September 1995): 551–78.

Taranto, Stacie. *Kitchen Table Politics: Conservative Women and Family Values in New York*. Philadelphia: University of Pennsylvania Press, 2017.

Waskey, A. J. L. "Tom Murphy (1924–2007)." *New Georgia Encyclopedia*. December 9, 2003; last edited August 26, 2013. https://www.georgiaencyclopedia.org/articles /government-politics/tom-murphy-1924-2007.

Watson, Elwood. "Guess What Came to American Politics? Contemporary Black Conservatism." *Journal of Black Studies* 29, no. 1 (September 1998): 73–92.

Wells, Jonathan Daniel, and Sheila R. Phipps, eds. *Entering the Fray: Gender, Politics, and Culture in the New South*. Columbia: University of Missouri Press, 2010.

Williams, Daniel K. *Defenders of the Unborn: The Pro-life Movement before Roe v. Wade*. New York: Oxford University Press, 2016.

———. *God's Own Party: The Making of the Christian Right*. New York: Oxford University Press, 2010.

Wright Rigueur, Leah. *The Loneliness of the Black Republican: Pragmatic Politics and the Pursuit of Power*. Princeton, N.J.: Princeton University Press, 2014.

———. "The Major Difference between Black Male and Female Voters." *Atlantic*, November 21, 2020. https://www.theatlantic.com/culture/archive/2020/11/why-black -men-and-women-vote-so-differently/617134.

Zarnow, Leandra Ruth. *Battling Bella: The Protest Politics of Bella Abzug*. Cambridge, Mass.: Harvard University Press, 2019.

INDEX

Pickett, Roscoe, Jr., 65, 68, 70–71
Pickett, Roscoe, Sr., 162–63n49
Ponder, Mrs. Carl, 55
Price, Tom, 157n33
Prince, Jack, 22, 138
Pro-Family Rally, 126–27
Pruett, Jane, 43

QAnon, 142–43

racist rhetoric traded for motherhood, household economics, and family values, 5, 73–74, 87–89, 105–6. *See also* Massive Resistance
Rath Packing Company, 50
Reagan, Maureen (Sills), 61, 66, 141
Reagan, Ronald, 71, 139–41, 166n36
Republican Congressional Committee (RCC), 46–47
Republican National Committee (RNC), 10, 74–75, 80
Republican Party: African American voters abandon, to Democratic Party, 90–91; Democratic Solid South and, 20; ERA platform and, 138–39; as party of Lincoln, 10; women candidates and, 145–46
Richardson, Eleanor, 131–32, 133
Richmond County, 29, 138
Robinson, Lee, 113
Rockefeller, Nelson, 15, 29
Rockefeller Commission, 108
Roe v. Wade (1973), 107–8
Romney, George, 72
Roosevelt, Edith Kermit, 66
Roughton, Naomi, 42–43
Ruckelshaus, Jill, 94
Russell, Richard, 23

Sandy Springs Women's Club, 116–17
Savannah Area Republican Women, 138
Scharmitzky, Margaret, 107
Schlafly, Fred, 65, 114, 135
Schlafly, Phyllis: on abortion, 107–8; *A Choice Not an Echo*, 36, 60–61; and Dunaway friendship, 36–37, 62, 63–64, 67–68, 95, 98, 131, 136; and Eagle Council, 67, 95, 114–15; empowerment, messages of, 62; ERA, overview of opposition to, 96–98; on foreign policy, 36; FRW network, building on, 95–96, 107; Georgia, visits to, 123, 133, 136; and GFRW, 62–64, 67–68, 107; *The Gravediggers*

(with Ward), 36, 62; and IWY, 122–27; and NFRW schism, 60–68; party credentials of, 61; *Phyllis Schlafly Report*, 67, 95–98, 106; as working woman, 97
school desegregation: *Brown v. Board of Education*, 15; Central High School (Little Rock, Ark.), 24, 72; federal overreach, conservative rhetoric of, 84, 103–4, 106; school busing, 84–86. *See also* Massive Resistance
Schroeder, Patricia, 103
Scott, C. A., 93
Scott, Marian, 10–11
Scott, Portia, 141
Scott, W. A., 11, 141
segregationists, feeling of abandonment by parties, 71–72. *See also* Maddox, Lester; Massive Resistance
sex discrimination, 101–2
Shapard, Virginia, 114, 133, 138
Shelton, Lee R., 16
Sherman, Erin, 107
Shields, Todd, 4–5
Silent Majority: minority voters and, 89, 91–93; Republican women's groundwork for, 80; tenets of, 84. *See also* racist rhetoric traded for motherhood, household economics, and family values
Smalley, Carolyn Wynn, 23
Smith, A. Edward, 41
Smith, George, 104
Smith, Margaret Chase, 10
Smith, Marilu, 41
South Carolina, 12, 37
Southern Black Republican Council, 141
Southern Christian Leadership Conference (SCLC), 55, 116; registration drives, 22
southern conservatism goes national, 80, 84–86, 125. *See also* Operation Lend-An-Ear
southern strategy: African American voters and, 90–93; Nixon's strategy, 72–73, 84–85, 90–91; Republican women as foundation for, 20, 28, 38, 70, 72–74, 84, 87, 123; scholarship on, 4–6
Southwest Fulton Federation of Republican Women, 140–41
Stanley, Charles, 118, 174n16
Stanton-King, Angela, 143
Statewide Registration Committee, 22
Steinem, Gloria, 105, 108
Stephens, Nancy, 29
Stoner, J. B., 105

Stop Taking Our Privileges Equal Rights Amendment (STOP ERA): baked goods for legislators, symbolism of, 110–11; conference in St. Louis, 130–31; ERA effects, expectations of, 102–4, 106–8; funding and, 122; GFRW grassroots tactics, use of, 95–96; grassroots organizing and voter outreach, 99, 101, 104, 107–9, 113–14, 115–16, 117–18, 134–35; IWY and, 121–22, 126–27; legislative path in Georgia, 104–6, 114; legislators, outreach to, 110–11, 112, 113, 117, 118–19, 131, 134–35; messaging and presentation, centralized, 105, 110–11, 114–15, 116, 122, 123; organizational structure, 99; Paschall support of, 127–31; pastors, recruitment of, 107, 118; as political outsiders, 118–19; pro-ERA boycotts of Atlanta, 120; Schlafly visit to Georgia, 113; tactics and success of, 127, 134. *See also* Dunaway, Kathryn; Schlafly, Phyllis

Student Nonviolent Coordinating Committee registration drives, 22

Suit, Hal, 89–90

Summerhill protests, 51–52

Sutton, Ralph, 23

Swann v. Charlotte-Mecklenburg (N.C.) Board of Education (1971), 84

Talmadge, Herman, 23, 92, 138

taxes: family values, framing of, 14, 130; racial discrepancies and, 5; for social programs, 102–3, 129–30, 132–33

Taylor, Mamie K., 100–101

Tea Party, 145

technology and data collection and analysis, 139–40

telephones: phone surveys, 39–40, 41–44; prevalence of, 41–42; robocalls, use of, 139–40

Tennessee, 12, 28

Texas, 12

Thomas County, 49–50

Thompson, Fletcher, 57, 77, 90, 93

Thompson, Ronnie, 70, 76

Thomson, Rosemary, 122–23, 124, 127

Thurmond, Strom, 25, 37, 66, 86

Tift County, 68

Towns County, 138

Troup County, 30, 36, 37, 45, 62, 70

Troutman, Frank, 68

Trump, Donald, 143, 145–46, 157n33

Turner, Herschel, 118

Tuten, James, 135

two-party system: African American identity within, 92–93; Deep South, Georgia women's work in, 37; as necessary for democracy, 18, 28; outsiders moving to Georgia and, 14, 69; rhetoric and ignoring of civil rights issues, 20

Two Party Tea Party, 18–19, 47–49

Unterman, Renee, 142, 145

UN World Conference on Women, 121

Vandiver, Ernest, 40, 43–45, 52

Victory Girls, 19, 23–24

Victory Squad, 26–27

Vietnam War, 44, 53, 70, 76, 102–4

Viguerie, Richard, 140

Virginia, 12, 28

Voluntary Action Program, 83

voter fraud, conservatives' allegations of, 27, 65–67, 125

voter registration drives in 2020 election, 144–46

voter suppression in 2020 election, 144

Voting Rights Act (1965), 4, 38, 39, 42, 52, 55, 73, 90–91; conservative shift away from discussion of, 50, 73

Wallace, Birdie, 10

Wallace, George, 71–72, 74–77, 79

Wallace, Lurleen, 163n52

Warnock, Raphael, 143

Warren, Earl, 72

Wash, Mrs. Lee, 23

Weddington, Sarah, 134

white girls, conservative use as symbol, 24, 56; "Go Bo Girls," 55–56; Victory Girls, 19, 23–24

Whittlesly, Faith Ryan, 140

Wilcox County, 22–23

Wilkinson County, 23

Williams, Hosea, 55

Williams, Nikema, 143

Williamson, Q. V., 42, 54

women candidates, 70, 71, 90, 129, 135, 141, 145–46; as elected officials, 112, 114, 141–46

Women for Nixon chapters, 74, 76, 77

Women in Your Political Life, The (L. A. Miller), 46–47

Women on the Warpath campaign, 49–51

women's church auxiliaries, 107, 137

Since 1970: Histories of Contemporary America

Jimmy Carter, the Politics of Family, and
the Rise of the Religious Right
       by J. Brooks Flippen

Rumor, Repression, and Racial Politics: How the Harassment
of Black Elected Officials Shaped Post–Civil Rights America
       by George Derek Musgrove

Doing Recent History: On Privacy, Copyright,
Video Games, Institutional Review Boards, Activist
Scholarship, and History That Talks Back
       edited by Claire Bond Potter and Renee C. Romano

The Dinner Party: Judy Chicago and the Power
of Popular Feminism, 1970–2007
       by Jane F. Gerhard

Reconsidering Roots: Race, Politics, and Memory
       edited by Erica L. Ball and Kellie Carter Jackson

Liberation in Print: Feminist Periodicals
and Social Movement Identity
       by Agatha Beins

Pushing Back: Women of Color–Led Grassroots
Activism in New York City
       by Ariella Rotramel

Remaking Radicalism: A Grassroots Documentary
Reader of the United States, 1973–2001
       edited by Dan Berger and Emily K. Hobson

Deep Cut: Science, Power, and the Unbuilt Interoceanic Canal
       by Christine Keiner

America's Other Automakers: A History of the Foreign-
Owned Automotive Sector in the United States
       by Timothy J. Minchin

Public Religions in the Future World: Postsecularism and Utopia
       by David Morris

Goldwater Girls to Reagan Women: Gender,
Georgia, and the Growth of the New Right
       by Robin M. Morris